Knowing and Teaching
Elementary Mathematics

*Teachers' Understanding of Fundamental
Mathematics in China and the United States*

The Studies in Mathematical Thinking and Learning Series
Alan Schoenfeld, Advisory Editor

Knowing and Teaching Elementary Mathematics

Teachers' Understanding of Fundamental Mathematics in China and the United States

Liping Ma
University of California, Berkeley

LEA   LAWRENCE ERLBAUM ASSOCIATES, PUBLISHERS

1999   Mahwah, New Jersey   London

Lawrence Erlbaum Associates, Inc., Publishers
10 Industrial Avenue
Mahwah, New Jersey 07430

Cover design by Kathryn Houghtaling Lacey

Library of Congress Cataloging-in-Publication Data

Ma, Liping.
    Knowing and teaching elementary mathematics : teachers'
understanding of fundamental mathematics in China and the United
States / Liping Ma.
        p. cm. -- (Studies in mathematical thinking and learning
series)
    Includes bibliographical references and indexes.
    ISBN 0-8058-2908-3 (cloth : alk. paper). -- ISBN 0-8058-2909-1
(pbk. : alk. paper)
    1. Mathematics--Study and teaching (Elementary) -- United States.
    2. Mathematics--Study and teaching (Elementary) -- China.
    3. Comparative education. I. Title. II. Series: Studies in
mathematical thinking and learning.
    QA135.5.M22 1999
    372.7'0973--dc21   99-17342
                                                                            CIP

Books published by Lawrence Erlbaum Associates are printed on acid-free paper,
and their bindings are chosen for strength and durability.

Printed in the United States of America

To Jianfeng, Sushu, and John,
and to Cathy Kessel,
with deepest love and appreciation

Contents

Foreword

Lee S. Shulman
The Carnegie Foundation for the Advancement of Teaching

This is a remarkable book. It is also remarkably easy to misunderstand its most important lessons. Liping Ma has conducted a study that compares mathematical understanding among U.S. and Chinese elementary school teachers as it relates to classroom teaching practices. What could be simpler? What could one possibly miscontrue? Let me count the ways.

- This book appears to be a comparative study of American and Chinese teachers of mathematics, but its most important contributions are not comparative, but theoretical.

- This book appears to be about understanding the *content* of mathematics, rather than its pedagogy, but its conception of content is profoundly pedagogical.

- This book appears to be about the practice of mathematics teaching, but it demands a hearing among those who set policy for teaching and teacher education.

- This book appears to be most relevant to the preservice preparation of teachers, but its most powerful findings may well relate to our understanding of teachers' work and their career-long professional development.

- This book focuses on the work of elementary school teachers, but its most important audience may well be college and university faculty members who teach mathematics to future teachers as well as future parents.

I shall try to clarify these somewhat cryptic observations in this foreword, but first a brief biographical note about Liping Ma.

Liping became an elementary school teacher courtesy of China's Cultural Revolution. An eighth-grade middle-school student in Shanghai, she was sent to "the countryside"—in her case a poor rural village in the mountainous area of South China—to be re-educated by the peasants working in the fields. After a few months, the village head asked Liping to become a teacher at the village school. As she has described it to me, she was a Shanghai teenager with but eight years of formal education struggling to teach all the subjects to two classes of kids in one classroom.

Over the next seven years, she taught all five grades and became principal of the school. A few years later, she would be hired as the Elementary School Superintendent for the entire county.

When she returned to Shanghai filled with curiosity about her new calling, she found a mentor in Professor Liu, who directed her reading of many of the classics of education—among them Confucius and Plato, Locke and Rousseau, Piaget, Vygotsky, and Bruner. Professor Liu eventually became president of East China Normal University where Liping earned a master's degree. She longed to study even more, and to pursue her further education in the United States. On the last day of 1988, she arrived in the United States to study at Michigan State University.

At Michigan State University, she worked with, among others, Sharon Feiman-Nemser and Suzanne Wilson in teacher education, with Deborah Ball and Magdalene Lampert in mathematics education, and with Lynn Paine in comparative education. She participated in the development and analysis of a national survey of elementary teachers' mathematical understandings, and marveled at the general misunderstandings that persisted among the U.S. teachers. They struck her as quite unlike the teachers she had come to know in China.

After a few years, her family chose to live in California, and Liping was admitted to the doctoral program at Stanford University to complete her coursework and dissertation. I served as her advisor and the Spencer Foundation awarded her a dissertation-year fellowship to complete the study that forms the basis for this book. This support, along with continued help from Michigan State, made possible her travel to China to collect the data from Chinese teachers. After completing her Ph.D., Liping was awarded a two-year postdoctoral fellowship to work with Alan Schoenfeld at Berkeley, where she continued her research and where her dissertation was transformed into this superb book.

What are the most important lessons to be learned from this book? Let us return to the list of misconceptions I presented earlier and discuss them more elaborately.

This book appears to be a comparative study of American and Chinese teachers of mathematics, but its most important contributions are not comparative, but theoretical. The investigation compares Chinese and American teachers and the Chinese, once again, know more. What could be simpler? But the key ideas of this book are not comparisons between American teachers and their Chinese counterparts. The heart of the book is Dr. Ma's analysis of the kind of understanding that distinguishes the two groups. Chinese teachers are far more likely to have developed "profound understanding of fundamental mathematics." To say that they "know more" or "understand more" is to make a deeply theoretical claim. They actually may have studied far less mathematics, but what they know they know more profoundly, more flexibly, more adaptively.

This book appears to be about understanding the content of mathematics, rather than its pedagogy, but its conception of content is profoundly pedagogical. Liping Ma set out to account for the differences in content knowledge and understanding between U.S. and Chinese elementary teachers, but her conception of understanding is critical. She has developed a conception of mathematical understanding that emphasizes those aspects of knowledge most likely to contribute to a teacher's ability to explain important mathematical ideas to students. Thus, her stipulation of four properties of understanding—basic ideas, connectedness, multiple representations, and longitudinal coherence—offers a powerful framework for grasping the mathematical content necessary to understand and instruct the thinking of schoolchildren.

This book appears to be about the practice of mathematics teaching, but it demands a hearing among those who set policy for teaching and teacher education. Policymakers have become frantic in their insistence that future teachers demonstrate that they possess the knowledge of subject matter necessary to teach children. We are about to see tests of content knowledge for teachers proliferate among state licensing authorities. These cannot be tests that assess the wrong kind of knowledge. Liping Ma's work should guide policymakers to commission the development of assessments that tap profound understanding of fundamental mathematics among future elementary teachers, not superficial knowledge of procedures and rules.

This book appears to be most relevant to the preservice preparation of teachers, but its most powerful findings may well relate to our understanding of teachers' work and their career-long professional development. Liping was not satisfied to document the differences in understanding between Chinese and American teachers. She also inquired into the sources for those differences. A critical finding (echoed in the work on TIMMS by Stigler and Hiebert) is that Chinese teachers continue to learn mathematics and to refine their content understandings throughout their teaching careers. Teachers' work in China includes time and support for serious deliberations and seminars on the content of their lessons. These are absolutely essential features of teacher work. American teachers are offered no opportunities within the school day for these collaborative deliberations, and therefore can teach for many years without deepening their understandings of the content they teach. Chinese teachers, in contrast, work in settings that create learning opportunities on a continuing basis.

This book focuses on the work of elementary school teachers, but its most important audience may well be college and university faculty members who teach mathematics to future teachers as well as future parents. Given our understanding of mathematical understanding for teaching, where can future teachers initially learn such mathematics? In China, they learn such mathematics from their own elementary and middle-school teachers, enhance that understanding in the content courses at their normal colleges (teacher-education colleges), and further sustain and develop their knowledge in practice. The only place to break the vicious cycle that limits the mathematical knowledge of U.S. teachers is in the development of far more effective mathematics courses in U.S. undergraduate programs. But current undergraduate mathematics programs seem to have no place for teaching fundamental mathematics for profound understanding. If anything, such knowledge is misconstrued as remedial instead of recognizing that it is rigorous and deserving of university-level instruction. Mathematics departments must take responsibility for serving this national priority for both future teachers and future citizens.

Although only now being published, copies of earlier drafts of this manuscript have been circulating in the mathematics community for some time. In a recent letter, Liping's postdoctoral mentor, Professor Alan Schoenfeld of the University of California at Berkeley, described the response to prepublication copies of this book vividly.

> Liping's manuscript has already gotten an amazing amount of notice. It's an underground hit, perhaps the only manuscript I know that has the attention and favor of both sides of the "math wars." Many world class mathematicians are rhapsodic about it; at the annual mathematics meetings, people like [he lists several leading professional mathematicians] were walking advertisements for the book. That's because it says content knowledge makes a difference. But at the same time, those who have reform perspectives—those who value a deep and connected view of mathematical thinking, and who understand that teacher competence includes having a rich knowledge base that contains a wide range of pedagogical content knowledge—find that the book offers riches regarding content, teacher preparation, and teacher professionalism.

This is indeed a valuable, enlightening book. It attests to the talent of its author, and to the Chinese and American learning environments that have nurtured that talent. It attests to the value of welcoming scholars from other nations to study in the United States. I urge all those who are seriously concerned about the quality of mathematics education in the United States to read this book, and to take its lessons seriously.

Acknowledgments

About 30 years ago, China was undergoing the so-called "Cultural Revolution." Millions of students from cities were sent to rural areas. As one of them, I left Shanghai, where I was born and raised, and went to a small, poor village in a mountainous area of south China. Seven of us teenagers—with seven or eight years of formal education—formed a "co-op" family there. We were supposed to make our living by working in the fields, and be re-educated by the peasants at the same time. A few months later, the head of the village came to me. He surprised me by asking me to become a teacher at the village elementary school—to educate their children. Most of the peasants in that mountain area were illiterate. They eagerly wanted to change this fate for their next generation.

Today, holding the book manuscript in my hands and looking back, I can clearly see the starting point of my career—that Shanghai girl who struggled very hard to teach all subjects to two grades of rural kids. It has been a long journey with laughter as well as tears. All the value of this book, if there is any, has been fostered throughout this journey.

This book would not have been possible without help along the way. The work occurred in two stages—the research and writing of my dissertation and its revision as a book. Both stages were accomplished with the assistance of numerous people and institutions.

First of all, I am grateful to the Spencer Foundation and the McDonnell Foundation for doctoral and postdoctoral fellowships that supported the writing and revision of my dissertation.

At Michigan State University in East Lansing—my "home town" in the United States—I was especially indebted to Professors Sharon Feiman-Nemser, Lynn Paine, and their families. My intellectual home was the TELT project and I benefited greatly from my interactions with project members. My work builds on TELT, both intellectually and through my use of questions developed by Deborah Ball and data collected by Deborah Ball, Sharon Feiman-Nemser, Perry Lanier, Michelle Parker, and Richard Prawat.

When I arrived in the United States, I only had thirty dollars in my pocket. Sharon, my advisor, worked hard to help me to find a research assistantship so that I could focus on my academic development. Her outstanding scholarship in teaching and research, as it does for all her other students, enlightened, and will continue to enlighten my research on teacher education.

Before I met Professor Lynn Paine, I could not tell from her phone call in Chinese that she was an American. She gave me my first and solid training in how to conduct cross-national research on education. Later, as a member of my dissertation committee at Stanford, she carefully read my dissertation and gave detailed and thoughtful comments to improve it.

At MSU, I was also indebted to Professors Deborah Ball, Margret Buchmann, David Cohen, Helen Featherstone, Robert Floden, Mary Kennedy, David Labaree, William McDiarmid, Susan Melnick, Richard Navarro, John Schwille, and Mun Tsang for their significant guidance in the early stage of my doctoral program.

In addition, I would like to thank my colleagues and fellow graduate students Zhixiong Cai, Fanfu Li, Yiqnig Liu, Shirley Miskey, Michelle Parker, Jeremy Price, Neli Wolf, and Chuanguo Xu. Their welcome, help, and companionship warmed me in my first days in a foreign country.

At Stanford University, my advisor Lee Shulman deserves a special mention. Lee offered his support from the moment I presented my research topic. He always generously provided vital intellectual insights, warm words of encouragement, and perceptive advice. Under his direction, I learned how to sow the seed of a research idea and grow it into a thriving tree.

I also thank Professors Myron Atkin, Robbie Case, Larry Cuban, Elliot Eisner, James Greeno, Nel Noddings, Thomas Rohlen, Joan Talbert, and Decker Walker at Stanford, for their support throughout my research endeavors. Professor Harold Stevenson at the University of Michigan read my dissertation proposal and provided valuable suggestions. Professor Fonian Liu, the former president of East China Normal University, also expressed his enthusiastic encouragement for my research.

During my postdoctoral tenure I owed much to Miriam Gamoran Sherin, who was then a graduate student at the University of California at Berkeley and is now an assistant professor at Northwestern University. Miriam read major portions of the manuscript. She not only helped to edit my "Chinglish," but inspired me with her thoughtful comments. Two other graduate students, Kathy Simon and Glen Trager, at Stanford contributed to my work with their editing and their warm and enduring encouragement.

During my postdoctoral tenure I decided to turn the dissertation into a book. When the task was finally accomplished, on my way to mail the book manuscript to the publisher I felt like a mother before her daughter's wedding. Finishing the dissertation had merely seemed like giving birth to a baby. Making it into a book—bringing her up and educating her— was not an easy task at all. For me, who began learning English on my own in my twenties, it was particularly difficult. Fortunately, an excellent group of people gave their warm and powerful hands to me.

Professor Alan Schoenfeld, with whom I did my postdoctoral work at the University of California at Berkeley, is the first person I would like to thank at this stage. Alan gave the book a home in the series he edits. He read and commented on every chapter of the book, provided valuable suggestions for improvement, and even rewrote a few paragraphs. He was always there whenever I needed help. Working with Alan closely, I learned much about research. I also learned much more—a way of interacting with students and colleagues. As William Shawn, editor of the *New Yorker*, said of his community, "Love has been the controlling emotion and love is the essential word." Alan has created a community where students are treated as future colleagues and everyone is a potential colleague. He astutely suggested a community member to help with the book.

Doctor Cathy Kessel, a research fellow at Berkeley, served as the indispensable "nanny" of my "baby"—the book. She did the heavy editing of the manuscript, challenged weak arguments, pushed me to make them clear, and understood and expressed my ideas. For Chapter 7, she reviewed the literature and amplified, strengthened, and clarified my arguments. In addition to this intellectual labor, she has taken care of all the tedious, detailed drudgery that occurs in the process of preparing a book manuscript. Cathy's contribution to this book can never be too strongly emphasized. Without her help, I, the "mother," would never have been able to bring up the "baby." In fact, her passion for the book is no less than mine.

I would like to thank Rudy Apffel, Deborah Ball, Maryl Gearhart, Ilana Horn, and Susan Magidson for their comments on the introduction. Anne Brown's detailed and thoughtful comments on chapters 1 through 4 helped to improve their clarity. Alan Schoenfeld's research group, the Functions Group, spent two sessions discussing my manuscript. Julia Aguirre, Ilana Horn, Susan Magidson, Manya Raman, and Natasha Speer made valuable comments. Thanks to the Functions Group and to Anne Brown for comments on chapters 5, 6, and 7. Thanks again to Robert Floden for providing last-minute information from the NCRTE database.

I would also like to thank Naomi Silverman, senior editor at Lawrence Erlbaum Associates, for her helpful and patient support.

My sincere gratitude goes to Professor Richard Askey, whose interest and enthusiasm brought the book manuscript to the attention of many.

Back in China, my homeland, I would first thank the peasants of Cunqian, the village where I lived and taught, who had little education themselves but put me on the path that led to a doctorate at Stanford University. I sincerely appreciate the Chinese teachers whom I interviewed. I also particularly appreciate my own teachers who impressed great teaching on my young mind.

Finally, my family certainly deserves the ultimate thanks and greatest appreciation. Without their support, not only this book, but also my whole life would be impossible.

Introduction

Chinese students typically outperform U.S. students on international comparisons of mathematics competency. Paradoxically, Chinese teachers seem far less mathematically educated than U. S. teachers. Most Chinese teachers have had 11 to 12 years of schooling—they complete ninth grade and attend normal school for two or three years. In contrast, most U.S. teachers have received between 16 and 18 years of formal schooling—a bachelor's degree in college and often one or two years of further study.

In this book I suggest an explanation for the paradox, at least at the elementary school level. My data suggest that Chinese teachers begin their teaching careers with a better understanding of elementary mathematics than that of most U.S. elementary teachers. Their understanding of the mathematics they teach and—equally important—of the ways that elementary mathematics can be presented to students continues to grow throughout their professional lives. Indeed, about 10% of those Chinese teachers, despite their lack of formal education, display a depth of understanding which is extraordinarily rare in the United States.

I document the differences between Chinese and U.S. teachers' knowledge of mathematics for teaching and I suggest how Chinese teachers' understanding of mathematics and of its teaching contributes to their students' success. I also document some of the factors that support the growth of Chinese teachers' mathematical knowledge and I suggest why at present it seems difficult, if not impossible, for elementary teachers in the United States to develop a deep understanding of the mathematics they teach. I shall begin with some examples that motivated the study.

In 1989, I was a graduate student at Michigan State University. I worked as a graduate assistant in the Teacher Education and Learning to Teach Study (TELT) at the National Center for Research on Teacher Education (NCRTE) coding transcripts of teachers' responses to questions like the following:

> Imagine that you are teaching division with fractions. To make this meaningful for kids, something that many teachers try to do is relate mathematics to other things. Sometimes they try to come up with real-world situations or story-problems to show the application of some particular piece of content. What would you say would be a good story or model for $1\frac{3}{4} \div \frac{1}{2}$?

I was particularly struck by the answers to this question. Very few teachers gave a correct response. Most, more than 100 preservice, new, and experienced teachers, made up a story that represented $1\frac{3}{4} \times \frac{1}{2}$, or $1\frac{3}{4} \div 2$. Many other teachers were not able to make up a story.

The interviews reminded me of how I learned division by fractions as an elementary student in Shanghai. My teacher helped us understand the relationship between division by fractions and division by positive integers—division remains the inverse of multiplication, but meanings of division by fractions extend meanings of whole-number division: the measurement model (finding how many halves there are in $1\frac{3}{4}$) and the partitive model (finding a number such that half of it is $1\frac{3}{4}$).[1] Later, I became an elementary school teacher. The understanding of division by fractions shown by my elementary school teacher was typical of my colleagues. How was it then that so many teachers in the United States failed to show this understanding?

Several weeks after I coded the interviews, I visited an elementary school with a reputation for high-quality teaching that served a prosperous White suburb. With a teacher-educator and an experienced teacher, I observed a mathematics class when a student teacher was teaching fourth graders about measurement. During the class, which went smoothly, I was struck by another incident. After teaching measurements and their conversions, the teacher asked a student to measure one side of the classroom with a yardstick. The student reported that it was 7 yards and 5 inches. He then worked on his calculator and added, "7 yards and 5 inches equals 89 inches." The teacher, without any hesitation, jotted down "(89 inches)" beside the "7 yards and 5 inches" that she had just written on the chalkboard. The apparent mismatch of the two lengths, "7 yards and 5 inches" and "89 inches," seemed conspicuous on the chalkboard. It was obvious, but not surprising, that the student had misused conversion between feet and inches in calculating the number of inches in a yard. What surprised me, however, was that the apparent mismatch remained on the chalkboard until the end of the class without any discussion. What surprised me even more was that the mistake was never revealed or corrected, nor even mentioned after the class in a discussion of the student teacher's teaching. Neither the cooperating teacher nor the teacher-educator who was supervising the student teacher even noticed the mistake. As an elementary teacher and as a researcher who worked with teachers for many years, I had developed certain expectations about elementary teachers' knowledge of mathematics. However, the expectations I had developed in China did not seem to hold in the United States.

---

[1] For more information about the two models, see chapter 3, p. 72.

The more I saw of elementary mathematics teaching and research in the United States, the more intrigued I became. Even expert teachers, experienced teachers who were mathematically confident, and teachers who actively participated in current mathematics teaching reform did not seem to have a thorough knowledge of the mathematics taught in elementary school. Apparently, the two incidents that had amazed me were only two more examples of an already widespread and well-documented phenomenon.[2]

Later, I read international studies of mathematics achievement.[3] These studies found that students of some Asian countries, such as Japan and China, consistently outperformed their counterparts in the United States.[4] Researchers have described various factors that contribute toward this "learning gap": differences in cultural contexts, such as parental expectations or number-word systems[5]; school organization, or amount of time spent learning mathematics; content and content allocation in mathematics curricula.[6] As I read this research, I kept thinking about the issue of teachers' mathematical knowledge. Could it be that the "learning gap" was not limited to students? If so, there would be another explanation for U.S. students' mathematical performance. Unlike factors outside of classroom teaching, teachers' knowledge might directly affect mathematics

---

[2]For more information about research on teacher subject matter knowledge, see Ball (1988a), Cohen (1991), Leinhardt and Smith (1985), NCRTE (1991), Putnam (1992), and Simon (1993).

[3]The International Association for the Evaluation of Educational Achievement (IEA) conducted the First International Mathematics Study in 1964. The study measured achievement in various mathematical topics in each of 12 different countries at Grades 8 and 12. In the early 1980s, IEA carried out another study. The Second International Mathematics Study compared 17 countries in the Grade 8 component and 12 in the Grade 12 component. The Third International Mathematics and Science Study (TIMSS), in which more than 40 countries participated, has recently started to release its reports. (For more information about the three studies, see Chang & Ruzicka, 1986; Coleman, 1975; Crosswhite, 1986; Crosswhite et al., 1985; Husen, 1967a, 1967b; LaPointe, Mead, & Philips, 1989; Lynn, 1988; McKnight et al., 1987; National Center for Education Statistics, 1997; Robitaille & Garden, 1989; Schmidt, McKnight, & Raizen, 1997.)

[4]TIMMS results follow this pattern. For example, five Asian countries participated in the Grade 4 mathematics component. Singapore, Korea, Japan, and Hong Kong had the top average scores. These were significantly higher than the U.S. score. (Thailand was the fifth Asian country participating.)

[5]For example, the Chinese word for the number 20 means "two tens," the Chinese word for the number 30 means "three tens," and so on. The consensus is that the Chinese number-word system illustrates the relationship between numbers and their names more straightforwardly than the English number-word system.

[6]For more information, see Geary, Siegler, and Fan (1993); Husen (1967a, 1967b); Lee, Ichikawa, and Stevenson (1987); McKnight et al. (1987); Miura and Okamoto (1989); Stevenson, Azuma, and Hakuta (1986); Stevenson and Stigler (1991, 1992); Stigler, Lee, and Stevenson (1986); Stigler and Perry (1988a, 1988b); Stigler and Stevenson (1981).

teaching and learning. Moreover, it might be easier to change than cultural factors, such as the number-word system[7] or ways of raising children.

It seemed strange that Chinese elementary teachers might have a better understanding of mathematics than their U.S. counterparts. Chinese teachers do not even complete high school; instead, after ninth grade they receive two or three more years of schooling in normal schools. In contrast, most U.S. teachers have at least a bachelor's degree. However, I suspected that elementary teachers in the two countries possess differently structured bodies of mathematical knowledge, that aside from subject matter knowledge "equal to that of his or her lay colleague" (Shulman, 1986), a teacher may have another kind of subject matter knowledge. For example, my elementary teacher's knowledge of the two models of division may not be common among high school or college teachers. This kind of knowledge of school mathematics may contribute significantly to what Shulman (1986) called pedagogical content knowledge—"the ways of representing and formulating the subject that make it comprehensible to others" (p. 9).

I decided to investigate my suspicion. Comparative research allows us to see different things—and sometimes to see things differently. My research did not focus on judging the knowledge of the teachers in two countries, but on finding examples of teachers' sufficient subject matter knowledge of mathematics. Such examples might stimulate further efforts to search for sufficient knowledge among U.S. teachers. Moreover, knowledge from teachers rather than from conceptual frameworks might be "closer" to teachers and easier for them to understand and accept.

Two years later, I completed the research described in this book. I found that although U.S. teachers may have been exposed to more advanced mathematics during their high school or college education,[8] Chinese teachers display a more comprehensive knowledge of the mathematics taught in elementary school.

In my study, I used the TELT interview questions. The main reason for using these instruments is their relevance to mathematics teaching. As Ed Begle recounts in *Critical Variables in Mathematics Education*, earlier studies often measured elementary and secondary teachers' knowledge by the number and type of mathematics courses taken or degrees obtained—and found little correlation between these measures of teacher knowledge and various measures of student learning. Since the late 1980s, researchers have

---

[7]However, instruction can successfully address irregularities in number-word systems. See Fuson, Smith, and Lo Cicero (1997) for an example of instruction that addresses the irregularities of the English and Spanish number-word systems.

[8]For information on the preparation of U.S. teachers, see Lindquist (1997).

been concerned with teachers' mathematics subject matter knowledge for teaching (Ball, 1988b) "the knowledge that a teacher needs to have or uses in the course of teaching a particular school-level curriculum in mathematics," rather than "the knowledge of advanced topics that a mathematician might have" (Leinhardt et al., 1991, p. 88). The TELT mathematics instruments developed by Deborah Ball for her dissertation research (Ball, 1988b), were designed to probe teachers' knowledge of mathematics in the context of common things that teachers do in the course of teaching. The interview tasks were structured by weaving a particular mathematical idea into a classroom scenario in which that idea played a crucial role. For example, in the question I mentioned earlier for which teachers' responses had been so striking, the mathematics of division by fractions was probed in the context of a familiar task of teaching—generating some sort of representation, real-world context, or diagram for this specific topic. This strategy has been useful for examining teachers' knowledge of the kind needed to teach in ways quite different from straight subject matter questions, like a mathematics test. The recent analysis of Rowan and his colleagues supports this strategy. Their 1997 *Sociology of Education* article describes a model based on data from the National Education Longitudinal Study of 1988. In this model a teacher's correct responses to another TELT item, developed according to the same conceptual framework, had a strong positive effect on student performance.

Another reason to use the TELT instruments is their broad coverage of elementary mathematics. While most of the research on teachers' mathematics knowledge focused on single topics, TELT was dedicated to the whole field of elementary teaching and learning. The TELT instruments for mathematics concerned four common elementary topics: subtraction, multiplication, division by fractions, and the relationship between area and perimeter. The wide distribution of these topics in elementary mathematics promised a relatively complete picture of teachers' subject matter knowledge of this field.

Yet another reason to use TELT instruments was that the TELT project had already constructed a sound database of teacher interviews. Drawing on this database, NCRTE researchers had accomplished substantial and influential research. With the picture of U.S. teachers' mathematics knowledge painted by the TELT study and other research, my comparative study would not only be more efficient but more relevant to mathematics education research in the United States.

Using the TELT questions and data, I studied teachers from the two countries (see Table I.1). The 23 teachers from the United States were considered "better than average." Eleven of them were experienced teachers who were participating in the SummerMath for Teachers Program at Mount

TABLE I.1
The Teachers in the Study[a]

	Teaching Experience	Pseudonym	N
	Beginning	*Begins with Ms. or Mr.*	
U.S.[b]	1 year	Name	12
Chinese	Less than 5 years	Initial[c]	40
	Experienced	*Begins with Tr.*	
U.S.[d]	Average 11 years	Name	11
Chinese	More than 5 years	Initial	24
Chinese with PUFM	Average 18 years	Chinese surname	8

[a]The U.S. teachers' views of their mathematical knowledge and the number of years taught by each experienced U.S. teacher are given in the Appendix.

[b]After completing the New Mexico State Department of Education certification requirements, these teachers took graduate courses in the summers before and after their first year of teaching. The research data used for this study were collected during the second summer.

[c]Although NCRTE gave each U.S. teacher a given name as a pseudonym, I did not do the same for the Chinese teachers. In Chinese there are no words that are considered given names as there are in English. Instead, Chinese parents make up a name for each child. A Chinese name is usually very informative, reflecting social status, education, and political attitude of the family; the epoch and place of birth; parental expectations; status in family tree; etc. So, it seems improper to me to make up names in Chinese for 72 people about whom I know very little except their knowledge of mathematics. In Chinese, surnames are comparatively neutral. However, the number of commonly used surnames is small, so I decided only to use surnames in the pseudonyms of the teachers whom I identified as having PUFM.

[d]These teachers were enrolled in the Educational Leaders in Mathematics program, an additional NSF-funded project in SummerMath. This program is longer and more intense than the regular summer program. Its goal is to prepare excellent classroom mathematics teachers to be in-service leaders in their own school districts or regions. (For more information, see NCRTE, 1988, pp. 79-85.) Teachers participate over two summers and three school years. The data used in this study were collected at the beginning of this program in July and August of 1987.

Holyoke College. They were considered "more dedicated and more confident" mathematically. TELT project members had interviewed them at the beginning of SummerMath. The other 12 were participating in the Graduate Intern Program run jointly by a school district and the University of New Mexico. TELT project members had interviewed them during the summer after their first year of teaching. They were to receive master's degrees at the end of this summer.

Although the U.S. teachers interviewed by TELT were considered above average, I attempted to obtain a more representative picture of Chinese teachers' knowledge. I chose five elementary schools that ranged from very high to very low quality[9] and interviewed all the mathematics teachers in each school, a total of 72 teachers.

Chapters 1 through 4 paint a picture of the teachers' mathematics subject matter knowledge revealed by the interviews. Each of these chapters is devoted to a standard topic in elementary mathematics: subtraction with regrouping, multidigit multiplication, division by fractions, and perimeter and area of a closed figure. Each chapter starts with a TELT interview question designed to present the mathematics through a hypothetical classroom scenario weaving mathematical knowledge with one of four common teaching tasks: teaching a topic, responding to a student's mistake, generating a representation of a certain topic, and responding to a novel idea raised by a student. For example, the division by fractions scenario given earlier asks teachers to represent $1\frac{3}{4} \div \frac{1}{2}$ in a way that would be meaningful for their students.

In each of these data chapters I describe the responses of the U.S. teachers, then those of the Chinese teachers, and conclude with a discussion of the data. Examples depict specific pictures of different understandings of elementary mathematics, including those of profound understanding of fundamental mathematics.

Studies of teacher knowledge abound in examples of insufficient subject matter knowledge in mathematics (Ball, 1988a, 1990; Cohen, 1991; Leinhardt & Smith, 1985; Putnam, 1992; Simon, 1993), but give few examples of the knowledge teachers need to support their teaching, particularly the kind of teaching demanded by recent reforms in mathematics education.[10]

Researchers have created general conceptual frameworks describing what teachers' subject matter knowledge of mathematics should be. Deborah Ball is among those who have done significant work in this area. She identified teachers' understanding of mathematics as "interweaving

---

[9]These schools were chosen from schools with which I was familiar before coming to the United States. Three schools were located in Shanghai, a large metropolitan area. Teaching quality at these schools varied; one was considered very high quality, one moderate, and one very low. The other two schools were in a county of middle socioeconomic and educational status. One was a high-quality county-town school. The other one was a low-quality rural school, with sites at three villages in a mountain area.

[10]Leinhardt and Ball are the two main researchers in this field. For more information on the work of Leinhardt and her colleagues, see Leinhardt and Greeno (1986); Leinhardt and Smith (1985); Leinhardt (1987); Leinhardt, Putnam, and Baxter (1991); and Stein, Baxter, and Leinhardt (1990). For more information on the work of Ball and her colleagues, see Ball (1988a, 1988b, 1988c/1991, 1988d, 1989, 1990), and Schram, Nemser, and Ball (1989).

ideas *of* and *about* the subject (1988b, 1991). By knowledge *of* mathematics she meant substantive knowledge of the subject: comprehension of particular topics, procedures, and concepts, and the relationships among these topics, procedures, and concepts. By knowledge *about* mathematics she meant syntactic knowledge, say, comprehension of the nature and discourse of mathematics. In addition, she proposed three "specific criteria" for teachers' substantive knowledge: correctness, meaning, and connectedness. In spite of expanding and developing conceptions of what teachers' subject matter knowledge of mathematics should be, Ball and other researchers have been limited by their data in the development of a concrete vision of such knowledge.

Chapter 5 begins to address this issue. In it I survey the various understandings depicted in the data chapters, discuss what I mean by fundamental mathematics, and discuss what it means to have a profound understanding of fundamental mathematics (PUFM). Profound understanding of fundamental mathematics goes beyond being able to compute correctly and to give a rationale for computational algorithms. A teacher with profound understanding of fundamental mathematics is not only aware of the conceptual structure and basic attitudes of mathematics inherent in elementary mathematics, but is able to teach them to students. The first-grade teacher who encourages students to find what five apples, five blocks, and five children have in common, and helps them to draw the concept of 5 from these different kinds of items, instills a mathematical attitude—using numbers to describe the world. The third-grade teacher who leads a discussion of why $7 + 2 + 3 = 9 + 3 = 12$ cannot be written as $7 + 2 + 3 = 9 + 12$ is helping students to approach a basic principle of mathematics—equality. The teacher who explains to students that because $247 \times 34 = 247 \times 4 + 247 \times 30$, one should move the second row one column to the left when using the standard multiplication algorithm is illustrating basic principles (regrouping, distributive law, place value) and a general attitude (it is not enough to know how, one must also know why). The students who enthusiastically report the different methods they used to find a number between $\frac{1}{4}$ and $\frac{1}{5}$ are excitedly experiencing the notion that one problem can be solved in multiple ways. In planning the students' lesson and orchestrating the discussion, their teacher has drawn on knowledge of how to teach (pedagogical content knowledge), but in understanding the students' responses and determining the goal of the lesson the teacher must also draw on subject matter knowledge.

Chapter 6 gives the results of a brief investigation of when and how teachers in China attain profound understanding of fundamental mathematics. The factors that support Chinese teachers' development of their mathematical knowledge are not present in the United States. Even worse, conditions in the United States militate against the development of elementary teachers' mathematical knowledge and its organization for teaching. The final chapter suggests changes in teacher preparation, teacher support, and mathematics education research that might allow teachers in the United States to attain profound understanding of fundamental mathematics.

Subtraction With Regrouping: Approaches To Teaching A Topic

Scenario

Let's spend some time thinking about one particular topic that you may work with when you teach, subtraction with regrouping. Look at these questions ($\frac{52}{-25}$, $\frac{91}{-79}$ etc.). How would you approach these problems if you were teaching second grade? What would you say pupils would need to understand or be able to do before they could start learning subtraction with regrouping?

When students first learn about subtraction, they learn to subtract each digit of the subtrahend from its counterpart in the minuend:

$$\begin{array}{r} 75 \\ -12 \\ \hline 63 \end{array}$$

To compute this, they simply subtract 2 from 5 and 1 from 7. However, this straightforward strategy does not work all the time. When a digit at a lower place value of the subtrahend is larger than its counterpart in the minuend (e.g., 22 – 14, 162 – 79), students cannot conduct the computation directly. To subtract 49 from 62, they need to learn subtraction with regrouping:

$$\begin{array}{r} {}^{5}\!\!\not{6}^{1}2 \\ -49 \\ \hline 13 \end{array}$$

Subtraction, with or without regrouping, is a very early topic anyway. Is a deep understanding of mathematics necessary in order to teach it? Does such a simple topic even involve a deep understanding of mathematics? Would a teacher's subject matter knowledge make any difference in his or her teaching, and eventually contribute to students' learning? There is only one answer for all these questions: Yes. Even with such an elementary mathematical topic, the teachers displayed a wide range of subject matter knowledge, which suggests their students had a corresponding range of learning opportunities.

THE U.S. TEACHERS' APPROACH: BORROWING VERSUS REGROUPING

Construing the Topic

When discussing their approach to teaching this topic, the U.S. teachers tended to begin with what they expected their students to learn. Nineteen of the 23 U.S. teachers (83%) focused on the procedure of computing. Ms. Fawn, a young teacher who had just finished her first year of teaching, gave a clear explanation of this procedure:

> Whereas there is a number like 21 – 9, they would need to know that you cannot subtract 9 from 1, then in turn you have to borrow a 10 from the tens space, and when you borrow that 1, it equals 10, you cross out the 2 that you had, you turn it into a 10, you now have 11 – 9, you do that subtraction problem then you have the 1 left and you bring it down.

These teachers expected their students to learn how to carry out two particular steps: taking 1 ten from the tens place, and changing it into 10 ones. They described the "taking" step as *borrowing*. By noting the fact that "1 ten equals 10 ones," they explained the step of "changing." Here we can see the pedagogic insight of these teachers: Once their students can conduct these two key steps correctly, they will very likely be able to conduct the whole computation correctly.

The remaining four teachers, Tr. Bernadette, Tr. Bridget, Ms. Faith, and Ms. Fleur, however, expected their students to learn more than the computational procedure. They also expected their students to learn the mathematical rationale underlying the algorithm. Their approach emphasized two points: the regrouping underlying the "taking" step and the exchange underlying the "change" step. Tr. Bernadette, an experienced teacher, said:

They have to understand what the number 64 means . . . I would show that the number 64, and the number 5 tens and 14 ones, equal the 64. I would try to draw the comparison between that because when you are doing the regrouping it is not so much knowing the facts, it is the regrouping part that has to be understood. The regrouping right from the beginning.

Ms. Faith, another teacher at the end of her first year of teaching, indicated that students should understand that what happens in regrouping is the exchange within place values:

They have to understand how exchanges are done . . . with the base 10 blocks when you reach a certain number—10, in base 10, in the ones column that is the same as, say, 10 ones or 1 ten . . . they have to get used to the idea that exchanges are made within place values and that it does not alter the value of the number. . . . Nothing happens to the actual value, but exchanges can be made.

What teachers expected students to know, however, was related to their own knowledge. The teachers who expected students merely to learn the procedure tended to have a procedural understanding. To explain why one needs to "borrow" 1 ten from the tens place, these teachers said, "You can't subtract a bigger number from a smaller number." They interpreted the "taking" procedure as a matter of one number getting more value from another number, without mentioning that it is a within-number re-arrangement:

You can't subtract a bigger number from a smaller number . . . You must borrow from the next column because the next column has more in it. (Ms. Fay)

But if you do not have enough ones, you go over to your friend here who has plenty. (Tr. Brady)

"We can't subtract a bigger number from a smaller one" is a false mathematical statement. Although second graders are not learning how to subtract a bigger number from a smaller number, it does not mean that in mathematical operations one cannot subtract a bigger number from a smaller number. In fact, young students will learn how to subtract a bigger number from a smaller number in the future. Although this advanced skill is not taught in second grade, a student's future learning should not be confused by emphasizing a misconception.

To treat the two digits of the minuend as two friends, or two neighbors living next door to one another, is mathematically misleading in another way. It suggests that the two digits of the minuend are *two* independent numbers rather than two parts of *one* number.

Another misconception suggested by the "borrowing" explanation is that the value of a number does not have to remain constant in computation, but can be changed arbitrarily—if a number is "too small" and needs to be larger for some reason, it can just "borrow" a certain value from another number.

[In contrast, the teachers who expected students to understand the rationale underlying the procedure showed that they themselves had a conceptual understanding of it.] For example, Tr. Bernadette excluded any of the above misconceptions:

> What do you think, the number, the number 64, can we take a number away, 46? Think about that. Does that make sense? If you have a number in the sixties can you take away a number in the forties? OK then, if that makes sense now, then 4 minus 6, are we able to do that? Here is 4, and I will visually show them 4. Take away 6, 1, 2, 3, 4. Not enough. OK, well what can we do? We can go to the other part of the number and take away what we can use, pull it away from the other side, pull it over to our side to help, to help the 4 become 14.

For Tr. Bernadette, the problem 64 – 46 was not, as suggested in the borrowing explanation, two separate processes of 4 – 6 and then 60 – 40. Rather, it was an entire process of "taking away a number in the forties from a number in the sixties." Moreover, Tr. Bernadette thought that it was not that "you can't subtract a bigger number from a smaller number," rather, that the second graders "are not able to do that." Finally, the solution was that "we go to *the other part of the number*" (italics added), and "pull it over to our side to help." The difference between the phrases "other number" and "the other part of the number" is subtle, but the mathematical meanings conveyed are significantly different.

Instructional Techniques: Manipulatives

Teachers' knowledge of this topic was correlated not only with their expectations about student learning, but also with their teaching approaches. When discussing how they would teach the topic, all except one of the teachers referred to manipulatives. The most popular material was bundles of sticks (popsicle sticks, straws, or other kinds of sticks). Others were beans, money, base 10 blocks, pictures of objects, and games. The teachers said that by providing a "hands-on" experience, manipulatives would facilitate better learning than just "telling"—the way they had been taught.

A good vehicle, however, does not guarantee the right destination. The direction that students go with manipulatives depends largely on the steering of their teacher. The 23 teachers had different ideas that they wanted to get across by using manipulatives. A few teachers simply wanted students to have a "concrete" idea of subtraction. With the problem 52 − 25 for example, Tr. Belinda proposed "to have 52 kids line up and take 25 away and see what happens." Ms. Florence reported that she would use beans as "dinosaur eggs" which might be interesting for students:

> I would have them start some subtraction problems with maybe a picture of 23 things and tell them to cross out 17 and then count how many are left . . . I might have them do some things with dinosaur eggs or something that would sort of have a little more meaning to them. Maybe have them do some concrete subtraction with dinosaur eggs, maybe using beans as the dinosaur eggs or something.

Problems like 52 − 25 or 23 − 17 are problems of subtraction with regrouping. However, what students would learn from activities involving manipulatives like taking 25 students away from 52 or taking 17 dinosaur eggs away from 23 is not related to regrouping at all. On the contrary, the use of manipulatives removes the need to regroup. Tr. Barry, another experienced teacher in the procedurally directed group, mentioned using manipulatives to get across the idea that "you need to borrow something." He said he would bring in quarters and let students change a quarter into two dimes and one nickel:

> A good idea might be coins, using money because kids like money. . . . The idea of taking a quarter even, and changing it to two dimes and a nickel so you can borrow a dime, getting across that idea that you need to borrow something.

There are two difficulties with this idea. First of all, the mathematical problem in Tr. Barry's representation was 25 − 10, which is not a subtraction with regrouping. Second, Tr. Barry confused borrowing in everyday life—borrowing a dime from a person who has a quarter—with the "borrowing" process in subtraction with regrouping—to regroup the minuend by rearranging within place values. In fact, Tr. Barry's manipulative would not convey any conceptual understanding of the mathematical topic he was supposed to teach.

Most of the U.S. teachers said they would use manipulatives to help students understand the fact that 1 ten equals 10 ones. In their view, of the two key steps of the procedure, taking and changing, the latter is harder to carry out. Therefore, many teachers wanted to show this part visually or let students have a hands-on experience of the fact that 1 ten is actually 10 ones:

> I would give students bundles of popsicle sticks that are wrapped in rubber bands, with 10 in each bundle. And then I'd write a problem on the board, and I would have bundles of sticks, as well, and I would first show them *how I would break it apart* (italics added), to go through the problem, and then see if they could manage doing the same thing, and then, maybe, after a lot of practice, maybe giving each pair of students a different subtraction problem, and then they could, you know, demonstrate, or give us their answer. Or, have them make up a problem using sticks, breaking them apart and go through it. (Ms. Fiona)

What Ms. Fiona reported was a typical method used by many teachers. Obviously, it is related more to subtraction with regrouping than the methods described by Ms. Florence and Tr. Barry. However, it still appears procedurally focused. Following the teacher's demonstration, students would practice how to break a bundle of 10 sticks apart and see how it would work in the subtraction problems. Although Ms. Fiona described the computational procedure clearly, she did not describe the underlying mathematical concept at all.

Scholars have noted that in order to promote mathematical understanding, it is necessary that teachers help to make connections between manipulatives and mathematical ideas explicit (Ball, 1992; Driscoll, 1981; Hiebert, 1984; Resnick, 1982; Schram, Nemser, & Ball, 1989). In fact, not every teacher is able to make such a connection. It seems that only the teachers who have a clear understanding of the mathematical ideas included in the topic might be able to play this role. Ms. Faith, the beginning teacher with a conceptual understanding of the topic, said that by "relying heavily upon manipulatives" she would help students to understand "how each one of these bundles is 10, it is 1 ten or 10 ones," to know that "5 tens and 3 ones is the same as 4 tens and 13 ones," to learn "the idea of equivalent exchange," and to talk about "the relationship with the numbers":

> What I would do, from that point, is show how each one of these bundles is 10, it is 1 ten or 10 ones. I would make sure that was clear. And what would happen if we undid this little rubber band and put 10 over here, how many ones would we have? And to get to the next step, I would show that now you have 1, 2, 3, 4 tens and 13 ones and then subtract in that fashion . . . I would say to the child so you are telling me that we have not added anything or subtracted anything to the 53, right? Right . . . Five tens and 3 ones is the same as 4 tens and 13 ones, and what happens when you take 25 from that?

Unlike the other teachers who used manipulatives to illustrate the computational procedure, Ms. Faith used them to represent the mathematical concept underlying the procedure. The only reason that Ms. Faith's use of manipulatives could take her students "further" than that of other teachers was that she understood the mathematical topic in a deeper way than others. Using a similar method, teachers with different views of the subject matter would lead students to different understandings of mathematics.

THE CHINESE TEACHERS' APPROACH: "DECOMPOSING A HIGHER VALUE UNIT"

Some of the Chinese teachers' understandings of the topic overlapped these of the U.S. teachers. The group of Chinese teachers who held a "borrowing" conception had a focus very similar to that of their U.S. counterparts:

> I will tell students that when you compute problems like 53 – 25, you first line up the numbers and start the subtraction from the ones column. Since 3 is not big enough for you to subtract 5 from it, you should borrow a ten from the tens column and turn it into 10 ones. Adding the 10 ones to 3 you get 13. Subtract 5 from 13 you get 8. Put 8 down in the ones column. Then you move to the tens column. Since 5 on the tens column has lent a 10 to the ones column, there are only 4 tens left. You take 20 from 40 and get 20. Put it down in the tens column. (Ms. Y.)

Ms. Y. was in the middle of her second year of teaching. Her explanation was a variant of Ms. Fawn's. She focused on the specific steps of the algorithm and did not show any interest in its rationale. The proportion of Chinese teachers who held such procedurally directed ideas, however, was substantially smaller than that of the U.S. teachers (14% vs. 83%). Figure 1.1 shows the teachers' different understandings of the topic.

Most of the Chinese teachers focused on regrouping. However, in contrast to the U.S. teachers, about 35% of the Chinese teachers described more than one way of regrouping. These teachers not only addressed the rationale for the standard algorithm, but also discussed other ways to solve the problem that were not mentioned by the U.S. teachers. Let's first take a look at the catchphrase of the Chinese teachers: decomposing a unit of higher value.

"*Decomposing a unit of higher value* [*tui yi* *]" is a term in Chinese traditional arithmetic reckoning by the abacus. Each wire on an abacus represents a certain place value. The value of each bead on the abacus depends on the position of the wire that carries the bead. The farther to the left a wire is located on the abacus, the larger the place value it represents. Therefore, the values of beads on left wires are always greater than those on right wires.

---

*The Chinese characters for this and other Chinese words appear in Appendix Fig. A.2.

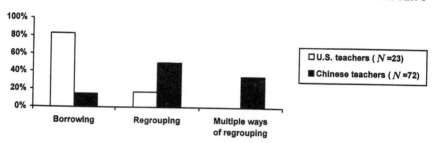

FIG. 1.1. Teachers' understanding of subtraction with regrouping.

When subtracting with regrouping on the abacus, one needs to "take" a bead on a left wire and change it into 10 or powers of 10 beads on a wire to the right. This is called "decomposing a unit of higher value."

Eighty-six percent of the Chinese teachers described the "taking" step in the algorithm as a process of "decomposing a unit of higher value." Instead of saying that "you borrow 1 ten from the tens place," they said that "you decompose 1 ten."[1]

The reason that one cannot compute 21 – 9 directly lies in the form of the number 21. In the decimal system, the numbers are composed according to the rate of 10. Given that a number gets 10 units at a certain place value (e.g., ones place or tens place), the 10 units should be organized into 1 unit of the next higher place value (e.g., tens place or hundreds place). Theoretically, no more than 9 "scattered" (*un*composed) units exist in the decimal number system. Now we want to subtract 9 scattered ones units from 21. The latter only has 1 ones unit. The solution, then, is to decompose a unit of higher value, a 10, and subtract 9 individual ones units from the recomposed 21.

During the interviews, the teachers tended to discuss the idea of "decomposing a higher valued unit" in connection to addition with carrying— "composing a unit of higher value [*jin yi*]." In describing how she would teach this topic, Tr. L., an experienced teacher who teaches first through third grades, said:

> I would start with a problem of straightforward subtraction, like 43 – 22 = ? After they solve it, I would change the problem into 43 – 27 = ? How does the new problem differ from the first one? What will happen when we compute the second problem? They will soon find that 7 is bigger than 3 and we do not have enough ones. Then I would say, OK, today we don't have enough ones. But sometimes we have too many ones. You must remember that last week when we did addition with carrying we had too many

---

[1]This aspect has also been observed by other scholars. Stigler and Perry (1988a) reported that Chinese teachers emphasize "the composition and decomposition of numbers into groups of ten."

ones. What did we do at that time? They will say we composed them into tens. So when we have too many ones, we compose them into tens, what can we do when we don't have enough ones? We may decompose a 10 back to ones. If we decompose a 10 in 40, what will happen? We will have enough ones. In this way I will introduce the concept of "decomposing a unit of higher value into 10 units of a lower value."

Some teachers indicated that the term "decomposing" suggests its relationship with the concept of "composing."

How come there are not enough ones in 53 to subtract 6? Fifty-three is obviously bigger than 6. Where are the ones in 53? Students will say that the other ones in 53 have been composed into tens. Then I will ask them what can we do to get enough ones to subtract 7. I expect that they will come up with the idea of decomposing a 10. Otherwise, I will propose it. (Tr. P.)

In China, as in the United States, the term "borrowing" used to be a traditional metaphor in subtraction.[2] Ms. S., a third-grade teacher in her second year of teaching, explained why she thought that the concept of "decomposing a higher value unit" made more sense than the metaphor of borrowing:

Some of my students may have learned from their parents that you "borrow one unit from the tens and regard it as 10 ones [*jie yi dang shi*]." I will explain to them that we are not borrowing a 10, but decomposing a 10. "Borrowing" can't explain why you can take a 10 to the ones place. But "decomposing" can. When you say decomposing, it implies that the digits in higher places are actually composed of those at lower places. They are exchangeable. The term "borrowing" does not mean the composing–decomposing process at all. "Borrowing one unit and turning it into 10" sounds arbitrary. My students may ask me how can we borrow from the tens? If we borrow something, we should return it later on. How and what are we going to return? Moreover, when borrowing we should get a person who would like to lend to us. How about if the tens place does not want to lend to the ones place? You will not be able to answer these questions that students may ask.

To construe the "taking" step as decomposing a unit of higher value reflects an even more comprehensive understanding than the explanation that draws on "regrouping." Although the rationale of the algorithm is

---

[2]Early versions of modern Chinese arithmetic textbooks used the term "subtraction with borrowing" translated from the West. During the past few decades, the textbooks have used instead "subtraction with decomposing."

regrouping the minuend, regrouping, however, is a mathematical approach that is not confined to subtraction. It is fundamental to a variety of mathematical computations. There are various ways of regrouping. For example, when conducting addition with carrying, the sum at a certain place may be more than 10 units. Then we regroup it by composing the units into one, or more, unit(s) of a higher place value. Again, doing multidigit multiplication we regroup the multiplier into groups of the same place value (e.g., in computing 57×39, one regroups 39 into $30 + 9$ and conducts the computation as $57 \times 30 + 57 \times 9$). In fact, each of the four arithmetical operations applies some kind of regrouping. Therefore, explaining the "taking" procedure in terms of "regrouping" is correct, because regrouping is less relevant to the topic of subtraction than "decomposing a unit of higher value." The former fails to indicate the specific form of regrouping occurring in the subtraction.

Moreover, in using the concept of decomposing a higher value unit, the subtraction procedure is explained in a way that shows its connection with the operation of addition. It not only provides more conceptual support for the learning of subtraction, but reinforces students' previous learning.

The Rate of Composing a Higher Value Unit. With the concept of "decomposing 1 ten into 10 ones," the conceptually directed Chinese teachers had actually explained both the "taking" and the "changing" steps in the algorithm. However, many of them further discussed the "changing" aspect of the procedure. About half of them, like the U.S. teachers in the "regrouping" group, emphasized that 1 ten is composed of 10 ones and can be decomposed into 10 ones. The other half, however, referred to a more basic mathematical idea—the rate for composing a higher value unit [*jin lu*]—as a concept that students need to know before learning regrouping, and that should be reinforced throughout teaching.

These teachers asserted that students should have a clear idea about "the rate for composing a higher value unit" so that they can better understand why a higher value unit is decomposed into 10, or powers of 10, lower value units. This understanding, according to these teachers, will facilitate students' future learning. Tr. Mao, a fifth-grade teacher who had taught elementary mathematics for thirty years, made this comment:

> What is the rate for composing a higher value unit? The answer is simple: 10. Ask students how many ones there are in a 10, or ask them what the rate for composing a higher value unit is, their answers will be the same: 10. However, the effect of the two questions on their learning is not the same. When you remind students that 1 ten equals 10 ones, you tell them the fact that is used in the procedure. And, this somehow confines them to the fact. When you require them to think about the rate for composing a higher value unit, you lead them to a theory that explains the fact as well

as the procedure. Such an understanding is more powerful than a specific fact. It can be applied to more situations. Once they realize that the rate of composing a higher value unit, 10, is the reason why we decompose a ten into 10 ones, they will apply it to other situations. You don't need to remind them again that 1 hundred equals 10 tens when in the future they learn subtraction with three-digit numbers. They will be able to figure it out on their own.

Ms. N. had taught lower grade classes at an elementary school in a rural area for three years. She said:

> To discuss the rate for composing a higher value unit here is not only helpful for them to deal with subtraction of multidigit numbers, but also other more complicated versions of problems. To decompose a ten into 10 ones or to decompose a hundred into 10 tens is to decompose 1 unit into 10 units of the next lower value. But sometimes we need to decompose one unit into one 100, one 1,000 or even more units of lower value. For example, to compute $302 - 17$, we need to decompose one hundred into 100 ones. Again, conducting the subtraction $10,005 - 206$, we need to decompose one unit into ten-thousand lower-valued units. If our students are limited to the fact that 1 ten equals 10 ones, they may feel confused when facing these problems. But if at the beginning of learning, they are exposed to the rate for composing a higher value unit, they may be able to deduce the solutions of these new problems. Or at least they have a key to solving the problems.

Teachers like Tr. Mao and Ms. N. shared a keen foresight in students' learning. Their approach to teaching subtraction with two-digit numbers foresaw the related skills needed for subtraction with multidigit numbers. Multidigit subtraction includes problems of decomposing a hundred into tens, or decomposing a thousand into hundreds. It may also include problems of decomposing a unit not into 10, but into a power of ten lower units, such as decomposing a thousand into 100 tens, etc. This "foresight," obviously, is based on these teachers' thorough understanding of this topic.

When learning addition with carrying, students of these teachers are exposed to the idea of the rate for composing a higher value unit. When teaching subtraction these teachers lead their students to revisit the idea from another perspective—the perspective of decomposing a unit. This visit is certainly an enhancement of their earlier learning of the basic idea.

Compared with the concept of exchanging 1 ten and 10 ones, the idea of the rate for composing a higher value unit reaches a more profound layer of mathematical understanding. Bruner (1960/1977), in *The Process of Education*, said, "The more fundamental or basic is the idea he has learned, almost by definition, the greater will be its breadth of applicability to new problems" (p. 18). Indeed, the rate for composing a higher value unit is a basic idea of the number system. Connecting the "changing" step with the idea of composing a unit in the number system reflects these teachers' insight into the basic ideas underneath the facts, and their capacity to embody a fundamental idea of the discipline in a single fact.

Multiple Ways of Regrouping. The previous discussion has been confined to the standard algorithm for solving subtraction problems. The algorithm has a procedure for regrouping the minuend in a certain way, for example, 53 is regrouped as 40 and 13. Although none of the U.S. teachers went beyond this standard way, some Chinese teachers did. These teachers pointed out that the algorithm is not the only correct way to conduct the subtraction. There are also other ways that will work. The standard way works best in most cases, but not in all cases. Around the principle of "decomposing a higher value unit," the teachers discussed various ways of regrouping:

> Actually there are several ways of grouping and regrouping that we can use to think about the problem 53 − 26. First of all, we can regroup 53 in this way:

$$53$$
$$/ \ \backslash$$
$$40 \quad 13$$

> In this way, we can subtract 6 from 13, 20 from 40, and get 27. This makes sense. However, we also may want to regroup 53 in another way:

$$53$$
$$/ \ | \ \backslash$$
$$40 \ 10 \ 3$$

> We subtract 6 from 10 and get 4, add the 4 to 3 and get 7, subtract 20 from 40, add the 7 to 20 and get 27. The advantage of this second way of regrouping is that it is easier to subtract 6 from 10 than from 13. The addition included in this procedure does not involve carrying so it is simple too. There is still another way to regroup. We may want to regroup the subtrahend 26 as:

$$26$$
$$/ \ | \ \backslash$$
$$20 \ 3 \ 3$$

> We first subtract one 3 from 53 and get 50. Then we subtract the other 3 from 50 and get 47. Finally we subtract 20 from 47 and get 27. (Tr. C)

The teachers referred to three main ways of regrouping. One was the standard way: decompose a unit at a higher value place into units at a lower value place, combine them with the original units at the lower place, and then subtract.

Another way was to regroup the minuend into three parts, rather than two parts, before subtracting. In other words, leave the unit split from the tens place, instead of combining it with the units at the ones place. Then subtract the subtrahend's digit at the ones place from the split unit. Finally, combine the difference with the minuend's units at the ones place. Although the additional part of the number seems to create some complexity, this computation is even easier than in the standard way. One simply needs to subtract the minuend from 10, rather than from a number larger than 10.

Subtraction with the third way of regrouping may be even easier. First, split from the ones place of the subtrahend the same number that is at the ones place of the minuend. Next, subtract the split number from the minuend, which makes the ones place of the minuend zero. Then subtract the rest of the subtrahend from the minuend that is now composed of whole tens.

The second and third ways are actually used frequently in daily life. These approaches are also usually more acceptable to young children because of their limited capacity in mathematics. In addition to describing these alternative ways of regrouping, the Chinese teachers also compared them—describing the situations when these methods may make the computation easier. Some teachers said that the second way of regrouping is used more often when the lowest placed digit of the subtrahend is substantially larger than that of the minuend. For example, $52 - 7$, or $63 - 9$. These problems are easy to solve if one first subtracts 7 from 50 and adds 2 to the first difference 43, or first subtracts 9 from 60 and adds 3 to the first difference 51. For in this kind of problem, the subtrahends are usually close to 10.

The third way is particularly easy when the value of the digits of the minuend and of the subtrahend at the lower place are close to each other. For example, $47 - 8$, or $95 - 7$. It is easy to subtract 7 from 47 and then subtract 1 from the first difference 40, or, to subtract 5 from 95 and then subtract 2 from the first difference 90.

Despite the number of ways to subtract, the standard way is still the best one for most problems, in particular, those that are more complicated. Tr. Li, a recognized teacher, described what happens in her classroom when she teaches subtraction:

> We start with the problems of a two-digit number minus a one-digit number, such as $34 - 6$. I put the problem on the board and ask students to solve the problem on their own, either with bundles of sticks or other learning aids, or even with nothing, just thinking. After a few minutes, they finish. I have them report to the class what they did. They might report a variety of ways. One student might say "$34 - 6$, 4 is not enough to subtract 6. But I

can take off 4 first, get 30. Then I still need to take 2 off. Because $6 = 4 + 2$. I subtract 2 from 30 and get 28. So, my way is $34 - 6 = 34 - 4 - 2 = 30 - 2 = 28$." Another student who worked with sticks might say, "When I saw that I did not have enough separate sticks, I broke 1 bundle. I got 10 sticks and I put 6 of them away. There were 4 left. I put the 4 sticks with the original 4 sticks together and got 8. I still have another two bundles of 10s, putting the sticks left all together I had 28." Some students, usually fewer than the first two kinds, might report, "The two ways they used are fine, but I have another way to solve the problem. We have learned how to compute $14 - 8$, $14 - 9$, why don't we use that knowledge. So, in my mind I computed the problem in a simple way. I regrouped 34 into 20 and 14. Then I subtracted 6 from 14 and got 8. Of course I did not forget the 20, so I got 28." I put all the ways students reported on the board and label them with numbers, the first way, the second way, etc. Then I invite students to compare: Which way do you think is the easiest? Which way do you think is most reasonable? Sometimes they don't agree with each other. Sometimes they don't agree that the standard way I am to teach is the easiest way. Especially for those who are not proficient and comfortable with problems of subtraction within 20,[3] such as $13 - 7$, $15 - 8$, etc., they tend to think that the standard way is more difficult.

Students may actually come upon various ways of regrouping if they try to solve the problems by themselves. This was reported by other teachers as well. To lead a thoughtful discussion once students have expressed all their ideas, a teacher needs a thorough comprehension of this topic. He or she should know these various solutions of the problem, know how and why students came up with them, know the relationship between the non-standard ways and the standard way, and know the single conception underlying all the different ways. Tr. G., a second-grade teacher in her early thirties, concluded, after describing the various ways her students might solve a problem using manipulatives:

> I would lead the class to discover that there is one process underlying all various ways of subtraction: to un-binding one bundle. This would bring them to understand the concept of decomposing a ten, which plays the key role in the computation.

It is important for a teacher to know the standard algorithm as well as alternative versions. It is also important for a teacher to know why a certain method is accepted as the standard one, while the other ways can still play

---

[3]By the term "subtraction within 20," Chinese teachers mean subtraction with regrouping with minuends between 10 and 20, such as $12 - 6$ or $15 - 7$. By the term "addition within 20," Chinese teachers mean addition with carrying where the sum is between 10 and 20, such as $7 + 8$ or $9 + 9$.

a significant role in the approach to the knowledge underlying the algorithm. With a broad perspective in comparing and contrasting the various ways of regrouping in subtraction, the concept underlying the procedure is revealed thoroughly. Supported by a comprehensive understanding of the conception, these teachers were able to show a flexibility in dealing with the nonstandard methods not included in textbooks.

Knowledge Package and Its Key Pieces

Another interesting feature of the Chinese teachers' interviews was that they tended to address connections among mathematical topics. For example, most of the Chinese teachers mentioned the issue of "subtraction within 20" as the conceptual, as well as procedural, "foundation" for subtraction with regrouping.

They said that the idea of regrouping in subtraction, to decompose a higher value unit into lower value units, is developed through learning three levels of problems:

The first level includes problems with minuends between 10 and 20, like $15 - 7$, $16 - 8$, etc. At this level, students learn the concept of decomposing a 10 and the skill derived from it. They learn that by decomposing a 10, they will be able to subtract one-digit numbers from "teen-numbers" with ones digits smaller than the subtrahend. This step is critical because before that, subtraction was straightforward—one subtracted small one-digit numbers from larger one-digit numbers or from "teen-numbers" with ones digits larger than the subtrahend.[4] The conception and the skill learned at this level will support regrouping procedures at the other levels.

The second level includes problems with minuends between 19 and 100, like $53 - 25$, $72 - 48$, etc. At the second level, the ten to be decomposed is combined with several tens. The new idea is to split it from the other tens.

The third level includes problems with larger minuends, that is, minuends with three or more digits. The new idea in the third level is successive decomposition. When the next higher place in a minuend is a zero, one has to decompose a unit from further than the next higher place. The problems involve decomposing more than once, and sometimes even several times. For example, in the problem $203 - 15$, working at the ones place, one needs to decompose 1 hundred into 10 tens, and moreover, decompose 1 ten into 10 ones.

---

[4]The Chinese number-word system may contribute to Chinese teachers' particular attention to composing and decomposing a 10. In Chinese, all the "teen-numbers" have the form "ten, a one-digit number." For example, eleven is "ten-one," twelve is "ten-two," and so on. (Twenty is "two tens," thirty is "three tens," and so on. Twenty-one is called "two tens-one," twenty-two is "two tens-two" and so on.) Therefore, "decomposing the 10" tends to be an obvious solution for the problem of "How one can subtract 5 from ten-two?"

According to the Chinese teachers, the basic idea of subtraction with regrouping develops through the three levels. However, the conceptual "seed" and the basic skill throughout all levels of the problems occur as early as the first level—subtraction within 20.

Here is a very interesting difference in understanding between the two countries. In the United States, problems like "5 + 7 = 12" or "12 − 7 = 5" are considered "basic arithmetic facts" for students simply to memorize. In China, however, they are considered problems of "addition with composing and subtraction with decomposing within 20."[5] The learning of "addition with composing and subtraction with decomposing within 20" is the first occasion when students must draw on previous learning, in this case their skill of composing and decomposing a 10 is significantly embedded.[6]

Tr. Sun was in her late thirties. She had taught for eighteen years at elementary schools in several cities. She even questioned my interview question, thinking that it was not relevant enough:

> The topic you raised was subtraction with regrouping. But the problems you showed me here, which all have minuends bigger than 20 and less than 100, are only one kind of problem in learning this topic. In fact, this is not the crucial kind of problem for learning this topic. It is hard for me to talk about how to teach the topic only drawing on the approach to these problems.

After discussing the three levels of problems for learning subtraction with regrouping, she continued to explain why she thought my question was problematic:

> There are new aspects in each of the other levels of learning, but they are actually developed forms of the basic idea introduced when one learns subtraction within 20. The skill one learns at the first level is applied in all the higher levels of subtraction. Once students have a firm grasp of the conception and skill for solving problems of subtraction within 20, their further learning of subtraction will have a sound foundation to build on. For example, many of them will be ready to figure out how to solve the problems you are showing me here largely on their own, or with a little hint from me or from their peers. So, subtraction within 20 is crucial for learning subtrac-

---

[5]In China, addition with carrying is called "addition with composing" and subtraction with regrouping is called "subtraction with decomposing." "Addition with composing and subtraction with decomposing within 20" is taught during the second semester of first grade.

[6]In Chinese elementary mathematics textbooks, before the section on "addition with composing and subtraction with decomposing within 20" there is a section on the composition of a 10. Until students reach the section of addition and subtraction within 20, however, the mathematical meaning of composing and decomposing a 10 is not clear to them.

tion with decomposing. This is the knowledge that weighs most among the three levels. Addition and subtraction within 20 is where we substantially focus our teaching efforts. So it seems to me impossible to talk about how to approach teaching subtraction with regrouping starting from the problems you presented.

The remarks of Tr. E. were very typical of the Chinese teachers:

Given that my students do not have a firm grasp of problems within 20, how could they solve problems like 37 – 18 = ? and 52 – 37 = ? Whenever they follow the algorithm, they will face problems like 17 – 8 = ? and 12 – 7 = ? Are we going to rely on counting sticks all the time? All the subtraction procedures in problems with bigger numbers, after all, are transformed into subtraction within 10 and within 20. That is why the first level is so important.

While the Chinese teachers talked about the importance of learning subtraction within 20, they did not assume that it was the only thing that one should learn before learning the problems that I showed them. The items they mentioned as necessary for students to learn this topic comprised a substantially longer list that those mentioned by the U.S. teachers. On average, Chinese teachers mentioned 4.7 items, while U.S. teachers mentioned 2.1 items.

Tr. Chen was a teacher in his late fifties. He had taught at a school in a county town for more than thirty years. He had described the three levels of learning regrouping in subtraction and I asked him if he assumed that mathematical learning is a sequence that goes step-by-step. He said:

I would rather say that learning a mathematical topic is never isolated from learning other topics. One supports the other. The connections among the three levels are important, but there are other important ideas included in subtraction as well. For example, the meaning of subtraction, etc. The operation of subtraction with decomposition is the application of several ideas rather than a single one. It is a package, rather than a sequence, of knowledge. The knowledge package I see when I teach the problems you presented is more expansive than the three levels I just discussed. It may also include addition within 20, subtraction of two-digit numbers without decomposing, addition of two-digit numbers with carrying, the idea of the rate for composing a higher valued unit, subtraction with decimals, etc. etc. Some of them support the present knowledge and some of them are supported by the present knowledge.

I asked Tr. Chen further about "knowledge package" and its size and the components. He responded:

There is not a firm, rigid, or single right way to "pack" knowledge. It is all up to one's own viewpoint. Different teachers, in different contexts, or the same teacher with different students, may "pack" knowledge in different ways. But the point is that you should see a knowledge "package" when you are teaching a piece of knowledge. And you should know the role of the present knowledge in that package. You have to know that the knowledge you are teaching is supported by which ideas or procedures, so your teaching is going to rely on, reinforce, and elaborate the learning of these ideas. When you are teaching an important idea that will support other procedures, you should devote particular efforts to make sure that your students understand the idea very well and are able to carry out the procedure proficiently.

Most of the Chinese teachers, like Tr. Chen, talked about a group of pieces of knowledge rather than a single piece of knowledge. The following network sketch was drawn based on their discussion of subtraction with regrouping. As Tr. Chen said, to "pack" knowledge—to see mathematical topics group-by-group rather than piece-by-piece—is a way of thinking. The teachers' opinions of what and how many knowledge pieces should be included in the "package" differed somewhat. What they shared were the principles of how to "pack" the knowledge and what the "key" pieces were. Figure 1.2 illustrates the main ideas the Chinese teachers use when they "pack" the knowledge pieces related to subtraction with regrouping. The rectangle represents the topic I raised in the interview. The ellipses represent the related knowledge pieces. The shaded ellipses represent the key pieces of knowledge. An arrow from one topic to another indicates that the first topic supports the second, thus, according to the teachers, should occur prior to the second in teaching.[7]

At the middle of the figure there is a sequence of four topics: "addition and subtraction within 10," "addition and subtraction within 20," "subtraction with regrouping of numbers between 20 and 100," and "subtraction with regrouping of large numbers." According to the Chinese teachers, the concept and procedure of subtraction with regrouping develops step-by-step through this sequence, from a primary and simple form to a complex and advanced form. The topic of "addition and subtraction within 20" is considered the key piece of the sequence to which the teachers devote most effort in the whole process of teaching subtraction with regrouping. They believe that the concept as well as the computational skill introduced with the topic "addition and subtraction within 20" constitute the basis for later learning of more advanced forms of subtraction with

---

[7]During interviews the Chinese teachers often commented that the relationship is two-way: first learning of a basic topic supports the learning of a more advanced topic, but the learning of a basic topic is also reinforced by the latter. Because the focus of this study is teaching, I did not put two-way arrows in the knowledge package figures.

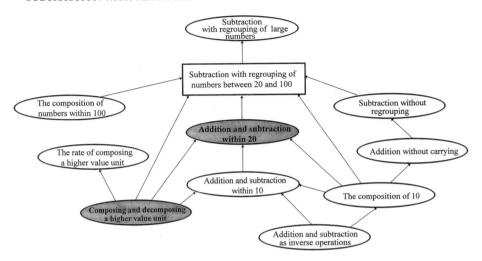

FIG. 1.2. A *knowledge package* for subtraction with regrouping.

regrouping. Therefore, it will provide powerful support to students' later learning of subtraction, both conceptually and procedurally.

Besides the central sequence, the knowledge package also contains a few other topics. Directly connected to one or more links in the sequence, directly or indirectly, these topics encircle the sequence. During their interviews, some teachers discussed a "sub-sequence" of this "circle"—from "the composition of 10" to "addition without carrying" to "subtraction without regrouping." We can imagine that with a change of perspective, for example, if our topic is how to teach subtraction without regrouping, this subsequence might become the central sequence in the teachers' knowledge package. One topic in the "circle," "composing and decomposing a higher value unit," is considered to be another key piece in the package because it is the core concept underlying the subtraction algorithm.

The purpose of a teacher in organizing knowledge in such a package is to promote a solid learning of a certain topic. It is obvious that all the items in the subtraction package are related to the learning of this topic, either supporting, or supported by it. Some items, for example, subtraction without regrouping, are included mainly to provide a procedural support. Other items, for example, composing and decomposing a higher value unit, are considered mainly as a conceptual support. Still others, for example, the concept of inverse operation, were referred to as conceptual support as well as procedural support.[8] Individual teacher's networks varied according to the size and the specific items included. However, the relationships between the items and some core items were common.

---

[8] A few Chinese teachers mentioned that they would remind students to "think about addition when doing subtraction" to facilitate their learning.

Manipulatives and Other Teaching Approaches

Although mentioned less frequently than among the U.S. teachers, manipulatives were also a strategy often reported by the Chinese teachers. What differed was that most Chinese teachers said that they would have a class discussion following the use of manipulatives. In these discussions students may report, display, explain, and argue for their own solutions. Through the discussions, "the explicit construction of links between understood actions on the objects and related symbol procedures" claimed by Hiebert (1984, p. 509) would be established.

Leading a discussion after using manipulatives, however, demands more breadth and depth in a teacher's subject matter knowledge. Through the manipulatives, various issues may be raised by the students. If a teacher does not know very well the different ways to solve a problem, how can he or she lead a discussion about the different ways students report to the class?

Sometimes a class discussion must deal with more intriguing problems that cannot be solved in one lesson. Ms. S. reported a discussion in her class that started at the beginning of the school year and concluded at the end:

> Last fall when my students worked on this kind of problems with manipulatives, we found a problem. We found that the manipulative procedure was not the same as we do it on paper with columns. Say we are doing the problem 35 − 18. With manipulatives we start from the higher value place. We take the 10 in 18 first and then take the 8 out. With columns we start with the ones place, subtracting the 8 first. The way with manipulatives, in fact, is the way we do most subtraction in our everyday life. When we think about how much change we will get after paying 2 Yuans[9] for something that costs 1 Yuan and 63 cents, we first subtract 1 Yuan and then 60 cents and then the 3 cents. But with the standard method in columns we do it the opposite way. We subtract 3 cents first, then 60 cents, and finally 1 Yuan. From the perspective of students' life experience, the way they learn in school seems to be more complex and makes less sense. We tried it on the board to see what would happen if we started from the higher place. We found that starting with the tens place we will first get a difference of 2 at the tens place:
>
> $$\begin{array}{r} 35 \\ -18 \\ \hline 2 \end{array}$$
>
> Then when we worked at the ones place, it happened that we had to change the difference at the tens place that we just got:

---

[9]Yuan is a unit for Chinese money. One Yuan is 100 cents.

$$
\begin{array}{r}
35 \\
-18 \\
\hline
2 \\
17
\end{array}
$$

But if we started from the ones place, this trouble could be avoided. We would get a final difference directly. Yet this explanation only solved half of the problem—why with columns we need to start at the lower place. Students were still not convinced that they had to learn the standard way, since they did not see an obvious advantage in using the standard way. I suggested that we save the puzzle, probably we would come back to the issue sometime later on. At the end of the school year, we worked on subtraction with decomposing larger numbers. I raised the question again for a discussion. My students soon found that with larger numbers, the standard way is much easier with most problems. Then they agreed that the standard way is worthwhile to learn . . .

If Ms. S's knowledge had been limited to how to conduct the computational procedure, it would be hard to imagine that she could lead her students to such a mathematical understanding.

DISCUSSION

Making Connections: Consciously Versus Unconsciously

Certainly a teacher's subject matter knowledge of mathematics differs from that of a non-teaching person. Special features of a teacher's subject matter knowledge are derived from the task of promoting student learning. To facilitate learning, teachers tend to make explicit the connections between and among mathematical topics that remain tacit for non-teachers. In discussions of teaching subtraction with regrouping, teachers tended to make two kinds of connections. First, they tended to connect the topic with one or a few related procedural topics, usually those of lower status such as the procedure of subtraction without grouping and the fact that 1 ten equals 10 ones. Obviously, these are the basis for subtraction with regrouping. Second, the teachers tended to connect the procedure with an explanation. This also reinforces students' learning—by giving a reason for "taking" and "changing," the teacher provides more information to support the learning of the algorithm.

When they were asked what they thought pupils would need to understand or be able to do before learning subtraction with regrouping, all the teachers presented their own "knowledge package" including both kinds of connections. One difference, however, was that some teachers showed a definite consciousness of the connections, while others did not. This difference was associated with significant differences in teachers' subject knowledge. The teachers who tended to "pack" knowledge consciously could describe the elements they included in the package. In addition, they were clearly aware of the structure of the network, and the status of each element in it.

On the other hand, those teachers who packed knowledge unconsciously were vague and uncertain of the elements and the structure of the network. The knowledge packages in their minds were underdeveloped. Indeed, although connecting a topic that is to be taught to related topics may be a spontaneous intention of any teaching person, a fully developed and well-organized knowledge package about a topic is a result of deliberate study.

Models of Teachers' Knowledge of Subtraction: Procedural Understanding Versus Conceptual Understanding

Most knowledge packages that the teachers described during interviews contained the same kinds of elements—those providing procedural support and those providing explanations. Teachers with conceptual understanding and teachers with only procedural understanding, however, had differently organized knowledge packages.

A Model of Procedural Understanding of Subtraction With Regrouping. The knowledge packages of the teachers with only a procedural understanding of subtraction contained few elements. Most of these elements were procedural topics directly related to the algorithm of subtraction with regrouping. A brief explanation was usually included, but it was not a real mathematical explanation. For example, when a teacher told his or her students that the rationale of the algorithm is just like their mother goes to a neighbor to borrow some sugar, this arbitrary explanation doesn't contain any real mathematical meaning. Some teachers explained that because the digit at the ones column of the minuend is smaller than that of the subtrahend, the former should "borrow" a ten from the tens column and turn it into ten ones. This was not a real mathematical explanation either. As discussed earlier in this chapter, some explanations were even mathematically problematic. The understanding of these teachers appeared conceptual, but in fact was too faulty and fragmented to promote students' conceptual learning.

Figure 1.3 illustrates a knowledge package of a teacher with procedural understanding. The top rectangle represents procedural knowledge of the algorithm. The two ellipses represent related procedural topics. The trapezoid underneath the rectangle represents pseudoconceptual understanding.

Eighty-three percent of the U.S. teachers' and 14% of the Chinese teachers' knowledge about subtraction with regrouping fell into this pat-

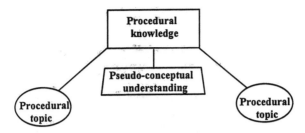

FIG. 1.3.   Procedural understanding of a topic.

tern. Their understanding of the topic contained a few procedural topics and a pseudoconceptual understanding. They made very few connections among mathematical topics and no mathematical arguments were involved in their explanations.

A Model of Conceptual Understanding of Subtraction. The knowledge of the teachers with a conceptual understanding of subtraction was differently considered and organized. Three kinds of mathematical knowledge are included in a fully developed and well-organized knowledge package of conceptual understanding: procedural topics, conceptual topics, and basic principles of the subject. *Procedural topics* are included to support the procedural learning, as well as the conceptual learning of the topic. For example, proficiency in composing and decomposing a 10 is such a procedural topic. Many Chinese teachers referred to it as a significant support for learning the addition and subtraction within 20, procedurally as well as conceptually. *Conceptual topics* are included mainly for a thorough understanding of the rationale underlying the algorithm. However, the teachers believed that conceptual topics also played an important role in promoting procedural proficiency. For instance, some teachers thought that a comprehensive understanding of the concept of regrouping helped students to choose an easy method of subtraction.

Some teachers' knowledge packages included *basic principles,* for example, the concept of *the rate of composing a higher value unit* and the concept of *inverse operations.* The rate of composing a higher value unit is a basic principle of understanding numeral systems. This concept is not only related to students' learning of subtraction with regrouping of large numbers when successive decomposition is necessary, but will also be related to students' later learning of the binary system—a completely different numeral system. Moreover, by revealing a principle of numeral systems, the concept will deepen one's understanding of the whole subject.

The concept of inverse operations is one of the main principles that underlie the relationships among the operations of mathematics. Though this concept is related to the learning of subtraction with its inverse operation, addition, it also supports the learning of other inverse operations in mathematics, such as multiplication and division, squaring and taking square roots, cubing and taking cube roots, raising to the n and taking nth roots, etc.

These two general principles are examples of what Bruner (1960/1977) called "the structure of the subject." Bruner said, "Grasping the structure of a subject is understanding it in a way that permits many other things to be related to it meaningfully. To learn structure, in short, is to learn how things are related" (p. 7).

Indeed, the teachers who tend to include "simple but powerful" basic ideas of the subject in their teaching would not only promote a conceptual learning in the present, but also prepare their students to relate their present learning to future learning.

A well-developed conceptual understanding of a topic also includes understanding of another dimension of structure of the subject—attitudes toward mathematics. Again, Bruner said, "Mastery of fundamental ideas of a field involves not only the grasping of general principles, but the development of an attitude toward learning and inquiry, toward guessing and hunches, toward the possibility of solving problems on one's own" (p. 20).

The teachers did not give any examples of attitudes toward mathematics in their knowledge packages. A few teachers, however, displayed their knowledge of general attitudes. Their discussions of the conventional and alternative ways of regrouping displayed an attitude of the subject—that of approaching a mathematical issue from various perspectives. Teachers' descriptions of encouraging students to present their own ways of doing subtraction with regrouping and leading them to a discussion of these ways showed the teachers' own attitudes toward mathematical inquiry. In addition, the teachers' intention of providing mathematical proof after raising an issue, their confidence and capacity in discussing the topic in a mathematical way, and their intention to promote such discussion among their students are all examples of general attitudes. In fact, though they were not explicitly included as particular items in any teacher's knowledge package, basic attitudes of mathematics have a strong influence on conceptual understanding of mathematics. As I note in later chapters, most of the specific topics mentioned in this chapter do not appear in discussions of multidigit multiplication, division by fractions, and area and perimeter. The attitudes the teachers presented in this chapter, however, will accompany us through the other data chapters and the remainder of the book.

Figure 1.2 displayed how a well-developed knowledge package for subtraction with regrouping was organized. Figure 1.4 illustrates a model of conceptual understanding of a topic. The uppermost gray rectangle represents procedural understanding of the topic. The central gray trapezoid represents conceptual understanding of the topic. It is supported by a few

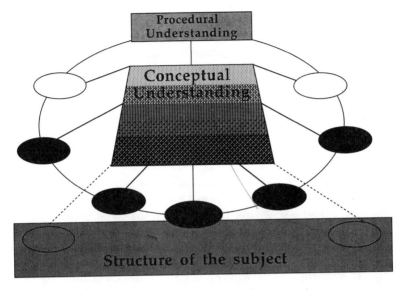

FIG. 1.4. Conceptual understanding of the topic.

procedural topics (white ellipses), regular conceptual topics (light gray ellipses), basic ideas of mathematics (dark ellipses as basic principles and dot-lined ellipses as basic attitudes of mathematics). The bottom rectangle represents the structure of mathematics.

An authentic conceptual understanding is supported by mathematical arguments. For example, the U.S. teachers who held a conceptual understanding elaborated the "regrouping" aspect of the operation. Many Chinese teachers explained that the main idea of the algorithm is "decomposing a higher value unit." Both explanations are based on mathematical arguments and reflected the teachers' conceptual understanding of the procedural topic.

The conceptual understanding of subtraction with regrouping, however, does not have "only one correct answer." There are various versions of conceptual explanations. For example, Teacher A might discuss the concept of *decomposing* a higher value unit. Teacher B might discuss the concept of decomposing relative to the concept of *composing*. Teacher C might introduce the concept of *rate* of composing a higher value unit. Teacher D might present the concept of *regrouping* using the regrouping suggested by the algorithm. Teacher E might present *several ways of regrouping* to elaborate the concept. All these teachers have authentic conceptual understandings. However, the breadth and depth of their understandings are not the same. The shading on the trapezoid is intended to display this feature of conceptual understanding.

We know very little about the quality and features of teachers' conceptual understanding. One thing that may be true is that the mathematical power of a concept depends on its relationship with other concepts. The closer a concept is to the structure of the subject, the more relationships it may have with other topics. If a teacher introduces a basic principle of the subject to explain the rationale of the procedure of subtraction with regrouping, he or she endows that explanation with a strong mathematical power.

Seventeen percent of the U.S. teachers and 86% of the Chinese teachers demonstrated a conceptual understanding of the topic. Among these teachers, the Chinese teachers presented a more sophisticated knowledge than their U.S. counterparts.

Relationship Between Subject Matter Knowledge and Teaching Method: Can the Use of Manipulatives Compensate for Subject Matter Knowledge Deficiency?

Compared with subject matter knowledge, other aspects of teaching usually receive more attention, perhaps because they seem to affect students more directly. In thinking of how to teach a topic a major concern will be what approach to use. During their interviews most teachers said that they would use manipulatives. However, the way in which manipulatives would be used depended on the mathematical understanding of the teacher using them. The 23 U.S. teachers did not have the same learning goals. Some wanted students to have a "concrete" idea of subtraction, some wanted students to understand that 1 ten equals 10 ones, and one wanted students to learn the idea of equivalent exchange. Those who wanted students to have a concrete idea of subtraction described uses of manipulatives that eliminated the need to regroup. Those who wanted students to understand that 1 ten equals 10 ones described a procedure with manipulatives that students could use for computation. The teacher who wanted students to learn the idea of equivalent exchange described how she would use manipulatives to illustrate the concept underlying the procedure. In contrast to the U.S. teachers, the Chinese teachers said they would have a class discussion following the use of manipulatives in which students would report, display, explain, and argue for their solutions.

In activities involving manipulatives, and particularly in the discussions described by the Chinese teachers, students may raise questions that would lead to a deeper understanding of mathematics. The realization of the learning potential of such questions may still largely rely on the quality of the teacher's subject matter knowledge.

SUMMARY

Subtraction with regrouping is so elementary that it is hard to imagine that teachers might not possess adequate knowledge of this topic. However, the interviews in this chapter revealed this was the case for some teachers.

Seventy-seven percent of the U.S. teachers and 14% of the Chinese teachers displayed only procedural knowledge of the topic. Their understanding was limited to surface aspects of the algorithm—the taking and changing steps. This limitation in their knowledge confined their expectations of student learning as well as their capacity to promote conceptual learning in the classroom.

This chapter also revealed different layers of conceptual understanding of subtraction with regrouping. Some U.S. teachers explained the procedure as regrouping the minuend and said that during instruction they would point out the "exchanging" aspect underlying the "changing" step. Most of the Chinese teachers explained the regrouping used in subtraction computations as decomposing a higher value unit. More than one third of the Chinese teachers discussed nonstandard methods of regrouping and relationships between standard and nonstandard methods.

Teachers with different understandings of subtraction with regrouping had different instructional goals. Although many teachers mentioned using manipulatives as a teaching approach, the uses they described, which would largely decide the quality of learning in class, depended on what they thought students should learn. In contrast with U.S. teachers, most Chinese teachers said that after students had used manipulatives they would have a class discussion—a teaching strategy that requires more breadth and depth of a teacher's subject matter knowledge.

Multidigit Number Multiplication: Dealing With Students' Mistakes

Scenario

Some sixth-grade teachers noticed that several of their students were making the same mistake in multiplying large numbers. In trying to calculate

$$\begin{array}{r} 123 \\ \times 645 \\ \hline \end{array}$$

the students seemed to be forgetting to "move the numbers" (i.e., the partial products) over on each line. They were doing this:

$$\begin{array}{r} 123 \\ \times 645 \\ \hline 615 \\ 492 \\ 738 \\ \hline 1845 \end{array}$$

instead of this:

$$\begin{array}{r} 123 \\ \times 645 \\ \hline 615 \\ 492 \\ 738 \\ \hline 79335 \end{array}$$

While these teachers agreed that this was a problem, they did not agree on what to do about it. What would you do if you were teaching sixth grade and you noticed that several of your students were doing this?

All of the teachers in the study considered the students' mistake in multidigit multiplication, lining up the partial products incorrectly, to be a problem of mathematical learning rather than a careless oversight. However, in identifying the problem and explaining how they would help students to correct the mistake, the teachers presented various ideas.

THE U.S. TEACHERS' APPROACH: LINING UP VERSUS SEPARATING INTO THREE PROBLEMS

Reasons for the Mistake

In identifying the students' mistake, sixteen of the U.S. teachers (70%) thought it was a problem of carrying out the lining-up procedure, whereas the other seven teachers (30%) concluded that the students did not understand the rationale of the algorithm. The second group of teachers included Tr. Bridget, Ms. Faith, and Ms. Fleur, who were also conceptually focused with respect to subtraction with regrouping. The same phrase—"the student did not have a good understanding of place value"—was heard frequently during most interviews. By the term "place value," however, the teachers in the two groups meant different things. What the procedurally directed teachers meant by "place value" was only the first half of the phrase, "place"—the location of the numbers. For instance, Tr. Bernice, an experienced teacher, gave this explanation:

> I see no problem with the multiplication by 5. In the next one, if they are multiplying the second one, the second in the tens column they would have to move over to the tens column to start putting their answer. And then they are multiplying the hundreds column so they would move over to the third spot.

When teachers like Tr. Bernice talked about the "tens column" or the "hundreds column," they did not focus on the value of the digits in these columns. They used the terms "tens" and "hundreds" as labels for the columns. In their view, these labels help one to verbalize the algorithm so that it can be carried out correctly. As long as students can identify a column and remember to put the relevant number in it, "they can't go wrong" (Tr. Baird). Other teachers used the numbers in the multiplier to identify columns. When they mentioned a part of the multiplier, 40 or 600, they did not mean its value, but used it to label a column. Addressing what was going on in the students' work, the beginning teacher Ms. Fay said:

> I think maybe they were just having a little bit of confusion about the place value. . . . First of all we are multiplying by one in the ones. Then we move over, and we are not multiplying by 4, we are multiplying by 40. *Therefore, you have to move the place value over. It is just remembering the process of where you put, where you start the column.* (italics added)

At first we might think that Ms. Fay had a conceptual focus. She used the term "place value," and said that the 4 in the tens place was not 4 but 40. However, she did not follow the conceptual direction one might expect from the first part of her statement. Her attention was on *how* to move over the numbers, not *why*. Neither "place value" nor "forty" focused on the value of the partial product. Nor were they used in order to reveal the concept underlying the algorithm. Recognizing 40 and 600 was simply a way of lining up the partial products: When you multiply by 40, remember to line up with 40; when you multiply by 600, remember to line up with 600. It is just a question of memorizing the procedure.

The teachers in the conceptually directed group, however, had a different interpretation of the students' mistake. Using the terms Ms. Fay used, another beginning teacher, Ms. Francesca, said:

> I would say the children, the students don't have an idea of, they really don't understand place value. They don't understand the concept, because they're doing 4 times 3, which is what that looks like, but you have got to take it as 40 times 3 and they are not understanding that. That's why they are not placing things accordingly . . . The problem is that they did not see how each number is established.

Ms. Francesca's concern, as well as that of the other teachers in the conceptually directed group, was not "where to put the answer." Rather, it was that the students did not understand why the reason the partial products are lined up in the way the algorithm requires. Tr. Belle, an experienced teacher, indicated that not understanding the concept underlying the procedure was the reason for the students' mistake:

> I don't think the kids understand what they are multiplying. I think if they really understood the concept, they'd remember where to put the number, they'd know where to put the numbers. I think very often kids are taught steps, you do this step and you do that step and you move in once and you move in twice; they don't really know why they're doing all that. I think if they really understand what they're doing, they'll move it in.

What the teachers believed to be the cause of the students' mistake determined the direction of the learning they intended to promote in dealing with the problem. The procedural or conceptual perspective of a teacher in defining the problem, however, seemed to be largely determined by the teacher's subject matter knowledge of multidigit multiplication.

All teachers in the conceptually directed group, but only two teachers in the procedurally directed group, showed a sound understanding of the rationale underlying the algorithm. The other fourteen procedurally directed teachers (61%) had limited knowledge of the topic. Although they were able to verbalize the "moving over" rule explicitly, none was able to explain it.

During their interviews, some teachers admitted they did not know the rationale. Tr. Beverly, an experienced teacher who considered mathematics her strength, replied that this was an area she had problems with and was not able to not explain "why moving over": "Now see, these are the kinds of things that I have problems [with]. Areas that I have, you know, problems on them."

Other teachers articulated an answer, but failed to provide a real mathematical explanation: "That's hard. . . . Because that's the way you always do it. . . . It is the fact. . . . I mean, this is the way we were told to do it" (Ms. Fay). "Because that's the correct way. That's what I learned. That's correct" (Ms. Fiona). "I can't remember that rule. I can't remember why you do that. It just like when I was taught, you just do it" (Ms. Felice).

Mathematical knowledge is based on both convention and logic. However, convention in this case serves as a shelter for those who don't have a conceptual understanding of a mathematical procedure.

Problematic features of the teachers' subject matter knowledge were also revealed in their opinions on the "hidden" zeros included in the computation. The staircase lining up that confused the erring students is, in fact, an abbreviation of the following:

$$
\begin{array}{r}
123 \\
\times 645 \\
\hline
615 \\
4920 \\
73800 \\
\hline
79335
\end{array}
$$

With the zeros included, the rationale of the algorithm becomes clear: 492 actually stands for 4920, and 738 stands for 73800. However, most teachers in the procedurally directed group did not see this meaning. The fourteen teachers with a procedural understanding of the algorithm had two different opinions about the role of the zeros in computation. Some thought the zeros were disturbing, while others saw them as useful place-holders. All considered the zeros as something alien to the computation. The teachers who held a negative position argued that the zeros are "artificial" and "not belonging in there":

> Well, some of the texts and some teachers use zeros and put a zero as a placekeeper in multiplication of each digit. But I've never liked that because it always seemed like there was, that it was artificial, that there was an addition of something in there that didn't really belong in there, to me, I felt personally uncomfortable with it. (Mr. Felix)

Other teachers thought that the zeros would confuse students more: "I would be afraid that [the zeros] would just confuse them more" (Tr. Bernice). "I do that [put an asterisk as placeholder] to pay attention, and also not to get confused with other zeros" (Tr. Belinda).

On the other hand, the teachers who considered the zeros as useful placeholders in carrying out the algorithm did not see a mathematical meaning in the zeros either. When probed about whether putting a zero after 492 would change the number, they became puzzled and confused:

> Oh, yeah, that's true, and, and for that matter, the reason I say a zero is because, um, it just, it's just helping me keep my place, it has no value in a number. Um, but it helps me keep my place and where, where I should be. (Ms. Fay)

> OK, I would not tell them I was adding zeros, I am putting down zeros as a placeholder. (Tr. Bernadette)

Not being able to explain the puzzle, Ms. Fay and Tr. Bernadette just wanted to avoid facing the challenge. Ms. Francine, however, argued that the number would not be changed because that "plus zero means plus nothing": "I would say well, what is 5 plus nothing? Is it adding anything? It is not."

Ms. Francine's argument suggests that she confused "adding zero" to a number ($5 + 0 = 5$ or $492 + 0 = 492$) with the role of a 0 in a numeral (50 or 4920). The teachers in the procedurally directed group used zero as a reminder for moving over. They did not see it as different from an arbitrary placeholder. Putting a zero is just like putting a meaningless x:

> I'd say that you are not changing them, you're just putting a space there to remind to move over. Or, maybe you could even put an x and not use a zero. Something to remind them to move it over. (Ms. Felice)

The conceptual probes exposed the limitations of these teachers' knowledge. They knew how to carry out the algorithm and how to verbalize the rule, but did not understand why the rule was created.

The seven teachers in the conceptually directed group, however, provided mathematical explanations of the algorithm. They explained that multiplying by 645 was actually multiplying by 5 and by 40 and by 600, so that the partial products were in fact 615, 4920, and 73800. Undergoing the same conceptual probes about the zeros, then, they withstood the trial. When asked if adding the zeros would change the number, some of them argued that it did, and some argued it did not. But both positions made sense. Ms. Fawn argued that if the 492 in the problem is seen as a regular 492, then adding a zero after that is changing the number, and, this changing is necessary:

> I would say yes, it is changing the number. Because 123 × 40 doesn't equal 492, this number isn't the right number, and we are changing the number because we are multiplying by more than 4, we are multiplying by 40.

Ms. Frances, from another point of view, argued that since the 492 is not a regular 492 but one starting from the tens column, adding a zero after it was not changing the number, but revealing its real value:

> Well, I would say that it was this number. Remember what you multiplied. . . . You would put a zero there, and that would be 4920, because they are multiplying by tens.

Still other teachers, like Ms. Faith and Ms. Fleur, indicated that by showing students "what was really going on in the procedure," the problem of whether putting a zero after the 492 would change the number would not be a problem, or, it would have already been solved:

> I'd already showed them that they're not just putting it (the zero) there, that there is a reason because that number is really 4,920, not 492 moved over. (Ms. Fleur)

> OK, I think by this process (separating the problem and listing the partial products) I would show that you are not just adding zeros. (Ms. Faith)

Teaching Strategies

Procedural

The two groups of teachers, who defined the students' mistake in two ways, had different approaches for addressing it. Procedurally directed teachers said they would teach students how to line up partial products correctly. They described three strategies.

Describing the Rule. Verbalizing the rule clearly was mentioned by five teachers, among them Tr. Bernice and Tr. Beverly:

> Well, if the child is aware of place value I might encourage them to put it under the number that they are multiplying as far as their place value. For instance, the 5 is in the ones column, so you would start on the ones column, the 4 is in the tens column, so you might start to move over and put it right underneath the 4 which is in the tens column. And then work in the hundreds column, put the 6. (Tr. Bernice)

> I would go back to place value and tell them that when they are multiplying by the ones, it is lined up with the numbers above. And that when they moved to the next number, which is the tens, it lines up with the tens. And then the next number would be lined up with the hundreds and so forth. (Tr. Beverly)

Tr. Bernice and Tr. Beverly's descriptions are two more examples of how a conceptual term can be used in a procedural way. The term "place value" was not introduced to students as a mathematical concept, but as labels for columns where they should put numbers.

Using Lined Paper. Another strategy to help students to carry out the rule was to use lined paper, or a grid:

> Well, probably the same way I do when I am teaching now. Is start with lined paper. And turn it around and have one number in each line, and get them to see how, this is a 40. Just put one number in each line, in each space. And then have them work it. And get them to see that when they multiply, well, 3 times 5 and that would come under the 5. . . . And then when they multiply 3 times 4, it would come in the same column as the 4. And when you multiply 3 times 6, it is in the same column as the 6. (Tr. Bridget)

The strategy suggested by most teachers was to put a placeholder in the blank spaces. Eight teachers proposed using zero as the placeholder. Of course, because most teachers did not understand the real meaning of the zeros, they did not even think to promote a deeper understanding of the particular format of lining up. They would suggest this to students just so numbers would be correctly positioned:

> What you might want to do to help remember is when you multiply you fill up the first line and then right away put a zero under the ones place so that you know you can't use that spot. (Ms. Francine)

Using Placeholders. Two teachers experienced in teaching this topic reported suggesting that their students use a placeholder other than zero, such as an asterisk. Tr. Barbara said that her way of teaching the topic was to use things that would "hit the student's eye" as placeholders:

> One thing that I would do is, well, I should say I have done, is when first teaching this on a felt board, I always put either an apple, orange or whatever, in the spaces . . . I mean, it could be some weird thing, even pictures of elephants. I do not care what it was. But the children memorized this and they said, oh I remember that [my teacher] said do not put anything there because that is where the orange was or that was the apple . . . Just put something different there so that it will hit their eye.

Tr. Barbara's strategy seemed to be drawn from the experience that putting an apple, an orange, an elephant, or anything unusual in the blank space was successful in teaching students to carry out the procedure correctly. Unfortunately, this does not appear to promote any meaningful mathematical learning. On the contrary, it is consistent with the idea that in learning mathematics it is unnecessary to understand the idea underlying a procedure—one should just follow the teacher's "interesting" but arbitrary commands. Aimed at solving the problem at the procedural level, this lining-up approach was not concerned with conceptual learning at all.

Conceptual

Explaining the Rationale. The teachers in the conceptually directed group, however, focused on disclosing the rationale of the lining-up rule. Two teachers reported that they would explain the rationale to students. Tr. Belle said:

> I'd talk about what the example itself means, what 123 times 645 means . . . We'd talk about 123 and what 123 really is, and what it means: it's 100, a 20, plus 3. And then we'd talk about 645 and what that means. And, then what does it mean to multiply, and I'd take a number like 123 times 5, and what does it mean to multiply 123 times 5; it means 123 five times. And then we'd do the same thing with the next part of the number, 40, and then the 600.

Separating the Problem into Three Subproblems. The other five teachers reported the strategy they would use: separate the problem into "small problems." They would separate the problem of $123 \times 645 =$ into three small problems in which 123 multiplied 5, 40, and 600, respectively. Then they would line up and add the three partial products, 615, 4920, and 73800. None of the five teachers justified this transformation in any way, for instance, with a reference to regrouping or to the distributive law. Three beginning teachers, Ms. Faith, Ms. Fleur, and Ms. Frances, reported the way they would demonstrate this. Taking Ms. Faith as an example:

> The way I would take them through this is I would start by multiplying 5 times 123 and *writing the answer to the side.* And then I would multiply 40 times 123, and then I would put the answer to the right. So that it is a part and they can visualize the zero is there . . . And then I would do 123 times 600. And then I would *add all of these together and I would, at the same time explain that what we are doing here is exactly the same thing.* (italics added)

As Ms. Faith indicated, through her demonstration and explanation students would see what is really going on through the procedure of multidigit multiplication. In particular, they would see that the numbers 492 and 738 in the procedure were actually 4920 and 73900 with the zeros left out. That would explain where the staircase columns came from, why the students are wrong, and also make sense of the lining-up rule. The following is another example:

> I'd review place value and show them that those partial products you can separate them out, just multiply 123 times 5 and then 123 times 40 and then 123 times 600 and then add them all up . . . *That is what you are doing in that problem.* And then I would have the kids put that zero placeholder in. (Ms. Fleur, italics added)

Some teachers in the conceptually directed group, such as Ms. Fleur, referred to procedural strategies as well, particularly to using a zero as a placeholder. No doubt teachers should pay attention to computational procedures. However, for the conceptually directed group procedural strategies were supplementary, while the procedurally directed group used them exclusively.

Relationship Between Subject Matter Knowledge and Teaching Strategy

Limited subject matter knowledge restricts a teacher's capacity to promote conceptual learning among students. Even a strong belief of "teaching mathematics for understanding" cannot remedy or supplement a teacher's disadvantage in subject matter knowledge. A few beginning teachers in the procedurally directed group wanted to "teach for understanding." They intended to involve students in the learning process, and to promote conceptual learning that explained the rationale underlying the procedure. However, because of their own deficiency in subject matter knowledge, their conception of teaching could not be realized. Mr. Felix, Ms. Fiona, Ms. Francine, and Ms. Felice intended to promote conceptual learning. Ironically, with a limited knowledge of the topic, their perspectives in defining the students' mistake and their approach to dealing with the problem were both procedurally focused. In describing his ideas about teaching, Mr. Felix said:

I want them to really think about it and really use manipulatives and things where they can see what they are doing here, why it makes sense to move it over one column. Why do we do that? I think that kids are capable of understanding a lot more rationale for behavior and actions and so on than we really give them credit for a lot of times. I think it is easier for anybody to do something and remember it once they understand why they are doing it that way.

Mr. Felix presented a distinct intention to encourage students to "really think about it." However, his own understanding of "why moving over" was that "you should line up with the digit you are multiplying." He did not understand the real value of the partial products and thought that the potential zeros "didn't really belong in there." Therefore, even though he intended to promote conceptual learning, his teaching strategy was to have students "do their problems sideways on the lined paper, using the lines of the paper to make the vertical columns," so as to make it clear "there is a column to skip"—no conceptual learning was evidenced at all.

Ms. Fiona insisted that her students needed to be able to answer the question "Why do you move those numbers over?" However, like Mr. Felix, she herself did not really understand why one has to move the numbers over. When questioned about this, she was not able to provide a convincing explanation. Then, what she wanted students to "understand" was "that's the correct way, that's what I learned."

Ms. Francine believed that for students' learning, understanding should come before memorization because "then they are set for life." However, when she said she would have students put zeros in so that they could line up the numbers correctly, she herself couldn't provide a mathematically legitimate explanation for why including the zeros makes sense. Consequently, even though Ms. Francine believed that students should understand a procedure before remembering it, her limited subject matter knowledge hindered her ability to help students understand the procedure.

Ms. Felice would use peer teaching. She believed that students could learn more math by working in heterogeneous groups with their peers. Again, however, her own limited subject matter knowledge would hinder her students:

Ms. Felice: OK, I would group them with children that were doing it in the right way . . . And I would have peer teaching going on. Then I would have them going up to the board with children that knew how, where they could be next to people that knew how. And then I would go over it, as they were doing it, I would be doing it, *so they could follow me and follow their peers* (italics added). We would discuss it, and if they still didn't get it, I would sit, and I would also

> sit down with them on a one-to-one basis and try to explain it to them.

Interviewer: Do you have an idea about how you'd like them to specifically explain how to do this problem, 123 by 645?

Ms. Felice: I'd have them explain why they were doing it like that, go through it verbally of, what, their steps. And then I would verbally go with them together and say, "This is how you do it," and we would both work it out together.

Interviewer: Could you tell me what you'd say?

Ms. Felice: I always, when I was young, I'd always put imaginary zeros there. Or I'd even put them in a different color and then, or I would erase them later on. But I'd always put something there to make me remember.

Although she mentioned that she would "have them explain why they were doing it like that," during the whole interview she never elaborated why. Instead, she emphasized *how* to carry out the procedure: to have students follow other students, go through their steps verbally, put imaginary zeros in, etc. She said she would discuss it with students, and explain to them on a one-to-one basis. Nevertheless, when a simulated conversation between Ms. Felice and students was suggested by the interviewer, she was not able to discuss the problem conceptually.

A teacher's subject matter knowledge may not automatically produce promising teaching methods or new teaching conceptions. But without solid support from subject matter knowledge, promising methods or new teaching conceptions cannot be successfully realized.

THE CHINESE TEACHERS' APPROACH: ELABORATING THE CONCEPT OF PLACE VALUE

The general picture of the Chinese teachers' approach to the problem has some aspects in common with that of the U.S. teachers. The Chinese case also showed correlations between the teachers' subject matter knowledge and their teaching strategies for this situation. The teachers who had a conceptual understanding of the topic tended to define the mistake as a problem of lacking conceptual understanding and tended to resolve it by addressing the students' understanding. The teachers who could merely verbalize the algorithm tended to just tell students to memorize the lining up rule.

Where the Chinese teachers differ from their U.S. counterparts is, again, in the size of the "camps" and in the variety of the "conceptually focused camp." Only six of the 72 Chinese teachers (8%) did not show a conceptual

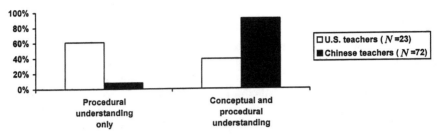

FIG. 2.1. Teachers' knowledge of the algorithm.

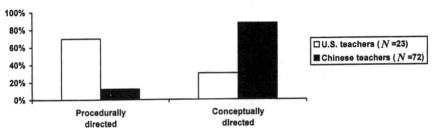

FIG. 2.2. Teaching strategies.

understanding of the algorithm. Nine Chinese teachers, the six who held a procedural understanding and three who understood the rationale, were procedurally focused in defining and dealing with the mistake. Sixty-three Chinese teachers took a conceptually directed position. A comparison between the "camp size" of the U.S. and Chinese teachers is displayed in the following two figures. Figure 2.1 illustrates the teachers' subject matter knowledge of the topic. Figure 2.2 illustrates the pedagogical direction in defining and dealing with the students' mistake.

These two figures illustrate the intriguing aspect discussed earlier: *slightly fewer teachers described a conceptually directed teaching strategy than had a conceptual understanding of the algorithm.*

Interpreting the Mistake

The conceptually directed Chinese teachers fell into three subgroups. One group drew on the distributive law.[1] Another group extended the conception of place value into place value system. The third group explained the problem from both perspectives.

---

[1]Students in China learn an arithmetic version of the commutative law, the associative law, and the distributive law. They are taught that these laws can make mathematical computations easier. For example, with the commutative law and the associative law, one can reorganize problems such as "12 + 29 + 88 + 11 =" into "(12 + 88) + (29 + 11) =" so that the computation becomes easier. With the distributive law, one can reorganize "35 × 102 =" as "35 × 100 + 35 × 2 =" to make the computation easier.

Distributive Law

The first subgroup contained about one third of the conceptually directed Chinese teachers. Their explanations paralleled those of the conceptually directed U.S. teachers. The Chinese teachers' arguments, however, were more mathematically "formal" than those of their U.S. counterparts. More than half of these teachers referred to the distributive law to justify their explanations, while none of the U.S. teachers mentioned this term. Rather than simply separating the problem into three smaller problems, the Chinese teachers tended to present the process of the transformation:

> The problem is that the student did not have a clear idea of why the numbers should be lined up in the way seemingly different from that in addition. The lining up is actually derived through several steps. First, I will put on the board an equation and work it through with students:

$$
\begin{aligned}
123 \times 645 &= 123 \times (600 + 40 + 5) \\
&= 123 \times 600 + 123 \times 40 + 123 \times 5 \\
&= 73800 + 4920 + 615 \\
&= 78720 + 615 \\
&= 79335
\end{aligned}
$$

> What allowed us to transform the problem? The distributive law. Then, I will suggest that the class rewrite the equation into columns:

$$
\begin{array}{r}
123 \\
\times 645 \\
\hline
615 \\
4920 \\
73800 \\
\hline
79335
\end{array}
$$

> I will ask students to observe the zeros in the equation as well as those in the columns. Do they affect the sum? Why yes, and why no? Can the zeros in the equation be eliminated? How about the zeros in the columns? If we erase the zeros in the columns, what will happen? Then I will erase the zeros in the columns and we will get staircase-like columns on the board:

$$
\begin{array}{r}
123 \\
\times 645 \\
\hline
615 \\
492 \\
738 \\
\hline
79335
\end{array}
$$

After such a discussion I believe that the lining-up way in multiplication will make sense to the students, and also, become impressive to them. (Tr. A.)

Tr. A.'s logic was very clear. First, she appealed to the distributive law to justify her transformation. She displayed the process of how the problem can be presented as a composition of three smaller problems. Second, she rewrote the operation into columns so that the three partial products were represented in the form of columns. She asked students to compare the two forms of the operation, in particular, to pay attention to the zeros in them. Then after a discussion of the role of the zeros, she erased the zeros in the columns because they did not make a difference in the computation. Finally, she transformed the original columns into the staircase-like columns in the algorithm. Compared with those of the U.S. teachers, Tr. A's explanation was closer to a conventional mathematical argument. The features of a mathematical argument—justification, rigorous reasoning, and correct expression—were reflected throughout her explanation.

A few other teachers, however, said that explanations like that of Tr. A. were still not rigorous enough. Another important mathematical property, multiplication by 10 and the powers of 10, should be included:

Besides the distributive law, there is another argument that should be included in the explanation. That is the multiplication of a number by 10 or a power of 10. Multiplying by 10 and a power of 10 is a special process that differs from regular multiplication—to get the product, we simply put the number of zeros in the multiplier at the end of the multiplicand. Multiplying a number by 10, we simply put one zero after the number, by 100, we simply put two zeros. This aspect also explains why $123 \times 40 = 4920$. Otherwise, if students treat 123×40 as a regular multiplication problem, they will get columns like these:

$$
\begin{array}{r}
123 \\
\times 40 \\
\hline
000 \\
492 \\
\hline
4920
\end{array}
$$

The problem of why 492 should be "moved over" will still be there. I think that is why in the textbook the multiplication by 10 and powers of 10 goes right before the multiplication by multidigit numbers in general. Since the procedure of multiplying 10 and the powers of 10 is so simple, we tend to ignore it. But in terms of the thoroughness of mathematics, it should be discussed, at least mentioned, in our explanation. (Tr. Chen)

Tr. Chen's concern was not gratuitous. Among the seven U.S. teachers who explained the rationale of the procedure, two showed ignorance of what Chen discussed. Although they separated the problem correctly into subproblems, they did not understand the particular procedures of ×10 and ×100 included in the subproblems ×40 and ×600. Rather, they treated them as regular computations:

Well what if we multiplied it by 10. And I would go through the whole concept. Well, 0 times this is 0. Now we are multiplying it by 40. I would show them that they needed to put the 0 there, because 0 times that was 0. So now we are going to be multiplying by the 4, 4 times this, and show them where the 0, how that holds the place value for them. (Ms. Fawn)

I would say how many 123 times 40 is . . . Go zero times that. Now, 0 times 3 is 0 and 0 times 2 is 0 and 0 times 1 is 0. (Ms. Frances)

In this sense, even though Ms. Fawn and Ms. Frances had a sound understanding of the rationale of the algorithm of multidigit multiplication, they did not show a thorough knowledge of this topic. Their explanations were not explicitly justified. Explanations like those of Tr. A. or Tr. Chen not only convey particular pieces of knowledge but the conventions of the discipline as well.

Transforming the problem 123×645 into $123 \times 600 + 123 \times 40 + 123 \times 5$ was one way to explain the rationale of the lining up procedure. The key elements in this explanation were first to reveal the "invisible" zeros in the procedure, and then to illustrate how they could be omitted.

The Place Value System

Other teachers, however, thought that revealing the zeros and then eliminating them again seemed to be an unnecessary detour. The other two thirds of the conceptually directed Chinese teachers described a more direct way to explain the procedure, which did not require introducing the zeros. Their argument was based on an elaboration of the concept of place value. Instead of saying that the 4 in 645 is *40* and 123×40 is *4920*, these teachers argued that the 4 in 645 is *4 tens* and 123 multiplied by 4 tens is *492 tens*. Then they explained why the 492 should be lined up with the tens place:

Since the 5 in 645 is at the ones place, it stands for 5 ones. $123 \times 5 = 615$, it is 615 ones. So we put the 5 at the ones place. The 4 in 645 is at the tens place, it stands for 4 tens. $123 \times 4 = 492$, it is 492 tens. So we put the 2 at the tens place. The 6 in 645 is at the hundreds place, so it stands for 6 hundreds. $123 \times 6 = 738$, it is 738 hundreds. So we put the 8 at the hundreds place. (Ms. S.)

By renaming 4920 as 492 tens and 73800 as 738 hundreds, the teachers avoided the "detour" of introducing zeros. In addition to the distributive law that provides the general rationale for the algorithm, the teachers drew on their sound understanding of place value system—the concept of basic unit and its place value, and the interdependence among place values.

The concept of the *basic unit* of a number plays a significant role in numeration. We usually use "one" as the basic unit of a number. When we say 123, we mean 123 ones. In daily life it is taken for granted that "one" is the basic unit of a number. However, we can also use other basic units for numerating if necessary, or even if we just want to. For example, using a ten, a hundred, a tenth, or even a two as basic unit, we can say that the number 123 is 12.3 tens, 1.23 hundreds, 1230 tenths, or even 61.5 twos. We can also change the value of a number by simply changing the place value of its basic unit. With the same three digits, 123 tenths, 123 tens, and 123 hundreds have significantly different values. Based on this observation, the teachers claimed that the 40 ones in 645 should actually be treated as 4 tens—a one-digit number—in the algorithm. Similarly, the 600 ones in 645 should be treated as 6 hundreds.

Indeed, in the place value system each place is related to the other. A single place value does not have an independent meaning. Each is defined by its relationship to other members in the system, so that all place values are interdependent. There would not be a "one," unless it were one tenth of a ten, one percent of a hundred, or ten tenths, etc. The place value of a basic unit determines how a number is presented.

Through discussions of the relationship between 4920 ones and 492 tens, students' previous understanding of place value would be developed:

> We need to deepen students' understanding of place value. Their concept of place value used to be pretty straightforward. The basic unit of a number is always the one at the ones place. When they saw a number 492, it always meant 492 ones. When they saw a number 738, it always meant 738 ones. But now, the place value of the basic unit is no longer a unique one. It changes according to the context. For example, the place value of the 4 in the problem is ten. When we multiply 123 by the 4, we regard it as 4 tens. Then tens becomes the place value of the basic unit of the product 492. It is not 492 ones, like it is in the students' work, but 492 tens. That is why we put the 2 at the tens place. The same happens when we multiply 123 by the 6, which we regard it as 6 hundreds. The place value of the basic unit of the product is the hundreds, 738 hundreds. So we should put 8 at the hundreds place. Instead of how many ones, now we are thinking about how many tens, how many hundreds, or even how many thousands, etc. . . . To correct the students' mistake we should expand their understanding of place value, to help them to think of the concept in a flexible way. Yes, it is 492, yet it is not 492 ones, but 492 tens. (Tr. Wang)

Tr. Mao regarded multidigit multiplication as a chance to develop students' concept of place value:

> We have taught students a basic rule that the digits should always be lined up with that of the same place value. Now they may get confused that the rule seems to be violated. But the confusion is actually a moment to elaborate their understanding of place value and the lining up rule. Why does it look like lining up in a different way? Does it violate the lining up rule we learned before? Through exploring these questions our students will see that the value of a number does not only depend on the digits it contains, but also the places where the digits are put. For example, the value of the three-digit numbers in the problem varies if we put them at different places. 123×4 is 492, no problem. But since the 4 is not 4 ones, but 4 tens, the 492 is also not 492 ones, but 492 tens. Or we can say that at this time, the tens place is the ones place of tens. The hundreds place becomes the tens place of tens. So it does for the number 738, it is 738 hundreds. Therefore, it is not that the lining up idea is changed or violated at all. Rather, a complex version is necessary to explain the rule.

These teachers presented clear descriptions of the various aspects of place value. They were also aware that the complicated aspects are derived from simple and elementary aspects of this concept. More important, they showed a sound understanding of the core idea of the concept—"what a digit at a certain place stands for." This core idea penetrates all stages of teaching and learning, and underlies different aspects of this concept. Moreover, the teachers were aware of how the concept of place value is interwoven with various mathematical operations and of the role it plays in these operations. With this awareness, the teachers prepare students to learn an idea even when it is not yet obvious in the content they are currently teaching. Tr. Li discussed how students' concept of place value develops step-by-step:

> Students cannot get a thorough understanding of place value in one day, but step-by-step. At first, when they begin to numerate and recognize two-digit, and then multidigit numbers, they get a preliminary idea of what is meant by a place in math, the names of the places, and limited aspects of the relation between places, like 1 ten equals 10 ones, etc. The most significant idea they learn at this stage is that digits at different places have different meanings, or stand for different values. We start to ask them the question, "What does this digit stand for?" They learn that a 2 at the ones place stands for 2 ones, a 2 at the tens place stands for 2 tens, and a 2 at the hundreds place stands for 2 hundreds, etc. Then when they learn regular addition and subtraction, place value becomes more meaningful for them, for they have to line up the digits with the same place value. After that, when learning

addition with composing and subtraction with decomposing,[2] students learn the aspect of composing and decomposing a unit of higher value. The composition and decomposition of a unit are also important aspects of the concept of place value. Now, in multiplication they encounter new aspects of the concept. They used to deal with several tens. Now they are dealing with several tens of tens, let's say 20 or 35 tens, or, even several hundreds of tens, like in this problem, 492 tens. They used to deal with several hundreds. Now they are dealing with several tens of hundreds, or, even several hundreds of hundreds, like 738 hundreds. To understand this aspect, they should know how to deal with place value in a systematic way.

Place Value and the Distributive Law

Tr. Li was one of the eleven teachers who claimed to expose students to two explanations—that with zeros as well as that without introducing the zeros. These teachers said that a comparison of the two ways will expand students' mathematical perspectives, as well as develop their capacity to make their own mathematical judgments.

Knowledge Package

As in the case of subtraction with regrouping, the Chinese teachers' response to the topic of multidigit multiplication evidenced their concern about the learning of related topics. The pieces in their knowledge packages included topics such as place value, the meaning of multiplication, the rationale of multiplication, multiplication by two-digit numbers, multiplication by one-digit numbers, multiplication by 10, multipliers and powers of 10, the distributive law, and the commutative law. There also were some key pieces in the package that the teachers thought carried more weight. Multiplication by two-digit numbers was the one that most stood out. It was considered the cornerstone that supported the learning of multiplication by three-digit numbers. The issue of "multiplication by two-digit numbers" was raised by the teachers in their first reactions to my question. About 20% of the Chinese teachers commented that their students had not made "such a mistake" in learning multiplication by three-digit numbers, for it should have been solved in the stage of learning multiplication by two-digit numbers:

> This mistake should have happened when students learn multiplication by two-digit numbers. The mathematical concept and the computational skill of multidigit multiplication are both introduced in the learning of the op-

---

[2]In China, addition with carrying is called "addition with composing" and subtraction with regrouping is called "subtraction with decomposing."

eration with two-digit numbers. So the problem may happen and should be solved at that stage. (Ms. F.)

Some teachers indicated that the topic I raised, multiplication by three-digit numbers, was not a key piece in the knowledge package. It is a "branch," not the "root" or the "trunk" of the tree. From the perspective of the Chinese teachers, multiplication by two-digit numbers weighs more than that by three-digit numbers. When analyzing the reason why the students had made such a mistake, some teachers said that "the students did not understand the concept when learning multiplication by two-digit numbers." Tr. Wang reported that multiplication by two-digit numbers was taken seriously and dealt with intensively in her instruction:

> To tell you the truth, I don't teach my students multiplication by three-digit numbers. Rather, I let them learn it by their own. My focus, though, is on multiplication by two-digit numbers. Multiplying by a two-digit number is the difficult point. Students need to learn a new mathematical concept as well as a new computational skill. You have to make sure they get both. I always have them discuss thoroughly, over and over. How to solve the problem? Why do you need to move over? They can have their own idea, they can also open the textbook and read what the book says. The main point is that they have to think over why, and to explain it. I usually have group discussions and class discussions. For the group discussion, I just pair two students who are sitting at the same desk,[3] or four students sitting at two desks one behind the other. The students at the front desk turn back to the other two students. The problem of group discussion is that some slow students may tend to rely on their classmates to explain the issue. So in class discussion I pay particular attention to them. I invite them to talk in the class and make sure that they understand the issue. Then, the class has to practice computation. Sometimes, even though they understand the rationale, they may still forget to move the numbers over because they had got used to lining up straightway when doing addition. So they need to practice. Once they have a clear idea of the concept and get enough practice, they become skillful in doing multiplication by two-digit numbers. I am pretty sure that then they will be able to learn multiplication by multidigit numbers on their own. That is why their understanding of the concept when working on two-digit multiplication is so important.

From the perspective of subject matter knowledge, Chinese teachers seem to have a clearer idea of what is the simplest form of a certain mathematical idea. From the perspective of student learning, they pay particular attention to the first time an idea is introduced to students in

---

[3]In China, two students share a student desk and all the desks are lined up row-by-row facing the teacher's desk.

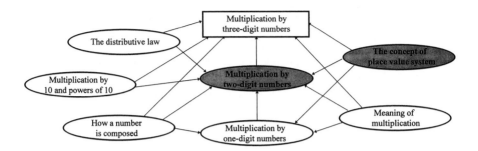

FIG. 2.3. A knowledge package for multiplication by three-digit numbers.

its simplest form. They believe that once students thoroughly understand the idea in its simple form, their later learning of its advanced and complex forms will have a solid basis on which to build. Later learning will also reinforce the idea learned in the simple form. In addition to the topic of multiplication with two-digit numbers, the concept of place value system was another key piece frequently mentioned by the teachers. Figure 2.3 illustrates the knowledge package of multidigit multiplication described by the teachers.

Teaching Strategies

The trend observed among the U.S. teachers was also evident among the Chinese teachers: How a teacher tended to help the students depended heavily on his or her own knowledge of the topic. The few Chinese teachers whose knowledge was limited to procedures reported that they would simply tell the students to remember to move over the columns. Most Chinese teachers, however, presented conceptually based strategies to help the students to understand the problem.

Explanation and Demonstration

Of the 72 teachers, 22 said they would explain a correct way to solve the problem to the students. Twenty teachers reported that they would do a demonstration as well as give an explanation. While these two approaches were also frequently seen among the U.S. teachers, the explanations and demonstrations of most Chinese teachers differed from their U.S. counterparts. For many U.S. teachers, explanation meant verbalizing the procedure of the algorithm and demonstration meant displaying the steps of computation. Most Chinese teachers, however, intended to illustrate the rationale of the algorithm by their explanations and demonstrations. The explanations were usually established on solid, conceptual grounds. The following is a typical example of an explanation by the Chinese teachers:

> I will tell the students that since the 4 in 645 represents 4 tens, therefore, 123 multiplied by the 4 equals 492 tens. 492 tens, where should the 2 be lined up? Of course with the tens place. Again, the 6 represents 6 hundreds, so that 123 times the 6 equals 738 hundreds. Where should the 7 be lined up? The hundreds place. The digits at the ones place of these three numbers (615, 492, and 738) actually represent three different values. One represents ones, one represents tens, and the other one represents hundreds. Your problem is that you didn't notice the difference and saw them all as representing ones. (Ms. G.)

Through her explanation, Ms. G. conveyed the concept included in the rationale underlying the procedure, as well as the vein of a mathematical argument. Most teachers who claimed to explain the algorithm by transforming the problem according to the distributive law reported they would demonstrate the transformation on the board. During the interviews, the teachers tended to display each step in the procedure as they would when teaching so that students could see the entire logical flow of the computation.

Students Find the Problem

Another 29 Chinese teachers intended to engage students in finding the problem on their own. Ms. Felice, a U.S. teacher, also expressed a similar intention, hoping that through peer teaching the erring students would find the problem on their own. However, because Ms. Felice's own knowledge of the topic was limited to the procedure, the problem she intended to lead the students to find was also at the procedural level. Many of the Chinese teachers, on the other hand, intended to lead students to an understanding of the rationale of the procedure as well as the associated mathematical concepts. During their interviews they reported several strategies they would like to use to engage and guide students to find the problem.

Observe, Examine, Analyze, and Discuss. Some Chinese teachers reported that they would expect students to find the problem through observation. They said they would put the error on the board and invite students to closely examine it, and then engage the class in discussing their findings:

> We will open our "little mathematical hospital." The students will be the "doctors" and the problem will be the "patient." The "doctors" are to diagnose if the "patient" is ill or not. Let them make the judgment. If it is "ill," what kind of illness? What is the cause of the illness? As a teacher, my responsibility is to lead them to find out *why* it is wrong . . . It is a problem

of place value, say, digits at different places express different meanings. (Tr. Sun)

I will put the problematic one on the blackboard and invite my students to observe carefully and see if it is correct or not. Then I will let them articulate where the problem is, why it is incorrect. Why should the 492 and 738 be lined up differently? What do these numbers now stand for, and what should they actually stand for? Then I will have a student, maybe the one who had made the mistake, come up to the board to correct it. After such a review of the rationale, we will summarize the rule. Finally, I give a few more problems and ask them to describe the procedure and explain it. (Ms. L.)

In contrast with Ms. Felice, the Chinese teachers did not stop at the stage when students saw the apparent problem. A discussion would follow to explore the underlying concept. What students learned through the discussion, then, was not merely to correct the flawed procedure, but also the underlying misconception.

Asking Questions to Set the Direction. Instead of directly displaying the problem, some teachers would set a direction before students observed the problem. Some teachers would use certain questions to guide students to uncover the problem. The questions would remind students of the concepts included in the explanation of the procedure, such as how a number is formed, place value of the digits in the multiplier, etc. These questions would usually be asked of the very students who made the mistake:

First of all, I will ask the students to tell me how the number 645 is formed. They will come up with 6 hundreds, 4 tens, and 5 ones. Or, they may say that it is 600 and 40 and 5. Then I will ask them to think about what 123×5 represents? What does 123×4 represent? What does 123×6 represent? So, were you correct in solving this problem? Why is it wrong? Go to correct it. (Tr. A.)

I will ask the students what the 4 in 645 stands for, they will say 4 tens, then I will ask them to estimate how many are 123 times 4 tens, can it be 492? Then I will ask them to go to do the rest of thinking, and come back to me with their work corrected and explain to me the problem they would have found. (Ms. F.)

I have taught more than twenty years of elementary math but never have met such a mistake. Given that it happens in my fifth grade students, I may want to say, OK, since you have learned the distributive law, who can rewrite the problem 123×645 according to the law, separating the multiplier according to place values? Once they rewrite it, they will soon see where the problem is. (Tr. Mao)

By asking the questions, the teachers gave students a hint of where the problem might be and let them find it on their own. Guided by these questions, students' attention would not be drawn to the surface aspects of the problem, but would go directly to its essence.

Diagnostic Exercises. To design relevant exercises to help students to "diagnose" the problem was another strategy the teachers used to set a direction to help students to find the problem. These exercises were also intended to raise the conceptual issues underlying the procedure:

> I think the reason that the students made such a mistake is that they do not understand the meaning each digit expresses when it is at each place. I will first have them solve some problems like these:
>
> $$123 = (\ ) \times 100 + (\ ) \times 10 + (\ ) \times 1$$
> $$645 = (\ ) \times 100 + (\ ) \times 10 + (\ ) \times 1$$
>
> Then, I will ask them to think if they were right or not, and why. (Tr. H.)

> First, I will ask them to do two problems:
>
> $$42 \times 40 = (\ ) \text{ tens}$$
> $$42 \times 400 = (\ ) \text{ hundreds}$$
>
> These problems will lead them to realize the rationale of multiplication. Second, I will ask students sharing the same desk to tell each other what 123 times each digit in 645 means, and in what places the products should be put. Then I will have them discuss if there is an error here, analyze the error drawing on the rationale of computation, and explain what is the correct way. (Ms. A.)

> Given that my students did it in this way, I will first have three students come up to the board, each computing one of the three problems: 123 × 5 = ?, 123 × 40 = ?, and 123 × 600 = ?, then ask the class to compare the results on the board with the problematic one, ask them, what do they find. In this way, they will soon discover the problem and how it was caused. (Tr. C.)

The teachers who would use "diagnostic exercises" indicated a direction to students, as did the teachers who would use questions, yet they left the task of approaching the problem to the students.

Check the Rule. Some Chinese teachers would have students review the procedure before discussing the rationale. These teachers said that they would like to have students check the rule to find the problem through comparing the error to the rule:

If my students have such a error, I will ask them to open the textbook and check with the procedure on their own. Then encourage them to think about why this is the rule, why the rule stipulates that the partial products should be lined up in this way. After that I will display the error on the blackboard. What do you think about these students' work? They will immediately find that it is wrong. I will ask them to say why it is wrong, how to correct it. (Mr. B.)

Even though they began from the procedural aspect of the rule, these teachers did not ignore this conceptual aspect. Based on their own conceptual understanding of the topic, they managed to achieve their intention of helping students "to remember the rule based on understanding it."

The teachers who proposed different strategies to engage students in finding the problem shared some common characteristics. Most teachers expected students to find the problem on their own, and explain it at the conceptual level. Some teachers asked questions or designed diagnostic problems intended to set a conceptual direction. Other teachers attempted to let students find the procedural problem first, and then approach the underlying concept. In either case, the rationale of the procedure was the focus.

Mathematical discourse, which is constituted by investigating, challenging, and defending propositions, includes a discourse within oneself as well. This convention of mathematics is reflected in these teachers' strategies—to engage students in finding the problem and explaining it on their own.

Tr. Chen's Approach

In addition to the above approaches to deal with the students' mistake, Tr. Chen proposed his own way which was also impressive. He suggested using "nonconventional" ways of solving the problem to help students to understand the procedure. He said that he would inspire students to see that there is actually more than one correct way to line up the columns. He proposed that there may be five ways other than the conventional way of lining up:

$$
\begin{array}{ccccc}
123 & 123 & 123 & 123 & 123 \\
\times 645 & \times 645 & \times 645 & \times 645 & \times 645 \\
\hline
615 & 492 & 492 & 738 & 738 \\
738 & 615 & 738 & 492 & 615 \\
492 & 738 & 615 & 615 & 492 \\
\hline
79335 & 79335 & 79335 & 79335 & 79335
\end{array}
$$

Tr. Chen believed that guiding students to find these nonconventional ways would stimulate their understanding of the algorithm so that they would use it in a more flexible way.

DISCUSSION

"Conceptual Understanding": Not a Simple Story

For the topic of multidigit multiplication, the teachers' responses were distributed in a pattern similar to that of the previous chapter. Again, all the teachers reached the procedural level—they all knew how to *do* the multiplication correctly. However, 61% of the U.S. teachers and 8% of the Chinese teachers were not able to provide authentic conceptual explanations for the procedure. Ironically, they tended to use the term "place value" procedurally—to identify or label the columns for lining up the numbers.

The remaining 39% of the U.S. teachers and 92% of the Chinese teachers provided conceptual explanations for the algorithm of multidigit multiplication. Their explanations, however, were of various forms. The seven U.S. teachers said that the problem 123×645 is actually constituted of the three subproblems 123×600, 123×40, and 123×5, but didn't give explicit justifications for this statement. Therefore, the partial products were actually not 615, 492, and 738, but 615, 4920, and 73800. The Chinese teachers, however, tended to indicate that the concept underlying the algorithm is the distributive law. They not only frequently mentioned the term distributive law, but applied it to display and justify the transition:

$$123 \times 645 = 123 \times (600 + 40 + 5)$$
$$= 123 \times 600 + 123 \times 40 + 123 \times 5$$
$$= 73800 + 4920 + 615$$
$$= 79335$$

To explain why the zeros at the end of the partial products are omitted in the algorithm, the Chinese teachers elaborated the concept of place value system. They said that from the perspective of place value system, the three partial products can also be regarded as 615 ones, 492 tens, and 738 hundreds. Moreover, a few Chinese teachers included multiplication by 10 and the powers of 10 in their discussion to make the explanation more rigorous.

Although all the explanations mentioned above make sense of the computational procedure of multidigit multiplication, one can easily see conceptual differences among them. How are we going to understand these differences among teachers' conceptual understanding of a mathematical topic? Will these differences in teachers' understanding make a difference in students' learning? In 1998 there is much talk in mathematics education about conceptual understanding, in contrast to procedural understanding.

Yet little attention has been paid to more specific features of an adequate conceptual understanding, for example its thoroughness.

Knowledge Package and Its Key Pieces

The interview questions of the topic of the previous chapter, subtraction with regrouping, included a probe of related topics. The interviews discussed in this chapter did not include a similar probe. Without this probe, the U.S. teachers limited their discussions to the topic of multidigit multiplication. Most Chinese teachers, however, tended to mention a few related topics spontaneously. As with the topic of subtraction with regrouping, the knowledge package the Chinese teachers mentioned included a linear sequence of mathematical topics: multiplication by one-digit numbers, by two-digit numbers, and by multidigit numbers. The sequence of multiplication operations was supported by a few other topics, such as the concept of place value system, the distributive law, multiplication by 10 and powers of 10, etc.

Interestingly, as in the case of subtraction with regrouping, the Chinese teachers thought that the interview topic was not the key piece of the package. The multiplication of two-digit numbers, where the rationale for the topic is introduced for the first time, was considered as the key piece that deserves most effort from teachers, as well as from students. For the topic of subtraction with regrouping, the key piece was subtraction within 20. Chinese teachers tend to pay significant attention to the occasion when a concept is first introduced. They intend to establish a solid basis for later learning. According to them, the more solid the first and primary learning is, the more support it will be able to contribute to later learning of the concept in its more complex form. This support, in turn, will enhance the early learning of the primary form.

The Chinese teachers' perspective about the key piece in a knowledge sequence brings to mind a teaching approach in the United States. In the spiral curriculum, mathematical concepts reoccur throughout the school years. How does each appearance of a concept in the curriculum contribute to mathematical learning? How should successive appearances of a concept be related in order to produce consistent learning? None of the U.S. teachers in this study nor any of those I have met in other schools in the U.S. presented a concern regarding how a concept should be taught at each occasion when it appears. Given that teachers are not aware that there is a relationship among these occasions, and given that they don't know what the relationship should be, the mathematical teaching of the topic will be splintered and inconsistent.

Relationship Between Subject Matter Knowledge and Beliefs: Is the Intent of Teaching for Understanding Enough?

The data in this chapter reveal an interesting aspect of the relationship between teachers' subject matter knowledge and the learning they intend to promote through their teaching. Among the teachers of both countries, the percentage of those who showed a conceptual understanding of the topic was slightly higher than those who took a conceptual direction in helping the students to correct the mistake. On one hand, none of those teachers whose knowledge was procedural described a conceptually directed teaching strategy. On the other hand, a few teachers who held a conceptual understanding of the topic would take a procedural direction in teaching—they did not expect their students' learning to reach as far as theirs. Not a single teacher was observed who would promote learning beyond his or her own mathematical knowledge.

SUMMARY

Most teachers considered the students' mistake in multidigit multiplication, lining up the partial products incorrectly, as an indication of a problem in the students' mathematical understanding rather than as a careless error. However, the teachers had different views of the problem: Some considered it a problem of knowing the procedure; others thought it a problem of conceptual understanding. The teachers' perspectives on the problem paralleled their subject matter knowledge of the topic. Most of the U.S. teachers' knowledge of the topic was procedural. In contrast, most of the Chinese teachers displayed a conceptual understanding.

The teachers described instructional strategies to address the mistake. The focus of these strategies did not completely parallel the teachers' knowledge: Slightly fewer teachers described conceptually directed strategies than had a conceptual understanding of the topic. The Chinese teachers' explanations of the algorithm and their strategies for dealing with the mistake were well supported by their knowledge of the basic ideas of the discipline and of topics related to multidigit multiplication.

Generating Representations: Division By Fractions

Scenario

People seem to have different approaches to solving problems involving division with fractions. How do you solve a problem like this one?

$$1\frac{3}{4} \div \frac{1}{2} =$$

Imagine that you are teaching division with fractions. To make this meaningful for kids, something that many teachers try to do is relate mathematics to other things. Sometimes they try to come up with real-world situations or story-problems to show the application of some particular piece of content. What would you say would be a good story or model for $1\frac{3}{4} \div \frac{1}{2}$?

This time the teachers are required to accomplish two tasks: to compute $1\frac{3}{4} \div \frac{1}{2}$, and to represent meaning for the resulting mathematical sentence. The mathematical topics discussed in the previous two chapters are relatively elementary, but division by fractions is an advanced topic in arithmetic. Division is the most complicated of the four operations. Fractions are often considered the most complex numbers in elementary school mathematics. Division by fractions, the most complicated operation with the most complex numbers, can be considered as a topic at the summit of arithmetic.

THE U.S. TEACHERS' PERFORMANCE ON CALCULATION

The weaknesses of the U.S. teachers' subject matter knowledge were more noticeable in this advanced topic than in the two topics discussed earlier. Their discussions of whole number subtraction and multiplication had all displayed correct procedural knowledge, but even this was lacking in many of their discussions of division by fractions. Of the 23 U.S. teachers, 21 tried to calculate $1\frac{3}{4} \div \frac{1}{2}$. Only nine (43%) completed their computations and reached the correct answer. For example, Mr. Felix, a beginning teacher, gave this explanation:

> I would convert the $1\frac{3}{4}$ to fourths, which would give me $\frac{7}{4}$. Then to divide by $\frac{1}{2}$, I would invert $\frac{1}{2}$ and multiply. So, I would multiply $\frac{7}{4}$ by 2 and I would get $\frac{14}{4}$, and then I would divide 14 by 4 to get it back to my mixed number, $3\frac{2}{4}$ or then I would reduce that into $3\frac{1}{2}$.

For teachers like Mr. Felix, the computational procedure was clear and explicit: Convert the mixed number into an improper fraction, invert the divisor and multiply it by the dividend, reduce the product, $\frac{14}{4}$, and change it to a proper fraction, $3\frac{1}{2}$.

Two out of the 21 teachers (9%) correctly conducted the algorithm, but did not reduce their answer or turn it into a proper fraction. Their answer, $\frac{14}{4}$, was an incomplete one.

Four out of 21 teachers (19%) were either unclear about the procedure, or obviously unsure of what they were doing:

> The first thing you'd *have to do* is change them into sync. Well, you're supposed to multiply that and add that. So that's 4, plus it's $\frac{7}{4}$, and then you *have to make it the same*. Divided by $\frac{2}{4}$. Right? And then you just cross multiply like that. You get $\frac{28}{8}$? (Ms. Felice, italics added)

To change the dividend and divisor into like fractions and then perform the division is an alternative to the standard division by fractions algorithm. For example, by converting a problem of dividing $1\frac{3}{4}$ pizzas by $\frac{1}{2}$ pizza into dividing $\frac{7}{4}$ pizzas by $\frac{2}{4}$ pizza, one divides 7 quarters of pizza by 2 quarters of pizza. This "common denominator" approach converts division by a fraction into division by a whole number (7 pieces divided by 2 pieces). Ms. Felice's difficulty, however, was that she did not present a sound knowledge of the standard algorithm yet thought that you "have to" change the numbers into like fractions. She might have seen the common denominator approach before, but seemed to understand neither its rationale nor the relationship between the alternative approach and the standard algorithm.

She might also have confused the standard algorithm for division by fractions with that for adding fractions, which requires a common denominator. In any case she was not confident during computation. Moreover, she did not reduce the quotient and convert it into a proper fraction.

Tr. Blanche, an experienced teacher, was extremely unsure about what she remembered of the algorithm:

> It seems that you need to, you cannot work with a fraction and a mixed number, so the first thing I would do, I turn this into some number of fourths. So you would have $\frac{7}{4}$ divided by $\frac{1}{2}$. Is this, is being the same as multiplying it by 2 as my understanding. So that the steps that I would take, now I am starting to wonder if I am doing this right. Would be that I have $\frac{7}{4}$ that I have converted this divided by $\frac{1}{2}$ is the same as doing $\frac{7}{4}$ times 2, I think. So that gives you 14, let me see if this . . . wait a second—Now let me think through this process . . . I cannot tell if it makes sense because I cannot remember . . . And for some reason I thought that that was exactly the formula that I remembered. But I'm not sure if it is logical.

Tr. Blanche started to wonder if she was doing this right at the beginning of the computation and ended up with "I'm not sure if it is logical."

While the memories of teachers like Ms. Felice and Tr. Blanche were confused or unsure, those of five others (24%) were even more fragmentary. They recalled vaguely that "you should flip it over and multiply" (Ms. Fawn), but were not sure what "it" meant:

> For some reason it is in the back of my mind that you invert one of the fractions. Like, you know, either $\frac{7}{4}$ becomes $\frac{4}{7}$, or $\frac{1}{2}$ becomes $\frac{2}{1}$. I am not sure. (Ms. Frances)

These five teachers' incomplete memories of the algorithm impeded their calculations. Tr. Bernadette, the experienced teacher who was very articulate about the rationale for subtraction with regrouping, tried a completely incorrect strategy:

> I would try to find, oh goodness, the lowest common denominator. I think I would change them both. Lowest common denominator, I think that is what it is called. I do not know how I am going to get the answer. Whoops. Sorry.

Like Ms. Felice, Tr. Bernadette first mentioned finding a common denominator. Her understanding was more fragmentary than Ms. Felice's, however. She did not know what the next step would be.

TABLE 3.1
The U.S. Teachers' Computation of $1\frac{3}{4} \div \frac{1}{2}$ ($N = 21$)

Response	%	N
Correct algorithm, complete answer	43	9
Correct algorithm, incomplete answer	9	2
Incomplete algorithm, unsure, incomplete answer	19	4
Fragmentary memory of the algorithm, no answer	24	5
Wrong strategy, no answer	5	1

The remaining teacher simply admitted that she did not know how to do the calculation after taking a look at it. Table 3.1 summarizes the 21[1] U.S. teachers' performance in computing $1\frac{3}{4} \div \frac{1}{2}$.

THE CHINESE TEACHERS' PERFORMANCE ON CALCULATION

All of the 72 Chinese teachers computed correct and complete answers to the problem. Instead of "invert and multiply," most of the Chinese teachers used the phrase "dividing by a number is equivalent to multiplying by its reciprocal":

Dividing by a number is equivalent to multiplying by its reciprocal. So, to divide $1\frac{3}{4}$ by $\frac{1}{2}$ we multiply $1\frac{3}{4}$ by the reciprocal of $\frac{1}{2}$, $\frac{2}{1}$, and we get $3\frac{1}{2}$. (Ms. M.)

The reciprocal of a fraction with numerator 1 is the number in its denominator. The reciprocal of $\frac{1}{2}$ is 2. We know that dividing by a fraction can be converted to multiplying by its reciprocal. Therefore, dividing $1\frac{3}{4}$ by $\frac{1}{2}$ is equivalent to multiplying $1\frac{3}{4}$ by 2. The result will be $3\frac{1}{2}$. (Tr. O.)

Some teachers mentioned the connection between division by fractions and division by whole numbers. Tr. Q. explained why the rule that "dividing by a number is equivalent to multiplying by its reciprocal" is not taught to students until the concept of fraction is introduced:[2]

Dividing by a number is equivalent to multiplying by its reciprocal, as long as the number is not zero. Even though this concept is introduced when

---

[1]As indicated earlier, 21 of the 23 teachers attempted the calculation.

[2]According to the current national mathematics curriculum of China, the concept of fractions is not taught until Grade 4. Division by fractions is taught in Grade 6, the last year of elementary education.

learning how to divide by fractions, it applies to dividing by whole numbers as well. Dividing by 5 is equivalent to multiplying by $\frac{1}{5}$. But the reciprocal of any whole number is a fraction—a fraction with 1 as its numerator and the original number as its denominator—so we have to wait until fractions to introduce this concept.

"Dividing by a number is equivalent to multiplying by its reciprocal" is used in Chinese textbooks to justify the division by fractions algorithm. This is consistent with the Chinese elementary mathematics curriculum's emphasis on relationships between operations and their inverses. Most teachers did not refer to the property to remind themselves of the computational procedure. They referred to it to justify their calculations.

Making Sense of the Algorithm

The original interview question only asked teachers to calculate the division problem. During interviews, however, some Chinese teachers tended to elaborate how the algorithm would make sense. Then after interviewing two thirds of the Chinese teachers, I started to ask teachers if the algorithm made sense to them. Most fourth- and fifth-grade teachers were able to say more than "dividing by a number is equivalent to multiplying by its reciprocal." They elaborated their understanding from various perspectives. Some teachers argued that the rationale for the computational procedure can be proved by converting the operation with fractions into one with whole numbers:

We can use the knowledge that students have learned to prove the rule that dividing by a fraction is equivalent to multiplying by its reciprocal. They have learned the commutative law. They have learned how to take off and add parentheses. They have also learned that a fraction is equivalent to the result of a division, for example, $\frac{1}{2} = 1 \div 2$. Now, using these, to take your example, we can rewrite the equation in this way:

$$
\begin{aligned}
1\frac{3}{4} \div \frac{1}{2} &= 1\frac{3}{4} \div (1 \div 2) \\
&= 1\frac{3}{4} \div 1 \times 2 \\
&= 1\frac{3}{4} \times 2 \div 1 \\
&= 1\frac{3}{4} \times (2 \div 1) \\
&= 1\frac{3}{4} \times 2
\end{aligned}
$$

It is not difficult at all. I can even give students some equations with simple numbers and ask them to prove the rule on their own. (Tr. Chen)

Other teachers justified the algorithm by drawing on another piece of knowledge that students had learned—the rule of "maintaining the value of a quotient":[3]

> OK, fifth-grade students know the rule of "maintaining the value of a quotient." That is, when we multiply both the dividend and the divisor with the same number, the quotient will remain unchanged. For example, dividing 10 by 2 the quotient is 5. Given that we multiply both 10 and 2 by a number, let's say 6, we will get 60 divided by 12, and the quotient will remain the same, 5. Now if both the dividend and the divisor are multiplied by the reciprocal of the divisor, the divisor will become 1. Since dividing by 1 does not change a number, it can be omitted. So the equation will become that of multiplying the dividend by the reciprocal of the divisor. Let me show you the procedure:

$$1\tfrac{3}{4} \div \tfrac{1}{2} = (1\tfrac{3}{4} \times \tfrac{2}{1}) \div (\tfrac{1}{2} \times \tfrac{2}{1})$$
$$= (1\tfrac{3}{4} \times \tfrac{2}{1}) \div 1$$
$$= 1\tfrac{3}{4} \times \tfrac{2}{1}$$
$$= 3\tfrac{1}{2}$$

> With this procedure we can explain to students that this seemingly arbitrary algorithm is reasonable. (Tr. Wang)

There are various ways that one can show the equivalence of $1\tfrac{3}{4} \div \tfrac{1}{2}$ and $1\tfrac{3}{4} \times \tfrac{2}{1}$. Tr. Chen and Tr. Wang demonstrated how they used the knowledge that students had already learned to justify the division by fractions algorithm. Other teachers reported that their explanation of why $1\tfrac{3}{4} \div \tfrac{1}{2}$ equals $1\tfrac{3}{4} \times 2$ would draw on the meaning of the expression $1\tfrac{3}{4} \div \tfrac{1}{2}$:

> Why is it equal to multiplying by the reciprocal of the divisor? $1\tfrac{3}{4} \div \tfrac{1}{2}$ means that $\tfrac{1}{2}$ of a number is $1\tfrac{3}{4}$. The answer, as one can imagine, will be $3\tfrac{1}{2}$, which is exactly the same as the answer for $1\tfrac{3}{4} \times 2$. 2 is the reciprocal of $\tfrac{1}{2}$. This is how I would explain it to my students. (Tr. Wu)

Alternative Computational Approaches

The interview question reminded the teachers that "people seem to have different approaches to solving problems involving division with fractions." Yet the U.S. teachers only mentioned one approach—"invert and multi-

---

[3]In China, the rule of "maintaining the value of a quotient" is introduced as a part of whole number division. The rule is: While the dividend and the divisor are multiplied, or divided, by the same number, the quotient remains unchanged. For example, $15 \div 5 = 3$, so $(15 \times 2) \div (5 \times 2) = 3$ and $(15 \div 2) \div (5 \div 2) = 3$.

ply"—the standard algorithm. The Chinese teachers, however, proposed at least three other approaches: dividing by fractions using decimals, applying the distributive law, and dividing a fraction without multiplying by the reciprocal of the divisor.

Alternative I: Dividing by Fractions Using Decimals[4]

A popular alternative way of dividing by fractions used by the Chinese teachers was to compute with decimals. More than one third reported that the equation could also be solved by converting the fractions into decimal numbers:

$$1\tfrac{3}{4} \div \tfrac{1}{2} = 1.75 \div 0.5 = 3.5$$

Many teachers said that the equation was actually easier to solve with decimals:

> I think this problem is easier to solve with decimals. Because it is so obvious that $1\tfrac{3}{4}$ is 1.75 and $\tfrac{1}{2}$ is 0.5, and any number can be divisible by the digit 5. You divide 1.75 by 0.5 and get 3.5. It is so straightforward. But if you calculate it with fractions, you have to convert $1\tfrac{3}{4}$ into a improper fraction, invert $\tfrac{1}{2}$ into $\tfrac{2}{1}$, multiply, reduce numerators and denominators, and, at last, you need to convert the product from an improper fraction into a mixed number. The process is much longer and more complicated than that with decimals. (Ms. L.)

Not only may decimals make a fraction problem easier, fractions may also make a decimal problem easier. The problem is to know the features of both approaches and be able to judge according to the context:

> Even though dividing by a decimal is sometimes easier than dividing by a fraction, this is not always the case. Sometimes converting fractions into

---

[4]In the Chinese national curriculum, topics related to fractions are taught in this order:

1. Introduction of "primary knowledge about fractions" (the concept of fraction) without operations.
2. Introduction of decimals as "special fractions with denominators of 10 and powers of 10."
3. Four basic operations with decimals (which are similar to those of whole numbers).
4. Whole number topics related to fractions, such as divisors, multiples, prime number, prime factors, highest common divisors, lowest common multiples, etc.
5. Topics such as proper fractions, improper fractions, mixed numbers, reduction of a fraction, and finding common denominators.
6. Addition, subtraction, multiplication, and division with fractions.

decimals is complex and difficult, sometimes the decimal might not terminate. Still sometimes, it is easier to solve a division with decimals problem by converting it into fractions. Like, $0.3 \div 0.8$, it is easier to solve by fractions: you will easily get $\frac{3}{8}$. It is important for us and also for our students, though, to know alternative ways of approaching a problem, and to be able to judge which way is more reasonable for a particular problem. (Tr. B.)

Teachers' comprehensive knowledge of a topic may contribute to students' opportunities to learn it. The teachers reported that students were also encouraged to solve fraction problems with decimals:

We also encourage students to solve fraction problems with decimals, or vice versa for all four operations. There are several advantages in doing this. Since they have already learned operations with decimals, this is a chance for them to review knowledge learned before. In addition, converting between fractions and decimals will deepen their understanding of these two representations of numbers and foster their number sense. Moreover, it is a practice of solving a problem through alternative ways. (Tr. S.)

Alternative II: Applying the Distributive Law

Seven teachers said that the distributive law could be used to calculate $1\frac{3}{4} \div \frac{1}{2}$. Instead of considering $1\frac{3}{4}$ as a mixed number and converting it into an improper fraction, they wrote it as $1 + \frac{3}{4}$, divided each part by $\frac{1}{2}$, then added the two quotients together. Two slightly different procedures were reported:

A)
$$\begin{aligned}
1\tfrac{3}{4} \div \tfrac{1}{2} &= (1 + \tfrac{3}{4}) \div \tfrac{1}{2} \\
&= (1 + \tfrac{3}{4}) \times \tfrac{2}{1} \\
&= (1 \times 2) + (\tfrac{3}{4} \times 2) \\
&= 2 + 1\tfrac{1}{2} \\
&= 3\tfrac{1}{2}
\end{aligned}$$

B)
$$\begin{aligned}
1\tfrac{3}{4} \div \tfrac{1}{2} &= (1 + \tfrac{3}{4}) \div \tfrac{1}{2} \\
&= (1 \div \tfrac{1}{2}) + (\tfrac{3}{4} \div \tfrac{1}{2}) \\
&= 2 + 1\tfrac{1}{2} \\
&= 3\tfrac{1}{2}
\end{aligned}$$

After presenting version A, Tr. Xie commented that this seemingly complicated procedure actually made the computation simpler than the standard procedure:

In this case applying the distributive law makes the operation simpler. The computational procedure I put on paper looks complicated but I wanted to show you the logic of the process. But, when you conduct the operation, it is very simple. You just think that 1 times 2 is 2 and $\frac{3}{4}$ times 2 is $1\frac{1}{2}$, then you add them together and get $3\frac{1}{2}$. One can do it even without a pencil. When working on whole numbers my students learned how to solve certain kinds of problems in a simpler way by applying the distributive law. This approach applies to operations with fractions as well.

The teachers' use of the distributive law provided evidence of their comprehension of the law and their confidence in using it. It also demonstrated their comprehensive understanding of a mixed number, a concept which was as we shall see, an obstacle for some U.S. teachers during computations.

Alternative III: "You Don't Have to Multiply"

Three teachers pointed out that even though multiplying by the reciprocal of the divisor is the conventional way to perform division by fractions, one does not always need to do this. Sometimes division by fractions problems can be solved without using multiplication. The equation that I required them to solve was one such example:

$$
\begin{aligned}
1\frac{3}{4} \div \frac{1}{2} &= \frac{7}{4} \div \frac{1}{2} \\
&= \frac{7+1}{4+2} \\
&= \frac{7}{2} \\
&= 3\frac{1}{2}
\end{aligned}
$$

Again, the teachers who proposed this approach argued that for the equation presented in the interview, their method was easier than the standard method. Two steps, inverting the divisor and reducing the final answer, were eliminated. However, the teachers explained that this approach is only applicable to the problems in which both the numerator and denominator of the dividend are divisible by those of the divisor. For example, in $1\frac{3}{4} \div \frac{1}{2}$, 7 is divisible by 1, and 4 is divisible by 2. However, if the problem is $1\frac{2}{3} \div \frac{1}{2}$, since the denominator of the dividend, 3, is not divisible by the denominator, 2, this approach will not apply. Tr. T. said:

In fact, division is more complicated than multiplication. Just think about the cases when one number can't be divided by another number without a remainder. Even if you use decimals, you may encounter repeating decimals. But in multiplication you never have the problem of remainders. Probably that is why the way of multiplying by the reciprocal of the divisor was accepted as the standard way. But in this case, because 4 divided by 2 is easy and so is 7 divided by 1, conducting division directly is even simpler.

Tr. Xie was the first teacher I met who described this nonstandard method of solving a division by fractions problem without performing multiplication. I told him that I had never thought about it that way and asked him to explain how it worked. He said that it could be proved easily:

$$
\begin{aligned}
1\tfrac{3}{4} \div \tfrac{1}{2} &= \tfrac{7}{4} \div \tfrac{1}{2} \\
&= (7 \div 4) \div (1 \div 2) \\
&= 7 \div 4 \div 1 \times 2 \\
&= 7 \div 1 \div 4 \times 2 \\
&= (7 \div 1) \div (4 \div 2) \\
&= \tfrac{7 \div 1}{4 \div 2}
\end{aligned}
$$

Again, he deduced the result by drawing on basic principles such as that of the order of operations and the equivalence between a fraction and a division expression.

All the teachers who suggested alternative methods argued that their methods were "easier" or "simpler" for this calculation. In fact, they not only knew alternative ways of calculating the problem, but also were aware of the meaning of these ways for the calculation—to make the procedure of calculation easier or simpler. To solve a complex problem in a simple way is one of the aesthetic standards of the mathematical community. The teachers argued that not only should students know various ways of calculating a problem but they should also be able to evaluate these ways and to determine which would be the most reasonable to use.

THE U.S. TEACHERS' REPRESENTATIONS OF DIVISION BY FRACTIONS

The Mathematical Concepts that the Teachers Represented

Although 43% of the U.S. teachers successfully calculated $1\tfrac{3}{4} \div \tfrac{1}{2}$, almost all failed to come up with a representation of division by fractions. Among the 23 teachers, 6 could not create a story and 16 made up stories with misconceptions. Only one teacher provided a conceptually correct but pedagogically problematic representation. The teachers displayed various misconceptions about the meaning of division by fractions.

Confounding Division by $\tfrac{1}{2}$ with Division by 2

Ten U.S. teachers confounded division by $\tfrac{1}{2}$ with division by 2. The teachers with this misconception generated stories about dividing the quantity $1\frac{3}{4}$ evenly between two people, or into two parts. The most common subject of these stories was circular food, such as pie or pizza:

> You could be using pie, a whole pie, one, and then you have three fourths of another pie and *you have two people*, how will you make sure that this gets *divided evenly*, so that each person gets an equal share. (Ms. Fiona, italics added)

The phrases the teachers used, "divide evenly between two," or "divide into half," corresponded to division by 2, not division by $\frac{1}{2}$. When we say that we are going to divide ten apples evenly between two people, we divide the number of apples by 2, not by $\frac{1}{2}$. However, most teachers did not notice that this difference.

Confounding Division by $\frac{1}{2}$ with Multiplication by $\frac{1}{2}$

Six teachers provided stories that confused dividing by $\frac{1}{2}$ with multiplying by $\frac{1}{2}$. This misconception, although not as common as the previous one, was also substantial. Taking another example with pies:

> Probably the easiest would be pies, with this small number. It is to use the typical pie for fractions. You would have a whole pie and a three quarters of it like someone stole a piece there somewhere. But you would happen to divide it into fourths and then have to *take one half of the total*. (Tr. Barry, italics added)

While the teachers we discussed earlier talked about "dividing between two," Tr. Barry suggested "take half of the total." To find a certain portion of a unit we would use *multiplication by fractions*. Suppose we want to take $\frac{2}{3}$ of a two-pound sack of flour, we multiply 2 by $\frac{2}{3}$ and get $1\frac{1}{3}$ pounds of flour. What teachers like Tr. Barry represented was multiplying by a fraction: $1\frac{3}{4} \times \frac{1}{2}$, not $1\frac{3}{4} \div \frac{1}{2}$. The stories that confused dividing by $\frac{1}{2}$ with multiplying by $\frac{1}{2}$ also revealed weaknesses in the teachers' conceptions of multiplication by fractions.

Confusing the Three Concepts

Tr. Bernadette and Tr. Beatrice, who were not in either of the above two groups, confused the three concepts, dividing by $\frac{1}{2}$, dividing by 2, and multiplying $\frac{1}{2}$:

> Dividing the one and three-fourths into the half. OK. Let us see . . . You would have all of this whole, you would have the three fourths here. And then you want only half of the whole. (Tr. Bernadette)

You get one and three-quarters liquid in a pitcher, you want to divide it in half, to visually, each one of you is going to have, get half of it to drink. (Tr. Beatrice)

When Tr. Bernadette and Tr. Beatrice phrased the problem as "dividing the one and three-quarters into the half" or "divide it in half," they were confusing division by $\frac{1}{2}$ with division by 2. Then, when they proposed that "you want only half of the whole" or "get half of it," they confused division by $\frac{1}{2}$ with multiplication by $\frac{1}{2}$. For them, there seemed to be no difference among division by $\frac{1}{2}$, division by 2, and multiplication by $\frac{1}{2}$.

No Confusion, But No Story Either

Two other teachers failed to provide a story but noticed that dividing by $\frac{1}{2}$ is different from dividing by 2. Tr. Belinda, an experienced sixth grade teacher, was aware of the deficiency in her knowledge and the pitfall of the problem:

I am not quite sure I understand it well enough, except in terms of computation. I know how to do it, but I do not really know what it means to me.

Mr. Felix also noticed a difference between the two concepts. After trying and failing to invent a story, he explained:

Dividing something by one half and so I confused myself with the two, thinking it meant dividing by two, but it doesn't . . . It means something totally different . . . Well, for me what makes it difficult is not being able to envision it, what it represents in the real world. I can't really think of what dividing by a half means.

Although Tr. Belinda and Mr. Felix were not able to provide a representation of the conception of division by fractions, they did not confuse it with something else. They were the only U.S. teachers who did not confuse division by fractions with another operation.

Correct Conception and Pedagogically Problematic Representation

Tr. Belle, an experienced teacher, was the only one who provided a conceptually correct representation of the meaning of division by fractions. She said:[5]

---

[5]Tr. Belle used $2\frac{1}{4}$ instead of $1\frac{3}{4}$. However, her understanding of the concept of dividing by a fraction is correct.

Let's take something like, two and a quarter Twinkies. And, I want to give each child a half a Twinkie. How many kids can get, will get a piece of Twinkie. Of course, I've got a half a child there at the end, but. OK, that's the problem with using children there, because then you have four and a half kids. You know, four kids, and one child's only going to get half the amount of the others. I guess they could figure that out.

Tr. Belle represented the concept correctly. To divide the number A by the number B is to find how many Bs are contained in A. However, as Tr. Belle herself indicated, this representation results in a fractional number of children. The answer will be $3\frac{1}{2}$ students. It is pedagogically problematic because in real life a number of persons will never be a fraction.

Dealing with the Discrepancy:
Correct Computation Versus Incorrect Representation

Even though the stories created by the teachers illustrated misconceptions about division by fractions, there were opportunities during the interviews that might have led some of them to find the pitfall. Of the 16 teachers who created a conceptually incorrect story, 9 had computed correct or incomplete answers. Because most teachers discussed the results of their stories, these discrepancies between the answers from the conceptually wrong stories ($\frac{7}{8}$) and from computations ($3\frac{1}{2}$, $\frac{7}{2}$, or $\frac{28}{8}$) might call for their reflection. Although four teachers did not notice any discrepancy, the remaining five did. Unfortunately, none of the five was led to a correct conception by discovering the discrepancy.

The five teachers reacted in three ways to the discrepancy. Three teachers doubted the possibility of creating a representation for the equation and decided to give up. Ms. Fleur was frustrated that "the problem doesn't turn out the way you think it would." Tr. Blanche was "totally baffled" when she noticed that the two answers were different. Tr. Barry concluded that "[the story] is not going to work. I do not know what I did."

Ms. Felice, however, seemed to be more assertive. She created a story for $1\frac{3}{4} \times \frac{1}{2}$ to represent $1\frac{3}{4} \div \frac{1}{2}$: "That's one and three-fourths cups of flour and you'd want half of that, so you could make a half a batch of cookies."

In estimating the result of the story problem, she noticed that it would be "a little over three quarters" rather than three and a half. Because she had been unsure during her procedural calculations, she soon decided that $\frac{28}{8}$, the answer she had attained earlier, was wrong. She thought that "a real-world thing" that she came up with held more authority than a solution she obtained using the algorithm:

It makes, it [the calculation that she did] was wrong. Because you have a half of a one would be one half, and a half of three fourths would be

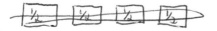

[lengthy pause] if you estimated it be a fourth and then a little bit more. Let's see, that the answer is a little over three fourths . . . When I did it in a real-world thing, I would realize that I had done it wrong, and then I'd just go over it again. When you do that without a real-world thing you might be doing them real wrong, and you might do the problem wrong that way.

Unfortunately, Ms. Felice's "real-world thing" represented a misconception. Because of her unsureness with computation and her blind inclination to "real-world things," finding the discrepancy did not lead her to reflect on the misconception, but to discard the correct, though incomplete, result that she had computed.

The remaining teacher, Ms. Francine, eventually found a way to explain away the discrepancy. The story problem she made up represented $1\frac{3}{4} \div \frac{1}{2}$:

So some kind of food, graham cracker maybe, because it has the four sections. You have one whole, four fourths, and then break off a quarter, we only have one and three fourths, and then we want, how are we going to divide this up so that let us say we have two people and we want to give half to one, half to the other, see how they would do it.

By dividing one and three fourths crackers between two people, she expected that she would get the same answer as she did with the equation $1\frac{3}{4} \div \frac{1}{2}$, "three and one half." However, it came out that each person would get three and one half quarters of crackers:

Would we get three and one half, did I do that right? [She is looking at what she wrote and mumbling to herself.] Let us see one, two, three, yes, that is right, one, two, three. *They would each get three quarters and then one half of the other quarter.* (italics added)

Even though Ms. Francine noticed that it was "two different [answers]," she finally explained how the latter, three and one half *quarters*, made sense with the previous answer, three and one half. She seemed to find this a satisfactory explanation of why the dividend $1\frac{3}{4}$ was smaller than the quotient $3\frac{1}{2}$:

You wonder how could one and three fourths which is smaller than three and a half see, so it is, here one and three quarters is referring to what you have completely, three and one half is, is according to the fraction of the one and the three fourths, so if you just took the equation, it would not make sense, I mean it would not make sense.

The way that Ms. Francine explained the discrepancy conflated the number $3\frac{1}{2}$ (the answer of $1\frac{3}{4} \div \frac{1}{2}$) with $3\frac{1}{2}$ quarters (the answer of $1\frac{3}{4} \div 2$).

Since the number $\frac{1}{2}$ is one quarter of the number 2, the quotient of a number divided by 2 will be one quarter of the quotient of the number divided by $\frac{1}{2}$. For instance, $2 \div 2 = 1$, $2 \div \frac{1}{2} = 4$, or $\frac{1}{2} \div 2 = \frac{1}{4}$, $\frac{1}{2} \div \frac{1}{2} = 1$. That is why $\frac{7}{8}$, the quotient of the equation $1\frac{3}{4} \div 2$, happened to be $3\frac{1}{2}$ quarters. Ms. Francine, of course, did not confuse them on purpose. She did not even notice the coincidence. Her inadequate knowledge of fractions and her ignorance that the result of dividing by a fraction less than 1 will be larger than the dividend led her to an incorrect explanation of the discrepancy.

The reason that finding discrepancies did not lead Ms. Francine or Ms. Felice to reflect on their representations was that their computational knowledge was limited and flimsy. Even though their calculations were correct, they were not solidly supported by conceptual understanding. As the teachers said during interviews, they did not understand why the computational algorithm worked. Therefore, results obtained from computation were unable to withstand a challenge, nor could they serve as a point from which to approach the meaning of the operation.

An Inadequate Understanding of Procedure
Impedes Creating a Representation

The case of Ms. Fay was another example of how knowledge of a computational skill may influence one's conceptual approach to the meaning of the operation. Ms. Fay seemed likely to reach an understanding of the meaning of division by fractions. While computing, she described the procedure clearly, and got a correct answer:

> I would copy the first fraction as it reads, then I would change the sign from division to multiplication. And then I would invert the second fraction. Then because the first fraction was a mixed fraction, I would change it from a mixed to a whole fraction. So I would take 1 times 4 which is 4 and then add it to 3 which would be $\frac{7}{4}$ times 2 . . . With fractions you multiply straight across so it would be 7 times 2 is $\frac{14}{4}$. And then I would reduce that.

Moreover, Ms. Fay phrased the problem correctly, using "dividing by one half" ($\div \frac{1}{2}$), rather than "into half" ($\div 2$). However, when she started to divide $1\frac{3}{4}$ pizza by $\frac{1}{2}$ pizza, she got "lost" and did not know where she "would go from there":

> Well, it would be one whole pizza and then three fourths of a pizza. Which would be kind of like this. And it would be divided by one half of a pizza. And then . . . I am lost after that, actually. If I combine those [the whole pizza and the three fourths of a pizza], I do not know what I would do next with a student. I would say that we would have to combine these because I know that you have to, that you need to. It is very hard, it is almost impossible

to divide a mixed fraction by whole fraction to me and I cannot explain why, but that is the way I was told. That you have to change the mixed numeral to a fraction . . . So you would have to show the student how to combine these two. And that is kind of hard. I do not know where I would go from there.

Ms. Fay had made an appropriate start. The story which she tried to make up, dividing $1\frac{3}{4}$ pizza by $\frac{1}{2}$ pizza, was likely to be a correct model for dividing $1\frac{3}{4}$ by $\frac{1}{2}$. However, she got "lost" in the middle and gave up finishing the story. What impeded Ms. Fay from completing the story was her inadequate understanding of the computational procedure that she wanted to use: change the mixed fraction into a improper fraction, and divide.

When computing, Ms. Fay dealt with the mixed number according to what she "was told." She executed the first part of the procedure, converting $1\frac{3}{4}$ into $\frac{7}{4}$. However, she could not explain why it should be changed. Moreover, she did not understand what was going on during the procedure of changing a mixed number into an improper fraction. This deficiency of understanding caused her to become "lost." If Ms. Fay had understood what is meant by changing a mixed number into an improper fraction—to change the whole number into an improper fraction with the same denominator as the fraction and combine it with the latter—she would have been able to conduct this procedure for the $1\frac{3}{4}$ pizzas. What she needed to do was only to cut the whole pizza into quarters so that the whole, 1, becomes $\frac{4}{4}$, and $1\frac{3}{4}$ pizza becomes $\frac{7}{4}$ pizza. It would take her at least one more step toward completing the representation. In addition to Ms. Fay, at least three other teachers reported that they had difficulty working with mixed numbers. Their inadequate knowledge of the computational procedure impeded their approach to the meaning of the operation.

Can Pedagogical Knowledge Make Up for Ignorance of the Concept?

The teachers' deficiency in understanding the meaning of division by fractions determined their inability to generate an appropriate representation. Even their pedagogical knowledge could not make up for their ignorance of the concept. Circular foods are considered appropriate for representing fraction concepts. However, as we have seen, the representations teachers generated with pizzas or pies displayed misconceptions. Ms. Francine's use of graham crackers with four sections was also pedagogically thoughtful in representing quarters. However, it did not remedy her misunderstanding of the meaning of division by fractions. To generate a representation, one should first know what to represent. During the interviews the teachers reported various pedagogical ideas for generating representations. Unfortunately, because of their inadequate subject matter knowledge, none of these ideas succeeded in leading them to a correct representation.

Ms. Florence was a teacher who claimed that she liked fractions. She would use "articles right in the classroom to represent a conception." The representation she proposed was:

> José has one and three fourths box of crayons and he wants to divide them between two people or divide the crayons in half, and then, first we could do it with the crayons and maybe write it on the chalkboard or have them do it in numbers.

Other contexts using measures, such as recipes, mileage, money, and capacity, were also used by teachers to represent fraction concepts. Ms. Francesca said she would use money: "I would tell them, 'You have got so much money, you have two people, and you have to divide it up evenly.' "

Tr. Blanche, an experienced teacher who was very confident in her mathematical knowledge, thought that she could use anything for the representation: "I would have one and three-quarters something, whatever it is, and if I needed to divide it by two I want to divide it into two groups . . ."

While the previously mentioned teachers represented the concept of dividing by 2, other teachers represented the concept of multiplying by $\frac{1}{2}$. Tr. Barbara was an experienced teacher who was proud of her mathematical knowledge and said she enjoyed "the challenge of math." She said she used to have a hard time with fractions when she was a student, but ever since one of her teacher taught her fractions by bringing in a recipe, she "got it" and "loved working" on it. She would teach her students in the way she was taught—using a recipe:

> Well if I were to have this type of equation, I would say well using one and three quarters cup of butter. And you want to *take a half of it*, how would you do it. Or it could be used in any, you know, I have flour or, or sugar or something like that.

Ms. Fawn, a beginning teacher, created several representations with different subjects, such as money, recipes, pies, apples, etc. However, all of her stories represented a misconception—that of multiplying by $\frac{1}{2}$ rather than dividing by $\frac{1}{2}$. There was no evidence that these teachers lacked pedagogical knowledge. The subjects of their stories—circular food, recipes, classroom articles, etc.—were suitable for representing fraction concepts. However, because of their misconceptions about the meaning of division by fractions, these teachers failed to create correct representations.

THE CHINESE TEACHERS' APPROACH
TO THE MEANING OF DIVISION BY FRACTIONS

The deficiency in the subject matter knowledge of the U.S. teachers on the advanced arithmetical topic of division by fractions did not appear among the Chinese teachers. While only one among the 23 U.S. teachers generated a conceptually correct representation for the meaning of the equation, 90% of the Chinese teachers did. Sixty-five of the 72 Chinese teachers created a total of more than 80 story problems representing the meaning of division by a fraction. Twelve teachers proposed more than one story to approach different aspects of the meaning of the operation. Only six (8%) teachers said that they were not able to create a story problem, and one teacher provided an incorrect story (which represented $\frac{1}{2} \div 1\frac{3}{4}$ rather than $1\frac{3}{4} \div \frac{1}{2}$). Figure 3.1 displays a comparison of teachers' knowledge about this topic.

The Chinese teachers represented the concept using three different models of division: measurement (or quotitive), partitive, and product and factors.[6] For example, $1\frac{3}{4} \div \frac{1}{2}$ might represent:

- $1\frac{3}{4}$ feet $\div \frac{1}{2}$ feet $= \frac{7}{2}$ (measurement model)
- $1\frac{3}{4}$ feet $\div \frac{1}{2} = \frac{7}{2}$ feet (partitive model)
- $1\frac{3}{4}$ square feet $\div \frac{1}{2}$ feet $= \frac{7}{2}$ feet (product and factors)

which might correspond to:

- How many $\frac{1}{2}$-foot lengths are there in something that is 1 and $\frac{3}{4}$ feet long?
- If half a length is 1 and $\frac{3}{4}$ feet, how long is the whole?
- If one side of a $1\frac{3}{4}$ square foot rectangle is $\frac{1}{2}$ feet, how long is the other side?

The Models of Division by Fractions

The Measurement Model of Division: "Finding How Many $\frac{1}{2}$s There Are in $1\frac{3}{4}$" or "Finding How Many Times $1\frac{3}{4}$ is of $\frac{1}{2}$"

Sixteen stories generated by the teachers illustrated two ideas related to the measurement model of division: "finding how many $\frac{1}{2}$s there are in $1\frac{3}{4}$" and "finding how many times $1\frac{3}{4}$ is of $\frac{1}{2}$." Eight stories about five topics corresponded to "finding how many $\frac{1}{2}$s there are in $1\frac{3}{4}$." Here are two examples:

---

[6]Greer (1992) gives an extensive discussion of models of multiplication and division. His category "rectangular area" is included in "product and factors."

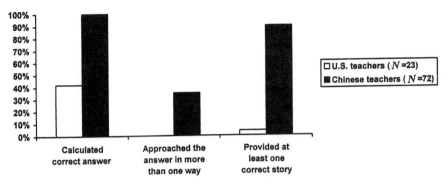

FIG. 3.1. Teachers' knowledge of division by fractions.

Illustrating it with the measurement model of division, $1\frac{3}{4} \div \frac{1}{2}$ can be articulated as how many $\frac{1}{2}$s there are in $1\frac{3}{4}$. To represent it we can say, for example, given that a team of workers construct $\frac{1}{2}$ km of road each day, how many days will it take them to construct a road of $1\frac{3}{4}$ km long? The problem here is to find how many pieces of $\frac{1}{2}$ km, which they can accomplish each day, are contained in $1\frac{3}{4}$ km. You divide $1\frac{3}{4}$ by $\frac{1}{2}$ and the result is $3\frac{1}{2}$ days. It will take them $3\frac{1}{2}$ days to construct the road. (Tr. R.)

Cut an apple into four pieces evenly. Get three pieces and put them together with a whole apple. Given that $\frac{1}{2}$ apple will be a serving, how many servings can we get from the $1\frac{3}{4}$ apples? (Ms. I.)

"Finding how many $\frac{1}{2}$s there are in $1\frac{3}{4}$" parallels the approach of Tr. Belle, the U.S. teacher who had a conceptual understanding of the topic. There were eight other stories that represented "finding how many times $1\frac{3}{4}$ is of $\frac{1}{2}$." For example:

It was planned to spend $1\frac{3}{4}$ months to construct a bridge. But actually it only took $\frac{1}{2}$ month. How many times is the time that was planned of the time that actually was taken? (Tr. K.)

"Finding how many $\frac{1}{2}$s there are in $1\frac{3}{4}$" and "finding how many times $1\frac{3}{4}$ is of $\frac{1}{2}$" are two approaches to the measurement model of division by fractions. Tr. Li indicated that though the measurement model is consistent for whole numbers and fractions when fractions are introduced the model needs to be revised:

In whole number division we have a model of finding how many times one number is of another number. For example, how many times the number 10 is of the number 2? We divide 10 by 2 and get 5. 10 is 5 times 2. This is what we call the measurement model. With fractions, we can still say, for example, what times $\frac{1}{2}$ is $1\frac{3}{4}$? Making a story problem, we can say for instance, there are two fields. Field A is $1\frac{3}{4}$ hectares, and field B is $\frac{1}{2}$ hectare. What times the area of field B is the area of field A? To calculate the problem we divide $1\frac{3}{4}$ hectares by $\frac{1}{2}$ hectare and get $3\frac{1}{2}$. Then we know that the area of the field A is $3\frac{1}{2}$ times that of the field B. The equation you asked me to represent fits this model. However, when fractions are used this division model of measurement need to be revised. In particular, when the dividend is smaller than the divisor and then the quotient becomes a proper fraction. Then the model should be revised. The statement of "finding what fraction one number is of another number," or, "finding what fractional times one number is of another number" should be added on the original statement. For example, for the expression $2 \div 10$, we may ask, what fraction of 10 is 2? Or, what fractional times is 2 of 10? We divide 2 by 10 and get $\frac{1}{5}$. 2 is $\frac{1}{5}$ of 10. Similarly, we can also ask: What is the fractional part that $\frac{1}{4}$ is of $1\frac{1}{2}$? Then you should divide $\frac{1}{4}$ by $1\frac{1}{2}$ and get $\frac{1}{6}$.

The Partitive Model of Division:
Finding a Number Such That $\frac{1}{2}$ of It is $1\frac{3}{4}$

Among more than 80 story problems representing the meaning of $1\frac{3}{4} \div \frac{1}{2}$, 62 stories represented the partitive model of division by fractions—"finding a number such that $\frac{1}{2}$ of it is $1\frac{3}{4}$":

Division is the inverse of multiplication. Multiplying by a fraction means that we know a number that represents a whole and want to find a number that represents a certain fraction of that. For example, given that we want to know what number represents $\frac{1}{2}$ of $1\frac{3}{4}$, we multiply $1\frac{3}{4}$ by $\frac{1}{2}$ and get $\frac{7}{8}$. In other words, the whole is $1\frac{3}{4}$, and $\frac{1}{2}$ of it is $\frac{7}{8}$. In division by a fraction, on the other hand, the number that represents the whole becomes the unknown to be found. We know a fractional part of it and want to find the number that represents the whole. For example, $\frac{1}{2}$ of a jump-rope is $1\frac{3}{4}$ meters, what is the length of the whole rope? We know that a part of a rope is $1\frac{3}{4}$ meters, and we also know that this part is $\frac{1}{2}$ of the rope. We divide the number of the part, $1\frac{3}{4}$ meters, by the corresponding fraction of the whole, $\frac{1}{2}$, we get the number representing the whole, $3\frac{1}{2}$ meters. Dividing $1\frac{3}{4}$ by $\frac{1}{2}$, we will find that the whole rope is $3\frac{1}{2}$ meters long . . . But I prefer not to use dividing by $\frac{1}{2}$ to illustrate the meaning of division by fractions. Because one can easily see the answer without really doing division by fractions. If we say $\frac{4}{5}$ of a jump-rope is $1\frac{3}{4}$ meters, how long is the whole rope? The division operation will be more significant because then you can't see the answer immediately. The best way to calculate it is to divide $1\frac{3}{4}$ by $\frac{4}{5}$ and get $2\frac{3}{16}$ meters. (Ms. G.)

Dividing by a fraction is finding a number when a fractional part of it is known. For example, given that we know that $\frac{1}{2}$ of a number is $1\frac{3}{4}$, dividing $1\frac{3}{4}$ by $\frac{1}{2}$, we can find out that this number is $3\frac{1}{2}$. Making a story problem to illustrate this model, let's say that one kind of wood weighs $1\frac{3}{4}$ tons per cubic meter, it is just $\frac{1}{2}$ of the weight of per cubic meter of one kind of marble. How much does one cubic meter of the marble weigh? So we know that $\frac{1}{2}$ cubic meter of the marble weighs $1\frac{3}{4}$ tons. To find the weight of one cubic meter of it, we divide $1\frac{3}{4}$, the number that represents the fractional part, by $\frac{1}{2}$, the fraction which $1\frac{3}{4}$ represents, and get $3\frac{1}{2}$, the number of the whole. Per cubic meter the marble weighs $3\frac{1}{2}$ tons. (Tr. D.)

My story will be: A train goes back and forth between two stations. From Station A to Station B is uphill and from Station B back to Station A is downhill. The train takes $1\frac{3}{4}$ hours going from Station B to Station A. It is only $\frac{1}{2}$ time of that from Station A to Station B. How long does the train take going from Station A to Station B? (Tr. S.)

The mom bought a box of candy. She gave $\frac{1}{2}$ of it which weighed $1\frac{3}{4}$ kg to the grandma. How much did the box of the candy originally weigh? (Ms. M.)

The teachers above explained the fractional version of the partitive model of division. Tr. Mao discussed in particular how the partitive model of division by integers is revised when fractions are introduced:

With integers students have learned the partitive model of division. It is a model of finding the size of each of the equal groups that have been formed from a given quantity. For example, in our class we have 48 students, they have been formed into 4 groups of equal size, how many students are there in each group? Here we know the quantity of several groups, 48 students. We also know the number of groups, 4. What to be found is the size of one group. So, *a partitive model is finding the value of a unit when the value of several units is known*. In division by fractions, however, the condition has been changed. Now what is known is not the value of several units, rather, the value of a part of the unit. For example, given that we paid $1\frac{3}{4}$ Yuan to buy $\frac{1}{2}$ of a cake, how much would a whole cake cost? Since we know that $\frac{1}{2}$ of the whole price is $1\frac{3}{4}$ Yuan, to know the whole price we divide $1\frac{3}{4}$ by $\frac{1}{2}$ and get $3\frac{1}{2}$ Yuan. In other words, *the fractional version of the partitive model is to find a number when a part of it is known*. (italics added)

Tr. Mao's observation was true. Finding a number when several units is known and finding a number when a fractional part of it is known are represented by a common model—finding the number that represents a unit when a certain amount of the unit is known. What differs is the feature of the amount: with a whole number divisor, the condition is that "*several times* the unit is known," but with a fractional divisor the condition is that "*a fraction* of the unit is known." Therefore, conceptually, these two approaches are identical.

This change in meaning is particular to the partitive model. In the measurement model and the factors and product model, division by fractions keeps the same meaning as whole number division. This may explain why so many of the Chinese teachers' representations were partitive.

Factors and Product: Finding a Factor That Multiplied
by $\frac{1}{2}$ Will Make $1\frac{3}{4}$

Three teachers described a more general model of division—to find a factor when the product and another factor are known. The teachers articulated it as "to find a factor that when multiplied by $\frac{1}{2}$ makes $1\frac{3}{4}$":

> As the inverse operation of multiplication, division is to find the number representing a factor when the product and the other factor are known. From this perspective, we can get a word problem like "Given that the product of $\frac{1}{2}$ and another factor is $1\frac{3}{4}$, what is the other factor?" (Tr. M.)

> We know that the area of a rectangle is the product of length and width. Let's say that the area of a rectangle board is $1\frac{3}{4}$ square meters, its width is $\frac{1}{2}$ meters, what is its length? (Mr. A.)

These teachers regarded the relationship between multiplication and division in a more abstract way. They ignored the particular meaning of the multiplicand and multiplier in multiplication and related models of division. Rather, they perceived the multiplicand and multiplier as two factors with the same status. Their perspective, indeed, was legitimized by the commutative property of multiplication.

The concept of fractions as well as the operations with fractions taught in China and U.S. seem different. U.S. teachers tend to deal with "real" and "concrete" wholes (usually circular or rectangular shapes) and their fractions. Although Chinese teachers also use these shapes when they introduce the concept of a fraction, when they teach operations with fractions they tend to use "abstract" and "invisible" wholes (e.g., the length of a particular stretch of road, the length of time it takes to complete a task, the number of pages in a book).

Meaning of Multiplication by a Fraction:
The Important Piece in the Knowledge Package

Through discussion of the meaning of division by fractions, the teachers mentioned several concepts that they considered as pieces of the knowledge package related to the topic: the meaning of whole number multiplication, the concept of division as the inverse of multiplication, models of whole number division, the meaning of multiplication with fractions, the concept of a fraction, the concept of a unit, etc. Figure 3.2 gives an outline of the relationships among these items.

The learning of mathematical concepts is not a unidirectional journey. Even though the concept of division by fractions is logically built on the previous learning of various concepts, it, in turn, plays a role in reinforcing and deepening that previous learning. For example, work on the meaning

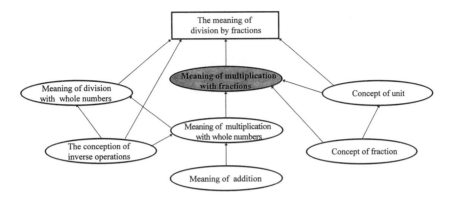

FIG. 3.2. A knowledge package for understanding the meaning of division by fractions.

of division by fractions will intensify previous concepts of rational number multiplication. Similarly, by developing rational number versions of the two division models, one's original understanding of the two whole number models will become more comprehensive:

> This is what is called "gaining new insights through reviewing old ones." The current learning is supported by, but also deepens, the previous learning. The meaning of division by fractions seems complicated because it is built on several concepts. On the other hand, however, it provides a good opportunity for students to deepen their previous learning of these concepts. I am pretty sure that after approaching the meaning and the models of division by fractions, students' previous learning of these supporting concepts will be more comprehensive than before. Learning is a back and forth procedure. (Tr. Sun)

From this perspective, learning is a continual process during which new knowledge is supported by previous knowledge and the previous knowledge is reinforced and deepened by new knowledge.

During the interviews, "the meaning of multiplication with fractions" was considered a key piece of the knowledge package. Most teachers considered multiplication with fractions the "necessary basis" for understanding the meaning of division by fractions:

> The meaning of multiplication with fractions is particularly important because it is where the concepts of division by fractions are derived . . . Given that our students understand very well that multiplying by a fraction means finding a fractional part of a unit, they will follow this logic to understand how the models of its inverse operation work. On the other hand, given that they do not have a clear idea of what multiplication with fractions means, concepts of division by a fraction will be arbitrary for them and very difficult to understand. Therefore, in order to let our students grasp the

meaning of division by fractions, we should first of all devote significant time and effort when teaching multiplication with fractions to make sure students understand thoroughly the meaning of this operation . . . Usually, my teaching of the meaning of division by fractions starts with a review of the meaning of multiplication with fractions. (Tr. Xie)

The concepts of division by fractions, such as "finding a number when a fractional part is known" or "finding what fraction one number is of another number," etc. sound complicated. But once one has a comprehensive understanding of the meaning of multiplication with fractions, one will find that these concepts are logical and easy to understand. Therefore, to help students to understand the meaning of division by fractions, many of our efforts are not devoted directly to the topic, but rather, to their thorough understanding of the meaning of multiplication with fractions, and the relationship between division and multiplication. (Tr. Wu)

The meaning of multiplication with fractions is also important in the knowledge package because it "connects several relevant conceptions":

The concept of multiplication with fractions is like a "knot." It "ties" several other important concepts together. As the operation of multiplication, it is connected with concepts of whole number addition and division. Moreover, in the sense that it deals with fractional numbers, it is related to the conception of a fraction, and those of addition and division with fractions. A grasp of the meaning of multiplication with fractions depends on comprehension of several concepts. At the same time, it substantially reinforces one's previous learning and contributes to one's future learning. (Ms. I.)

Indeed, from the teachers' perspective, the importance of pieces of knowledge in mathematics is not the same. Some of them "weigh" more than others because they are more significant to students' mathematical learning. In addition to "the power of supporting" that we have discussed earlier, another aspect that contributes to the importance of a piece of knowledge is its "location" in a knowledge network. For example, multiplication with fractions is important also because it is at an "intersection" of several mathematical concepts.

The Representations of the Models of Division by Fractions

The Chinese teachers' profound understanding of the meaning of division by fractions and its connections to other models in mathematics provided them with a solid base on which to build their pedagogical content knowledge of the topic. They used their vivid imaginations and referred to rich topics to represent a single concept of division by fractions. On the other hand, some teachers used one subject to generate several story problems to represent various aspects of the concept. Teachers also drew on knowledge of elementary geometry—the area of a rectangle—to represent division.

Rich Topics Representing the Partitive Model

Even though the operation of division has two models, it appears that the two models do not receive the same attention. For most of the teachers in our research, the partitive model was substantially more impressive than the measurement model. Teachers referred to about thirty subjects in generating more than sixty story problems to represent the fractional version of the partitive model of division. In addition to those discussed earlier, here are a few other examples:

A factory that produces machine tools now uses $1\frac{3}{4}$ tons of steel to make one machine tool, $\frac{1}{2}$ of what they used to use. How much steel did they used to use for producing one machine tool? (Ms. H.)

Uncle Wang ploughed $1\frac{3}{4}$ mus[7] in $\frac{1}{2}$ a day; with this speed, how many mus can he plough in a whole day? (Mr. B.)

Yesterday I rode a bicycle from town A to town B. I spent $1\frac{3}{4}$ hour for $\frac{1}{2}$ of my journey, how much time did I take for the whole journey? (Tr. R.)

A farm has $1\frac{3}{4}$ mus of experimental fields growing wheat. It is $\frac{1}{2}$ of the area of the experimental field growing cotton. How big is the field of cotton? (Tr. N.)

In a river with swift current a downriver boat takes only $\frac{1}{2}$ the time of an upriver boat to go the same long journey. Now we have a downriver boat which took $1\frac{3}{4}$ hour going from place A to place B, how long it will take an upriver boat to go from place B to place A? (Tr. Mao)

Given that we want to know how much vegetable oil there is in a big bottle, but we only have a small scale. We draw $\frac{1}{2}$ of the oil from the bottle, weigh it, and find that it is $1\frac{3}{4}$ kg. Can you tell me how much all the oil in the bottle originally weighed? (Ms. R.)

One day Xiao-Min went to downtown to see a movie. On his way he ran into his aunt. Xiao-Min asked her, "Do you know how far is it from our village to downtown?" His aunt said, "I am not going to tell you the number but I will give you a clue. You have walked $1\frac{3}{4}$ lis[8] and it is exactly $\frac{1}{2}$ of the whole distance. Figure out your question on your own." (Ms. K.)

While the U.S. teachers tended to use a concrete whole (such as round food) and its parts to represent a whole and a fraction, most Chinese teachers

---

[7]"Mu" is a Chinese measurement for area. Fifteen mus is one hectare.

[8]"Li" is a traditional measurement for distance. One li is $\frac{1}{2}$ kilometer.

represented these concepts in a more abstract way. Only 3 of the 72 teachers used round food as the subject of their representation. In many story problems created by the Chinese teachers, $3\frac{1}{2}$, the quotient of the division, was treated as a unit, and $1\frac{3}{4}$, the dividend, was regarded as $\frac{1}{2}$ of the unit.

While food and money were the two main subjects of U.S. teachers' representations, those used by the Chinese teachers were more diverse. In addition to topics in students' lives, those related to students' lives were also included, such as what happens in a farm, in a factory, in the family, etc. Teachers' solid knowledge of the meaning of division by fractions made them comfortable using a broad range of topics in representations.

Several Stories With a Single Subject

Among the teachers who created more than one story to illustrate various aspects of the concept of division by fractions, Ms. D. stood out. She generated three stories about the same subject:

> The equation of $1\frac{3}{4} \div \frac{1}{2} =$ can be represented from different perspectives. For instance, we can say, here is $1\frac{3}{4}$ kg sugar and we want to wrap it into packs of $\frac{1}{2}$ kg each. How many packs can we wrap? Also, we can say that here we have two packs of sugar, one of white sugar and the other of brown sugar. The white sugar is $1\frac{3}{4}$ kg and the brown sugar is $\frac{1}{2}$ kg. How many times is the weight of white sugar of that of brown sugar? Still, we can say that here is some sugar on the table that weighs $1\frac{3}{4}$ kg; it is $\frac{1}{2}$ of all the sugar we now have at home, so how much sugar do we have at home? All three stories are about sugar, and all of them represent $1\frac{3}{4} \div \frac{1}{2}$. But the numerical models they illustrate are not the same. I would put the three stories on the board and invite my students to compare the different meanings they represent. After the discussion I would ask them to try to make up their own story problems to represent the different models of division by fractions. (Ms. D.)

In order to involve students in a comparison of the different concepts associated with $1\frac{3}{4} \div \frac{1}{2}$, Ms. D. created several representations with a single subject. The similarity in the subject and the similarity in the numbers included in the operation would make the difference in the numerical models that the stories represented more obvious to students.

DISCUSSION

Calculation: How Did It Reveal Teachers' Understanding of Mathematics?

The difference between the mathematical knowledge of the U.S. teachers and that of the Chinese teachers became more striking with the topic of division by fractions. The first contrast was presented in calculation. The interview question of this chapter asked the teachers to calculate $1\frac{3}{4} \div \frac{1}{2}$. The process of calculation revealed features of teachers' procedural knowledge and of their understanding of mathematics, as well as of their attitude toward the discipline.

In the two previous chapters all teachers presented a sound procedural knowledge. This time, only 43% of the U.S. teachers succeeded in calculation and none of them showed an understanding of the rationale of the algorithm. Most of these teachers struggled. Many tended to confound the division by fractions algorithm with those for addition and subtraction or for multiplication. These teachers' procedural knowledge was not only weak in division with fractions, but also in other operations with fractions. Reporting that they were uncomfortable doing calculation with mixed numbers or improper fractions, these teachers' knowledge about the basic features of fractions was also very limited.

All of the Chinese teachers succeeded in their calculations and many of them showed enthusiasm in doing the problem. These teachers were not satisfied by just calculating and getting an answer. They enjoyed presenting various ways of doing it—using decimals, using whole numbers, applying the three basic laws, etc. They went back and forth across subsets of numbers and across different operations, added and took off parentheses, and changed the order of operations. They did this with remarkable confidence and amazingly flexible skills. In addition, many teachers made comments on various calculation methods and evaluated them. Their way of "doing mathematics" showed significant conceptual understanding.

Another interesting feature of the Chinese teachers' mathematics is that they tended to provide "proofs" for their calculation procedures. Most teachers justified their calculations by mentioning the rule that "dividing by a number is equivalent to multiplying by its reciprocal." Others converted the fraction $\frac{1}{2}$ into $1 \div 2$ and proved step by step that dividing by $\frac{1}{2}$ is equivalent to multiplying by 2. Still other teachers used the meaning of dividing by $\frac{1}{2}$ to explain the calculating procedure. Their performance is mathematician-like in the sense that to convince someone of a truth one needs to prove it, not just assert it.

"A Concept Knot": Why It is Important

In addition to their performance in "doing mathematics," the Chinese teachers showed a knowledge of fractions that was markedly more solid than that of the U.S. teachers in other ways. The Chinese teachers were aware of abundant connections between fractions and other mathematical topics. They were aware of how a fraction can be written as a division expression in which the numerator is the dividend and the denominator is the divisor. They were also aware of the relationship between decimals and fractions, and were very skillful in converting between the two number forms. Moreover, they were aware of how the models of division by fractions are connected to the meaning of multiplication with fractions and to whole number models of division.

As in the two previous chapters, the Chinese teachers did not regard the topic of this chapter as the key piece of the knowledge package in which it is included. The key piece in the package was the meaning of multiplication with fractions. The teachers regarded it as a "knot" that ties a cluster of concepts that support the understanding of the meaning of division by fractions. In the previous chapters we noted that the Chinese teachers tend to pay significant attention to the occasion when a concept is first introduced and tend to regard it as a key piece in a knowledge package. In addressing the key piece in the knowledge package of this chapter, they still adhered to this principle. However, since the mathematical topic discussed in this chapter is more advanced and complex, its stepping stone is not a single concept but a connection of several concepts.

One of the reasons why the U.S. teachers' understanding of the meaning of division of fractions was not built might be that their knowledge lacked connections and links. The understanding of most of the U.S. teachers was supported by only one idea—the partitive model of whole number division. Because other necessary concepts for understanding and their connections with the topic were missing, these teachers were not able to generate a conceptual representation of the meaning of division by fractions.

Relationship Between Teachers' Subject Matter Knowledge and Their Representations

Generating representations for a mathematical concept is a common teaching task. Most of the U.S. teachers tended to represent the meaning of division by fractions with a real-world example. The topics that the Chinese teachers used, however, were broader and less connected with students' lives. Doubtless connecting school mathematics learning with students' out-of-school lives may help them make more sense of mathematics. However, the "real world" cannot produce mathematical content by itself. Without a solid knowledge of what to represent, no matter how rich one's knowledge of students' lives, no matter how much one is motivated to connect mathematics with students' lives, one still cannot produce a conceptually correct representation.

SUMMARY

This chapter investigated teachers' subject matter knowledge of two aspects of the same topic—division by fractions. Teachers were asked to calculate $1\frac{3}{4} \div \frac{1}{2}$ and to illustrate the meaning of the operation, an aspect of subject matter knowledge not approached in previous chapters. The U.S. teachers' knowledge of division by fractions was obviously weaker than their knowledge of the two previous topics. Although 43% of the U.S. teachers succeeded in correctly calculating a complete answer, none showed an understanding of the rationale underlying their calculations. Only Tr. Belle, an experienced teacher, succeeded in generating a representation that correctly illustrated the meaning of division by fractions.

The Chinese teachers' performance on the task for this chapter was not noticeably different from that on the previous tasks. All of their calculations were correct and a few teachers went a step further to discuss the rationale underlying the algorithm. Most of the teachers generated at least one correct and appropriate representation. Their ability to generate representations that used a rich variety of subjects and different models of division by fractions seemed to be based on their solid knowledge of the topic. On the other hand, the U.S. teachers, who were unable to represent the operation, did not correctly explain its meaning. This suggests that in order to have a pedagogically powerful representation for a topic, a teacher should first have a comprehensive understanding of it.

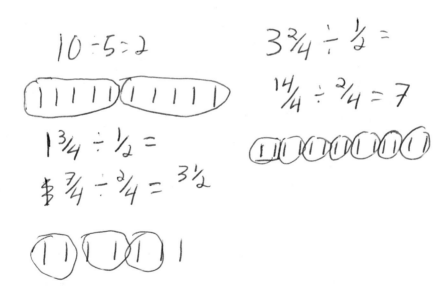

Exploring New Knowledge: The Relationship Between Perimeter And Area

Scenario

Imagine that one of your students comes to class very excited. She tells you that she has figured out a theory that you never told the class. She explains that she has discovered that as the perimeter of a closed figure[1] increases, the area also increases. She shows you this picture to prove what she is doing:

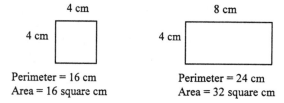

How would you respond to this student?

Students bring up novel ideas and claims in their mathematics classes. Sometimes teachers know whether a student's claim is valid, but sometimes they do not. The perimeter and area of a figure are two different measures. The perimeter is a measure of the length of the boundary of a figure (in

---

[1]The term "a closed figure" used in the scenario was intended to invite the teachers to discuss various kinds of figures. However, during the interviews teachers talked exclusively about squares and rectangles. A few Chinese teachers said that closed figure is a concept introduced at the secondary school level in China so they preferred to focus the discussion on the particular figure mentioned by the student.

the case of a rectangle, the sum of the lengths of the sides of the figure), while the area is a measure of the size of the figure. Because the calculations of both measures are related to the sides of a figure, the student claimed that they were correlated.

The immediate reactions of the U.S. and Chinese teachers to this claim were similar. For most of the teachers in this study, the student's claim was a "new theory" that they were hearing for the first time. Similar proportions of U.S. and Chinese teachers accepted the theory immediately. All the teachers knew what the two measures meant and most teachers knew how to calculate them. From this beginning, however, the teachers' paths diverged. They explored different strategies, reached different results, and responded to the student differently.

HOW THE U.S. TEACHERS EXPLORED THE NEW IDEA

Teachers' Reactions to the Claim

Strategy I: Consulting a Book. While two of the U.S. teachers (9%) simply accepted the student's theory without doubt, the remainder did not. Among the 21 teachers who suspected the theory was true, five said that they had to consult a book. Four of the five explained that they needed a book because they did not remember how to calculate perimeter and area:

> [Pause of about 5 seconds] I forgot my perimeters and my areas here. [Frank looked intently at the problem for about 10 seconds] Well, let's see now the area ... [pause of about 10 seconds] ... I have to look it up and I will get back to students. (Mr. Frank)

> I think I would be looking up formulas, first. To give me the basic formula, for the perimeter and area. And then see if they might even give some examples of the perimeter expanding in one way, and see how they formulated their problem, and see if hers meshed up with what they had in the book. I could also say maybe we could contact someone who has more background in that area, another teacher. (Ms. Fay)

With no idea how to calculate the perimeter and the area, these teachers found it difficult to investigate a claim about the relationship between the two measures. So they chose to consult a textbook or another authority.

Ms. Francesca, a beginning teacher, did know the formulas for calculating the perimeter and area of a rectangle. Believing that the student's claim would not hold in every case, she thought that the only way she could explain it to the student was "to take other examples that did not hold true." However, she explained that because she did not understand why the formulas worked, it was hard for her to develop a counterexample on her own. What she would do would be to find someone to tell her, or "go home and look it up and check it out":

> Let us see, perimeter is [she mumbles the formula to herself]. How would I explain it to her that, that does not hold true? I guess the only other way I would, right now from the top of my head, is to take other examples that did not hold true, and illustrate to her that . . . that it does not hold true. And I cannot remember exactly why . . . I would go back and research it and find out why, and then come back to her and show her. And probably if like somebody were to come up to me and tell me this right now. Because I, to be honest, I remember how to figure out perimeter and area, but I do not understand why right now. I would tell them, I do not believe this is true, but let me find out for sure and go out on my own and look it up and do problems, and then come back and tell her why.

It was obvious that Ms. Francesca knew more about the topic than the other four teachers. Yet she also noticed that she lacked specific knowledge related to the claim. She would turn to a textbook or to those with more knowledge, hoping that would help her to find a correct answer for the problem.

Strategy II: Calling for More Examples.   Thirteen U.S. teachers proposed another strategy to explore the claim—calling for more examples:

> I am not sure. I would say probably that it may work in some cases, but may not work in other cases. (Ms. Fiona)

> What I would need to do is probably have enough examples. (Tr. Blanche)

> We should talk about whether it worked in every case, if it proves true in every situation. (Ms. Florence)

These teachers' responses to the claim, that it needed more examples, were based on everyday experience, rather than mathematical insight. Most adults will not be persuaded to accept a proposition with only one example. The teachers' comments on the student's mathematical theory, in fact, paralleled general statements such as "Even though I see two white swans, I would not believe that all swans are white." However, how many white swans do we need to see in order to believe that all swans are white? Themselves concerned about *the number* of examples, these teachers ignored the fact that a mathematical statement concerning an infinite number of cases cannot be proved by finitely many examples—no matter how many. It should be proved by a mathematical argument. The role of examples is to *illustrate* numerical relationships, rather than *prove* them.

Although the teachers were able to point out that one example is not sufficient to prove a theory, they were not able to investigate the claim mathematically. A few of them suggested trying arbitrary numbers, for example, "one through ten," or "strange numbers such as threes and sevens." These suggestions were based on common sense, rather than mathematical insight.

Strategy III: Mathematical Approaches. The remaining three teachers investigated the problem mathematically. Ms. Faith was the only one who achieved a correct solution. Her approach was to present an example that disagreed with the student's theory:

> I would say, "Now tell me though what happens when you have got 2 inches on the one side and 16 inches on the other side." I would ask her what the perimeter is, then I would ask her to figure out the area. Aha!

The student used a square with sides of 4 inches and a rectangle with the width of 4 inches and the length of 8 inches to prove her statement. The perimeter of the square was 16 inches and that of the rectangle was 24 inches. The area of the former was 16 square inches and that of the latter was 32 square inches. The student concluded that "as the perimeter of a figure increased, the area increases correspondingly." Ms. Faith would ask her to try another example, a rectangle with a width of 2 inches and a length of 16 inches. The perimeter of Ms. Faith's rectangle was 36 inches, 12 inches longer than that of the student's rectangle. According to the student's claim, the area of Ms. Faith's rectangle should be bigger than that of the student's. However, it was not true. Ms. Faith's rectangle had the same area as that of the student's, 32 square inches. With a single counterexample, Ms. Faith disproved the claim.

Ms. Francine also tested the claim by trying a long, skinny rectangle. However, she was not as successful as Ms. Faith:

> I would say that by this picture that is right. How about, though, draw another picture, but skinny, long . . . then showing her that maybe it would not always work . . . Like that [she drew some figures on paper]. Four and 8 . . . I am trying . . . the area is when you multiply, 32. So, yes, that is right . . . Let us say this one, 4 by 4, and let us say this is 2 by 4 . . . oh, oh, wait a minute. I do not know. I do not know if she is right or not . . . I guess we would have to find out, . . . look it up in a book!

Ms. Francine came close to finding a counterexample. However, she failed because she followed the pattern in the student's example—changing the

TABLE 4.1
U.S. Teachers' Reactions to Student's Claim ($N = 23$)

Reactions	%	N
Simply accepted the claim	9	2
No mathematical investigation	78	18
Investigated the claim	13	3

perimeter by changing a pair of opposite sides and keeping the other pair of sides fixed. She reduced the perimeter by reducing the length of one pair of opposite sides from 4 inches to 2 inches, but kept the other pair of sides unchanged. Contrary to her expectation, the student's claim still held: the area of her new figure decreased as well. Then she was confused. She decided to give up her own approach and look it up in a book—the response of a layperson rather than the response of a mathematician.

Mr. Felix was the third teacher who approached the problem mathematically. He would explore why the student's claim was true:

> I would . . . confirm that indeed in the case of these rectangles and squares that is true; that it does get bigger. I would talk about why that is the case. What the relationship between the area and the perimeter is, and how to use something like a squaring off grid method, to talk about how adding that extra perimeter adds to the area.

Mr. Felix's approach explains why Ms. Francine failed to disprove the student's claim. When the increase (or decrease) of the perimeter is caused only by the increase (or decrease) of only one pair of opposite sides, the area of the figure will increase (or decrease) as well. The area of the increased (or decreased) new figure is the increased (or decreased) length times the length of the unchanged side. Using this pattern one can generate infinitely many examples that support the student's claim.

Mr. Felix, however, did not completely examine the student's claim. He stopped after explaining why the claim worked in this case and did not investigate the cases in which it would *not* work. Of the 23 U.S. teachers, Ms. Faith, a beginning teacher, was the only one to successfully examine the student's proposition and attain a correct solution. Table 4.1 summarizes the U.S. teachers' reactions to the student's claim.

Teachers' Responses to the Student

Ball (1988b) indicated three possibilities that teachers might use to respond when they are confronted with a new idea proposed by a student:

1. Divert the student from pursuing ideas outside the scheduled curriculum.

2. Be responsible for evaluating the truth of the student's claim.

3. Engage the student in exploring the truth of her claim.

The teachers in the study chose the second and third alternatives. The teachers who took the second alternative reported that they would "tell" or "explain" the solution to the student. The teachers who took the third alternative reported that they would invite the student to investigate or discuss the claim further. In addition, most teachers explained that they would first give a positive comment to the student. Therefore, the teachers' responses to the student fell into two main categories: *praise with explanation*, and *praise with engagement in further exploration*.

Sixteen U.S. teachers (72%) described an intention to engage the student in a further proof of the claim. However, without an understanding of the proof themselves, their attempts to engage the student in such a discussion could only be superficial. Three teachers reported that they would "look it up with the student":

> OK, what I would do is go, go with her to a math book and look up perimeter, look up area, and how, how perimeter and area are related, and go through it together. (Ms. Frances)

> I think I would say, "I am not real sure but let us look it up together, and see, and see if we can find a book that would show us whether you are—your discovery is correct or not." (Ms. Fay)

These teachers were the ones who did not remember how to calculate the two measures of a rectangle. What they suggested that the student should do was the same as what they themselves wanted to do—to find the knowledge that is stored in a book.

Six teachers said they would ask the student to try, or to show them more examples, to prove her own claim:

> She's right. Have her try, encourage her and say, I think you are right and have her maybe show the class or show me—try it with different examples and make sure that she can support her hypothesis. Put her in a position of that "I really found something out"—make her feel good. (Ms. Fleur)

> Oh, most likely, oh yes. Now I just want to make sure it is right. Well, I would praise her for doing work at home ... I would then use these as examples on the board. Maybe ask her to be my teacher's helper, give other examples. (Tr. Belinda)

> I'd be excited. I really do not have a comment on it. I'd probably like to have her do a few more to prove it. (Tr. Beatrice)

These teachers merely asked the student to try more examples, but did not think mathematically about the problem or discuss specific strategies. Five other teachers offered to try more examples with the student, but did not mention specific strategies either:

> I am not sure. I would say probably that it may work in some cases, but may not work in other cases. I would say, well you know, this is very interesting. Let us try it with some other numbers and see if this works as well. (Ms. Fiona)

> I think the best, you probably have to go through and start with, again, even a different group of numbers and bring her on all the way through. In other words, well maybe it would work with one case but it would not work with the next case. So maybe showing the girl working with not just the 4 by 4 and then the 4 by 8, but say 3 by 3 and try it with other numbers. Well, let us say she continues in this vein . . . (Tr. Bernadette)

Five teachers mentioned specific strategies for approaching the problem. However, except for that mentioned by Ms. Faith, the strategies were not based on careful mathematical thinking. When they suggested trying "different numbers" or "strange numbers," they were not considering different cases in a systematic way as we shall see the Chinese teachers did. Rather, the strategy they proposed was based on the idea that a mathematical claim should be proved by a large number of examples. This misconception, which was shared by many U.S. teachers, would be likely to mislead a student.

HOW THE CHINESE TEACHERS EXPLORED THE NEW IDEA

Teachers' Approaches to the Problem

The Chinese teachers' first reactions to the problem were very similar to those of the U.S. teachers. About the same proportion of the Chinese teachers (8%) as of the U.S. teachers (9%) accepted the claim immediately, without any doubt. The other Chinese teachers were not sure if the claim was valid or not. It took them a while to think about it before they began to respond. Of the four interview questions, this took them the longest time to think over. And, once they started to discuss the problem, their responses differed considerably from those of their U.S. counterparts.

The Chinese and the U.S. teachers' responses differed in three ways. First, many Chinese teachers showed an enthusiastic interest in *the topic*, the relationship between the perimeter and the area of a rectangle, while the U.S. teachers tended to be concerned with whether *the claim* that "as the perimeter increases, the area increases as well" was true or not.

Second, most Chinese teachers made mathematically legitimate explorations on their own, while most of their U.S. counterparts did not. No Chinese teacher said that he or she would need to consult a book or someone else,[2] and none ended up saying "I am not sure." The Chinese teachers' explorations, however, did not necessarily lead them to correct solutions. Consequently, most U.S. teachers who held a "not sure" opinion avoided a wrong answer, but 22% of the Chinese teachers, because of their problematic strategies, gave incorrect solutions. The remaining 70% solved the problem correctly.

Third, the Chinese teachers demonstrated a better knowledge of elementary geometry. They were very familiar with perimeter and area formulas. During their interviews, many discussed relationships among the various geometric figures that were not even mentioned by any of the U.S. teachers. For example, some Chinese teachers said that a square is a special rectangle. Some also pointed out that a rectangle is a basic figure—that perimeter and area calculations for various other figures rely on using rectangles.[3]

Figure 4.1 summarizes the reactions of the teachers of the two countries to the problem.

Justifying an Invalid Claim: Teachers' Knowledge and Pitfalls. Sixteen Chinese teachers who investigated the problem mathematically argued that the student's claim was correct. Twelve teachers justified the claim by discussing *why* it was the case, the other four teachers addressed *how* it was the case. These teachers tended to build their arguments on the correspondence formed by identifying the length, width, and area of the rectangle with two numbers and their product:

> I think the student is right. As the perimeter of a rectangle increases, its area increases as well. We know that the area of a rectangle is the product of its length and width. In other words, the length and the width are the two factors that produce the area. Unquestionably, as the factors increase, the product will increase as well. (Ms. H.)

Their strategy, although incorrect, was grounded in appropriate, although incorrect mathematics. First, the teachers identified the student's claim as a numerical relationship—the relationship between two factors

---

[2]Stigler, Fernandez, and Yoshida (1996) reported a similar tendency on the part of Japanese elementary teachers.

[3]In the Chinese curriculum the area formulas for other shapes such as squares, triangles, circles, and trapezoids are derived from that for rectangles.

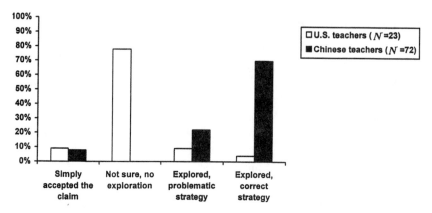

FIG. 4.1. A comparison of teachers' reactions to the student's claim.

and their product in multiplication. Then they drew on an established principle of this relationship—that between the factors and the product—to prove the claim. The flaw was, however, that they failed to notice that the claim involved *two* different numerical relationships, not just a multiplicative one. While the relationship of length, width, and area of a rectangle is multiplicative, that of its length, width, and perimeter is additive. The perimeter of a rectangle can increase while two of the sides of the rectangle decrease in length.

The teachers who said that the claim was true had explanations similar to Mr. Felix's:

> The student's claim is true. Let's have a look at how it is true. If we overlap the square on the rectangle, we will see another uncovered square. That will be the increased area. One pair of opposite sides of the increased area is actually the width of the two original figures, the other pair of opposite sides of the increased area is the difference between the length of the original rectangle and the side of the original square. Or, we can say that it is the increased piece of the length . . . (Ms. B.)

Like Mr. Felix, they failed to consider all the ways in which the perimeter of a rectangle may increase. Therefore, they only explained how the student's case was true, but did not explore the real problem: if it is always true.

Although these sixteen teachers did not attain correct solutions, they showed the intention to explore the problem mathematically. Instead of making general comments about the student's claim, they investigated the problem and reached their own conclusions. Moreover, these teachers were aware of an important convention in the discipline: any mathematical proposition has to be proved, and they tended to follow this convention. They did not just opine "the claim is right," rather, they gave proofs of their opinions. The arguments they made, although deficient, were grounded in legitimate mathematics. In addition to a solid knowledge of the calculation of the two measures, these teachers displayed sound attitudes toward mathematical investigation. Of course, their approaches also revealed an obvious weakness—the lack of thoroughness in their thinking.

Disproving the Claim: The First Level of Understanding. Fifty of the 72 Chinese teachers gave correct solutions but their different approaches displayed various levels of understanding. The first level was to disprove the student's claim. The 14 Chinese teachers' approach at this level was similar to Ms. Faith's—looking for counterexamples:

> Her claim was not true. I will say nothing but show the student a counterexample. For instance, under her square (with sides of 4 cm), I may want to draw a rectangle with the length of 8 cm and the width of 1 cm. She will soon find that my figure is of longer perimeter but smaller area than hers. So, without saying, her claim is wrong. (Ms. I.)

> This claim does not hold true in all cases. It is easy to find cases which can disprove the theory. For example, there is a rectangle, its length is 10 cm and its width is 2 cm. Its perimeter will be the same as that of the student's rectangle, 24 cm. But its area will be only 20 square cm, smaller than that of the student's rectangle. (Tr. R.)

To disprove the claim, the teachers created two kinds of counterexamples. One consisted of figures with longer perimeter but smaller area or shorter perimeter but bigger area, than one of the student's figures. The other kind consisted of figures with the same area but a different perimeter—or the same perimeter but a different area—as the student's figures.

Identifying the Possibilities: The Second Level of Understanding. Eight teachers explored the various possible relationships between perimeter and area. They gave different kinds of examples that supported, as well as opposed the claim, to show the various possibilities:

> I will present several figures to her and ask her to calculate their perimeter and area:

6

2 [c   ]

P = 16
A = 12

7

1 [d   ]

P = 16
A = 7

By comparing these figures, she will learn that as the perimeter increases, the area does not necessarily increase as well, such as in the case of figures *a* and *b*. Also, when the perimeter remains the same, the area may not be the same, such as in the case of figures *c* and *d*. So she will know that there is not a direct relationship between perimeter and area. What she has found is one of several solutions of the problem. (Ms. E.)

I will first praise her for her independent thinking. But I will also let her know that there may be two other situations as well. For example, when the perimeter increases, the area can increase, but it may also decrease, or even stay the same. Then I will show her an example of each case to compare with her rectangle (with length of 8 cm and a width of 4 cm). I will first give an example of her claim, like a rectangle with a length of 8 cm and width of 5 cm. The perimeter will increase from 24 cm to 26 cm, the area will increase from 32 square cm to 40 square cm. Now, the second example will be a rectangle with length 12 cm and width 2 cm. Its perimeter will increase to 28 cm, but its area will decrease to 24 square cm, only three quarters of the area of her rectangle. Another example might be a figure with length 16 cm and width 2 cm. Its perimeter will also increase, up to 36 cm, but the area will stay the same as that of her rectangle, 32 square cm. So I will tell her that mathematical thinking has to be thorough. This is one feature of our thinking that gets improved in learning mathematics. (Mr. A.)

Mr. A. revealed that increasing the perimeter may cause the area to increase, decrease, or stay the same. Ms. E. described two cases in which the two measures changed in different ways—while the perimeter increases, the area decreases, and while the perimeter stays the same, the area decreases. At this level of understanding, teachers discussed various facets of the relationship between the perimeter and the area of a figure. In particular, they examined different kinds of changes in the area of a rectangle that can be caused by changes in the perimeter. The teachers did not simply disprove the student's claim, rather, they presented a wider perspective in which the student's claim was included.

Clarifying the Conditions: The Third Level of Understanding. In addition to displaying the various possibilities, 26 teachers clarified the conditions under which these possibilities held. These teachers tended to explore numerical relationships between perimeter and area and elaborate specific examples:

It is obvious that in some cases the claim holds but in some other cases it does not hold true. Yet when does it hold true and when does it not? In other words, under what conditions does it hold up, and under what conditions does it not? We had better have a clear idea about it. To clarify the specific conditions that cause the various possibilities, we can first investigate the conditions that will cause an increase in the perimeter, and then explore how these conditions affect the change in the area. (Mr. D.)

Tr. R. articulated the strategy that she and several other teachers used to explore the conditions under which the student's claim held. They first examined the cause in the student's claim—an increase in the perimeter. They investigated the situations that would produce an increase in the perimeter of a rectangle and found three patterns. Then they analyzed the changes these patterns would produce in the area. Through a careful examination, Tr. R. attained a clear picture of how the area might be affected by an increase in the perimeter of the different ways:

I would say that the student's claim holds up under certain conditions. We know that changes in the length and width of a figure may cause an increase in perimeter. There are three ways to change the length and the width of a rectangle that would cause an increase in its perimeter. The first is when either the length or the width increases but the other measure remains the same. Under this condition, the area of the figure will increase accordingly. For example, given that the length of the student's rectangle increases to 9 cm and its width remains unchanged, the original area, 32 square centimeters, will increase to 36 square centimeters. Or, given that the width of the original rectangle increases to 5 cm but its length remains unchanged, its area will increase to 40 square centimeters. The second way to increase the perimeter is when both the length and the width increase at the same time. Under this condition, the area will also increase. For example, given that the length of the rectangle increases to 9 cm and the width increases to 5 cm at the same time, the area of the rectangle will increase to 45 square cm. The third condition that causes an increase in perimeter is when either the length or the width of a figure increases but the other measure decreases; however, the increased quantity is larger than the decreased quantity. Under this condition, the perimeter will also increase, but the change in area may go in three directions. It may increase, decrease, or stay the same. For example, given that the width increases to 6 cm and the length decreases to 7 cm, the perimeter will increase to 26 cm and area will increase to 42 square cm. Given that the length increases to 10 cm and the width decreases to 3 cm, the perimeter will also increase to 26 cm, but the area will decrease to 30 square cm. Given that the length increases to 16 cm and the width decreases to 2 cm, the perimeter will increase to 36 cm, yet the area will remain the same, 32 square cm. In brief, under the first two conditions, the student's claim holds true, but under the last condition, it does not necessarily hold. (Tr. R.)

The solution that these teachers attained was: when increase in the perimeter is caused by the increase in either or both the length and the width of a rectangle, the area of the figure will increase accordingly; but when the increase in perimeter is caused by increasing length and decreasing width, or vice versa, the area will not necessarily increase as well. About two thirds of the 26 teachers elaborated their discussion in the manner of Tr. R. They addressed both situations—when the claim holds and when it does not necessarily hold. The remaining third of the teachers focused on one of these situations. The teachers who reached this level of understanding did not regard the claim as absolutely correct or absolutely wrong. Rather, they referred to the concept of "conditional." They argued that the claim was conditionally correct:

> So, now we can say that the student's claim is not absolutely wrong, but it is incomplete or conditional. Under certain conditions it is tenable, but under other conditions it does not necessarily hold. I am glad that you raised the problem. I have figured out something new today which I haven't thought about before. (Tr. J.)

> After the discussion I may want to give her a suggestion to revise her claim by confining it to certain conditions. She may want to say that under the conditions that the increase of the perimeter is caused by the increase of either the length or the width but the other side remains unchanged, or by the increase of both the length and the width, the area of the rectangle increases as well. That will be a safe statement. (Ms. G.)

In clarifying the different conditions under which the student's claim would hold or not hold, the teachers developed different relationships between the perimeter and area of a rectangle. The student's claim was not simply abandoned; rather, it was revised and incorporated into one of the relationships.

Explaining the Conditions: The Fourth Level of Understanding. Six of the teachers who reached the third level of understanding went even further, explaining why some conditions supported the student's claim and why other conditions did not. Their approaches varied. After a detailed and well-organized discussion of the conditions under which the student's claim would hold, Tr. Mao said:

> At last, we can have an examination of why these conditions are tenable. Imagine how the area of a figure changes when its perimeter changes. Under the first two conditions, the original area remains but a new area is added to it. For instance, when the length increases but the width remains the same, there will be an extra area expanding horizontally from the original

one. On the other hand, when the width increases but the length remains the same, there will be an extra area expanding vertically from the original one. If both the length and the perimeter increase at the same time, the original area will expand in both directions. In any of these cases, the original area is still there but some other extra area is added to it. We can draw figures to display the cases. In fact, it can also be proved by using the distributive property. For example, when the length increases 3 cm, it becomes $(a + 3)$ cm.[4] The area will be $(a + 3)b = ab + 3b$. Now, compared to the original area, ab, we can see why it is larger. $3b$ is the increased quantity. However, given that one measure increases and the other one decreases, the original area of the first figure will be destroyed. There is no reason that guarantees the new area will be bigger than the previous one.

Tr. Mao's argument was based on a geometric representation of the situation. He also applied the distributive property to add another proof to his approach. Tr. Xie's argument about why rectangles with the same perimeter can have different areas was also very insightful. He first indicated that for the same perimeter one can form many rectangles of different lengths and widths, because there are many different pairs of addends that make the same sum. Then he argued that when these pairs of addends become factors, as in calculating the area of the figure, obviously they will produce very different products. Finally, using the fact that the closer the value of the two factors, the larger their product, he claimed that for a given perimeter, the square is the rectangle with the largest area:

> The area of a rectangle is determined by two things, its perimeter and its shape. The problem of the student was that she only saw the first one. Theoretically, with the same perimeter, let's say 20 cm, we can have infinite numbers of rectangles as long as the sum of their lengths and widths is 10 cm. For example, we can have $5 + 5 = 10$, $3 + 7 = 10$, $0.5 + 9.5 = 10$, even $0.01 + 9.99 = 10$, etc., etc. Each pair of addends can be the two sides of a rectangle. As we can imagine, the area of these rectangles will fall into a big range. The square with sides of 5 cm will have the biggest area, 25 square cm, while the one with a length of 9.99 cm and a width of 0.01 cm will have almost no area. Because in all the pairs of numbers with the same sum, the closer the two numbers are, the bigger the product they will produce . . . (Tr. Xie)

Tr. Xie and Tr. Mao did not draw on the same basic principles of mathematics for their arguments. However, both developed solid arguments. In fact, a basic principle of mathematics may be able to support various numerical models. On the other hand, a numerical model may

---

[4]In Chinese elementary math textbooks, a stands for length of a figure, and b stands for width of a figure.

also be supported by various basic principles. A profound understanding of a mathematical topic, at last, will include certain basic principles of the discipline by which the topic is supported. Passing through various levels of understanding of the student's claim, the teachers got closer and closer to a complete mathematical argument.

A Map of How Teachers' Exploration Was Supported

The teachers explored the student's claim and reached an understanding of the mathematical issues at various conceptual levels: finding a counter-example, identifying the possible relationships between area and perime-ter, clarifying the conditions under which those relationships hold, and explaining the relationships. While in the three previous chapters we were interested in teachers' existing knowledge of school mathematics, now we are interested in their capacity for exploring a new idea. The task required the teachers to "jump" from their current "home site" to a novel "site," to discover something they had not thought about before.

Figure 4.2 represents how the teachers' approach to the relationship between perimeter and area was supported. The rectangle at the top rep-resents the task: to explore a new mathematical idea on one's own. The rhombuses represent the affective factors. The other components of the figure represent aspects of teacher subject matter knowledge. The circle represents knowledge, calculation of perimeter and area, closely related to the new idea. The squares represent what Bruner (1960/1977) consid-

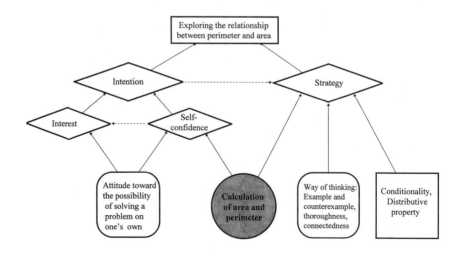

FIG. 4.2. A map of how teachers' exploration was supported.

ered basic ideas of a subject—basic principles (represented by squares with straight corners) and basic attitudes (represented by squares with round corners).

Teachers' explorations of the student's claim were affected by two factors: *intention* and *strategy*. Undoubtedly strategy plays a significant role in this task. However, the interviews revealed that teachers' intentions also played a critical role. Teachers who did not intend to examine the claim did not bother to think of a strategy. Most U.S. teachers did not evidence any intention to approach the new idea on their own, so they did not seriously consider a strategy.

The teachers' intention to approach the student's claim on their own relied on two subfactors—their *interest* in a new mathematical proposition and their *self-confidence* in their ability to understand it. The teachers who enthusiastically made a thorough study of the student's claim were those particularly interested in the mathematical topic raised. They were driven by a strong curiosity about the relationship between perimeter and area of a rectangle. A strong internal motivation for teaching mathematics could be observed in these teachers' responses. On the other hand, the teachers who were not interested in the claim were not motivated to examine it. Interest in exploring a mathematical proposition, however, is supported by one's attitude toward the possibility of solving a problem on one's own, and affected by one's confidence of solving the problem.

Confidence was the other factor determining whether or not a teacher investigated the claim. The teachers who were not confident of their own ability to solve the problem did not attempt it. Teachers' confidence drew on two aspects of their subject matter knowledge: their *attitudes toward the possibility of solving mathematical problems on their own* and their *knowledge of the particular topics related to the proposition.* Those who either did not believe that it was possible to solve the problem on their own, or did not know how to calculate the perimeter and area of a figure, would not further explore relationships between perimeter and area. Consequently, their intentions of solving the problem, if they existed, would be inhibited.

Teachers' strategies for investigating the problem drew on three aspects of their subject matter knowledge: their knowledge of the particular topic related to the new idea, *the ways of thinking in mathematics* and *basic principles of the discipline related to the approach.* All the teachers who successfully accomplished the task showed familiarity with the formulas for calculating perimeter and area, as well as understanding of their underlying rationales. Their proficiency in calculation, indeed, substantially supported their investigations which involved various procedures of calculation.

Teachers' knowledge of mathematical thinking played a key role in helping teachers to "jump" from their previous knowledge to a new discovery. Not all teachers who knew how to calculate perimeter and area of a rectangle conducted a mathematical approach on their own. However, those who also knew how to think of the claim in a mathematical way did. Although some did not reach a correct solution, their knowledge of how to think about the proposition in a mathematical way at least led them to a legitimate approach. In contrast, the teachers who knew the formulas but did not think of the claim in a mathematical way were not able to approach the problem mathematically.

Finally, teachers' knowledge of basic mathematical principles—for example, the conditionality of a mathematical proposition—contributed substantially to their approach. Acquaintance with the application of the distributive property, again, enhanced some teachers' explanations of the addition and multiplication relationships connected with the topic.

Teachers' Responses to the Student

The Chinese teachers' responses to the student fall into the same categories as those of the U.S. teachers—*praise with explanation* and *praise with engagement in further exploration*. However, because most of the Chinese teachers investigated the problem, their responses to the student were significantly more substantial and relevant than those of their U.S. counterparts. More appropriate examples were provided to illustrate the various aspects of the topic and more appropriate questions were raised to lead the student to further discovery.

In addition, the two groups of teachers were differently distributed in the two categories. Only two U.S. teachers (9%) reported that they would give the student an explanation, one immediately and one after "looking it up." Most of the U.S. teachers said they would explore the claim with the student who proposed it, but they generally did not have ideas about what that exploration would be. Most of the Chinese teachers (62%) after getting a clear solution would give the student a detailed explanation of the topic in contrast to those who would engage her in discovering the results on her own (30%). Most of the Chinese teachers' explanations during the interviews were clear, well organized, and complete. Generally, an explanation came after an assertion such as "Tell the student her claim was not true" or "Tell the student her claim was not complete." Most of the teachers who justified the student's claim would also explain to her why they thought she was right.

The Chinese teachers who would engage the student in a further discussion of the claim were those who presented a better understanding and were more comfortable in their own investigation of the problem. Most said they would raise questions or give other examples to lead the student to find the limitations of her claim and reach a further understanding of the relationship between the perimeter and area of a rectangle:

As for the student, first of all I will praise her. I will make nice comments about her independent thinking, and the consistency between her claim and her example. But then I will lead her to find the problem with her claim. I will first ask her to explain why in her case as the perimeter increases, the area increases as well, ask her to show me the increased part of the area and tell me how it was generated. Then I will say, your example showed a situation in which one pair of the opposite sides of the figure increased and the other pair of sides remained unchanged. This is one situation that causes the perimeter of a rectangle to increase. Have you thought of any other situations in which the perimeter will increase as well? Do you know what will happen in the other situations? Now we know that in at least one situation your claim holds. But to prove your claim you should make sure that it works in all situations, and provide an explanation for why it holds. She might easily find other situations in which the perimeter of a rectangle will increase. Very likely, she will find that when the other pair of sides increases, or when both pairs of sides increase, the perimeter will increase as well. And she will also find that in these cases her claim will hold. Then I will lead her to think of more situations. Probably she could find out that under certain conditions her claim does not hold. If she can't think of the other conditions on her own, I will give her some examples and let her think over what kinds of situations these examples illustrate and what will happen under these situations. In brief, I will lead her to investigate her claim on her own, and give her help whenever necessary. At the end, I expect her to have a clear idea of under which conditions her claim holds and under which conditions it does not hold. I also want to help her to see that the problem with her approach was the lack of thoroughness in her thinking. So I will close the conversation by emphasizing that it is very good for one to think independently, yet it is not enough. One should also learn how to think. As in her case, how to think in a thorough way. (Tr. T.)

Tr. T's response shows several interesting features presented in similar responses from many Chinese teachers. First of all, there was a subtle interweaving of praise and criticism. Although she started with praise for the student's independent thinking, after a discussion of the various facets of the topic, she ended the conversation by indicating that the student should work on improving the aspect of her thinking that was praised by the teacher—to think in a thorough way. This pattern was seen in a few other teachers' responses. For example:

I will first give a positive reaction to her initiative, tell her that I am glad about what she has found. Then I will suggest that we have more discussions about the claim. Based on her rectangle, I will give her a series of examples that present different situations that may cause an increase in the perimeter and a different change in the area ... [examples omitted]. Finally, I will encourage her again for her spirit of daring to initiate a study and explore a new idea on her own. But at the same time I will indicate to her that one

should not only dare to think, but also learn how to be good at thinking.
(Tr. Sun)

Most of the Chinese teachers reported that they would first of all praise the student's mental effort, such as "close observation," "inquiry into new knowledge," "independent thinking," and "the initiative to explore new knowledge on her own," etc. However, they would soon turn to a discussion of the problematic aspects of the student's claim, which they considered to be caused by a certain inadequacy in her way of thinking. At the end, the teachers would go back to what they had praised, confirming it again, and indicating what should be improved later on.

Moreover, the Chinese teachers' responses tended to interweave other elements: telling, explaining, raising questions, and displaying examples. Here is an example of a teacher who would first tell the student that her claim was problematic and then guide her further:

> I may want to tell her that her finding is not complete. Because it only illustrates one kind of relation between perimeter and area. I will suggest that she think of other cases. What will happen if the width increases but the length remains the same? What will happen if both the length and the width increase? What will happen if the length increases and the width decreases, or vice versa? I will ask her to continue thinking about these situations and to come back to tell me her new findings. If she can't find the complete solution after a new exploration, I will discuss it with her and show her other relevant examples in order to reveal the solution step-by-step. Finally, to urge her to further explore the relationship between perimeter and area of a rectangle, I will probably give her a problem to think about: Given that with a same perimeter, what kind of length and width will cause the largest area? (Tr. S.)

Although some teachers would engage the student in exploring the problem on her own, they would also be ready at any time to give specific suggestions about how to approach it:

> First of all I would ask her to look again at the figures she brought and tell me her idea of how the area increased. If she can't tell me, I may want to suggest that she can imagine that the square overlaps with the rectangle, and see where the increased area is and think where this area came from. It is caused by the increase in the length. It is obvious that the more the length increases, the bigger this increased area will be. Also, an increase in length will cause an increase in perimeter. Then I would ask her if there any other ways in which the area of a rectangle can increase. Following the logic of our discussion, she would probably say that when the width increases, the area increases as well. How about if both the length and width increase? Of course both the perimeter and area will increase. We don't even need any examples here. Then I would ask her if she knows another way to

increase the perimeter of a rectangle. This would be a hard step for her because she would have to change the way she has been thinking. I might ask her to think about it at home and come back to me the next day. Or, if I feel that she would not be likely to discover it on her own, I would give her some examples with longer perimeter than the figure she brought to me but less, or equal area. For example, a rectangle with a length of 10 cm and a width of 2 cm. In this way, I would lead her to a discussion of the conditions under which her claim will hold and the conditions under which it will not, and why. After clearing that up, we would come to a discussion of what the problem was with her original claim and how it was caused. (Tr. C.)

Some teachers seemed to be particularly good at using appropriate examples, while others were good at asking appropriate questions. However, these two elements were connected:

I will first comment on her attitude of thinking independently. Then I will ask her, "Are you sure that the theory you discovered from the two figures is true for all cases? Do you want to try some more examples? For example, do you want to draw different rectangles with a perimeter of 24 cm and calculate what their areas are? See what happens and come back again." She might come back with figures such as 1×11, 2×10, 3×9, 4×8, 5×7, 6×6, etc., each with the area she calculated. [Chen drew some rectangles on a sheet of paper.] It is very likely that she would have already found that with the same perimeter you get figures of different areas. I would hope that she could also find by herself that with rectangles of the same perimeter, the closer the lengths of the length and the width, the bigger the area. Or, at least, she would see that the square has the biggest area and the skinniest rectangle [on her paper] has the smallest area. Then I will ask her if she can see any pattern in the shape and the area of figures with the same perimeter. Through the discussion she will find out on her own that area and perimeter do not increase at the same time. (Tr. Chen)

While Tr. C. would guide the student to reflect on her previous thinking, Tr. Chen would guide the student to further investigation of the topic. Both of these thoughtful responses were heavily supported by the teachers' subject matter knowledge—their knowledge of how to investigate a new idea in mathematics as well as their knowledge of specific mathematical topics related to the idea.

DISCUSSION

Attitude Toward the Discipline: Promoter of Teachers' Mathematical Inquiry

The U.S. teachers did not show glaring weaknesses in their calculation of perimeter and area of rectangles. However, there was still a remarkable difference between the U.S. teachers and their Chinese counterparts. Only three U.S. teachers (13%) conducted mathematical investigations on their own and only one reached a correct answer. On the other hand, 66 Chinese teachers (92%) conducted mathematical investigations and 44 (62%) reached a correct answer.

Two main factors may have precluded the U.S. teachers from a successful mathematical investigation—their lack of computational proficiency and their layperson-like attitude toward mathematics. Although most of the U.S. teachers knew how to calculate the two measures, they were far less proficient than their Chinese counterparts. A few reported that although they could do the calculations, they did not understand their rationales, and that this deficiency hampered further exploration. This was not the case for the Chinese teachers. None reported that lack of knowledge about the formulas hindered their investigations.

The second factor, which may be even more significant, was the teachers' attitudes toward mathematics. In responding to the student's novel claim about the relationship between perimeter and area, the U.S. teachers behaved more like laypeople, while the Chinese teachers behaved more like mathematicians. This difference displayed their different attitudes toward mathematics. In discussing the structure of a subject, Bruner (1960/1977) wrote:

> Mastery of the fundamental ideas of a field involves not only the grasping of general principles, but also the development of an attitude toward learning and inquiry, toward guessing and hunches, toward the possibility of solving problems on one's own. (p. 20)

In this chapter, we saw that all the teachers who explored the claim showed sound attitudes toward mathematics. They may or may not have reached a correct answer, but their attitude toward the possibility of solving a mathematical problem independently and their ways of thinking mathematically promoted their inquiries.

Being Acculturated to Mathematics: Should It be a Feature of Mathematics Teachers?

Although the soundness of the Chinese teachers' attitudes toward mathematics has been a particular focus of this chapter, it was evident in the previous chapters as well. The reader may have noticed that in all four chapters quotations from the Chinese teachers have been generally longer than those of the U.S. teachers. In fact, the U.S. teachers did not say less than their Chinese counterparts during the interviews, but what they said was less mathematically relevant and mathematically organized.

One reason for the Chinese teachers' eloquence may be their teaching style. Chinese teachers' teaching is more lecture-like. Whenever they teach a new mathematics concept or a skill, they need to prepare a small "lecture"—a complete presentation of the concept or the skill. These small lectures that run through their mathematical teaching and compose a significant part of it, in fact, train them to talk in an organized way.

Yet there is another deep-seated factor which seems to play an even more important role. That is the acculturation of the Chinese mathematics teachers to the discipline. Obviously, these teachers are not mathematicians. Most of them have not even been exposed to any branch of mathematics other than elementary algebra and elementary geometry. However, they tend to think rigorously, tend to use mathematical terms to discuss a topic, and tend to justify their opinions with mathematical arguments. All these features contributed to the mathematical eloquence of the Chinese teachers.

Relationship Between Teachers' Subject Matter Knowledge and Positive Responses to Students' Proposals: How Can a Mathematical Inquiry be Promoted and Supported?

The moment when a student brings up a novel idea or claim is a special opportunity to promote mathematical learning and inquiry. To give the student positive comments and praise his or her initiative is certainly necessary. However, positive comments alone do not suffice to promote significant mathematics learning and inquiry. The student would need a teacher's particular support in further mathematical learning and inquiry. In this chapter, we have seen that a teacher may support the student by providing explanations about the claim, by showing the student how to examine the claim, or by leading the student step by step in her own inquiry. All these supports for mathematical learning, however, are based on the teacher's own knowledge of mathematical inquiry. Teachers who did not know how to conduct such an inquiry, though they would praise the student and ask her to bring more examples, only displayed supports that were too vague and too general to promote real mathematical learning. To empower students with mathematical thinking, teachers should be empowered first.

According to what I have presented in the four data chapters, one might expect that I would conclude that teachers tend not to and may be unable to promote mathematical learning beyond their own understanding. Is it true that students' mathematical learning cannot go beyond their teachers' mathematical knowledge? I asked this question of Ms. Lin, my own elementary teacher. She was not included in my research. However, I encountered her when I revisited my elementary school while collecting the data for this study. After telling me very proudly that some of her sixth-grade students had just won a mathematics contest, she said: "They did it! They solved problems that they never have learned before. They solved problems that even I myself don't know how to do! I am proud of them. But I am also proud of myself. Because I am convinced that it is me who fostered their ability to explore new problems on their own—the capacity to surpass their teacher!"

If Ms. Lin was right, it seems that students who are capable of exploring problems on their own may at times surpass their teacher. However, what kind of teacher can foster in students the ability to explore new mathematics problems? Must such teachers have this ability first? As yet this question has not been studied. Yet my assumption is that only teachers who are acculturated to mathematics can foster their students' ability to conduct mathematical inquiry. To foster such an ability in their students, the teachers must have it first.

SUMMARY

This chapter investigated how the teachers approached a mathematical idea that was new to them: the relationship between the perimeter and the area of a rectangle. Two aspects of subject matter knowledge contributed substantially to a successful approach: knowledge of topics related to the idea and mathematical attitudes. In contrast with previous chapters, the presence or absence of mathematical attitudes was a significant factor in completing the task for this chapter.

The U.S. teachers did not show major deficiencies in their knowledge of topics related to the new idea. More than half of them knew the formulas for calculating the perimeter and area of a rectangle. However, the U.S. teachers were particularly weak in their general attitude toward mathematics. Most behaved in an unmathematical way in approaching the new idea and did not investigate it independently. Only Ms. Faith, a beginning teacher, investigated the new idea and reached a correct solution. In contrast, most of the Chinese teachers investigated the new idea independently, but about one fifth did not reach a correct solution due to problematic strategies.

Teachers' Subject Matter Knowledge: Profound Understanding Of Fundamental Mathematics

The previous four chapters depicted U.S. and Chinese teachers' knowledge of four topics in elementary mathematics. There was a striking contrast in the knowledge of the two groups of teachers studied. The 23 "above average" U.S. teachers tended to be procedurally focused. Most showed sound algorithmic competence in two beginning topics, whole number subtraction and multiplication, but had difficulty with two more advanced topics, division by fractions, and perimeter and area of a rectangle. Although they came from schools whose quality ranged from excellent to mediocre, most of the 72 Chinese teachers demonstrated algorithmic competence as well as conceptual understanding of all four topics. This chapter is devoted to discussion of the teachers' knowledge across the particular topics.

Considered as a whole, the knowledge of the Chinese teachers seemed clearly coherent while that of the U.S. teachers was clearly fragmented. Although the four topics in this study are located at various levels and subareas of elementary mathematics, while interviewing the Chinese teachers I could perceive interconnections among their discussions of each topic. From the U.S. teachers' responses, however, one can hardly see any connection among the four topics. Intriguingly, the fragmentation of the U.S. teachers' mathematical knowledge coincides with the fragmentation of mathematics curriculum and teaching in the U.S. found by other researchers as major explanations for unsatisfactory mathematics learning in the United States (Schmidt, McKnight, & Raizen, 1997; Stevenson & Stigler, 1992). From my perspective, however, this fragmentation and coherence are effects, not causes. Curricula, teaching, and teachers' knowledge reflect the terrains of elementary mathematics in the United States

107

and in China. What caused the coherence of the Chinese teachers' knowledge, in fact, is the mathematical substance of their knowledge.

A CROSS-TOPIC PICTURE OF THE CHINESE TEACHERS' KNOWLEDGE: WHAT IS ITS MATHEMATICAL SUBSTANCE?

Let us take a bird's eye view of the Chinese teachers' responses to the interview questions. It will reveal that their discussions shared some interesting features that permeated their mathematical knowledge and were rarely, if ever, found in the U.S. teachers' responses.

To Find the Mathematical Rationale of an Algorithm

During their interviews, the Chinese teachers often cited an old saying to introduce further discussion of an algorithm: "Know how, and also know why." In adopting this saying, which encourages people to discover a reason behind an action, the teachers gave it a new and specific meaning—*to know how to carry out an algorithm and to know why it makes sense mathematically.* Arithmetic contains various algorithms—in fact it is often thought that knowing arithmetic means being skillful in using these algorithms. From the Chinese teachers' perspective, however, to know a set of rules for solving a problem in a finite number of steps is far from enough—one should also know why the sequence of steps in the computation makes sense. For the algorithm of subtraction with regrouping, while most U.S. teachers were satisfied with the pseudoexplanation of "borrowing," the Chinese teachers explained that the rationale of the computation is "decomposing a higher value unit."[1] For the topic of multidigit multiplication, while most of the U.S. teachers were content with the rule of "lining up with the number by which you multiplied," the Chinese teachers explored the concepts of place value and place value system to explain why the partial products aren't lined up in multiplication as addends are in addition. For the calculation of division by fractions for which the U.S. teachers used "invert and multiply," the Chinese teachers referred to "dividing by

---

[1]In teaching, Chinese teachers tend to use mathematical terms in their verbal explanations. Terms such as *addend, sum, minuend, subtrahend, difference, multiplicand, multiplier, product, partial product, dividend, divisor, quotient, inverse operation,* and *composing* and *decomposing,* are frequently used. For example, Chinese teachers do not express the additive version of the commutative law as "The order in which you add two numbers doesn't matter." Instead, they say "When we add two addends, if we exchange their places in the sentence, the sum will remain the same."

a number is equivalent to multiplying by its reciprocal" as the rationale for this seemingly arbitrary algorithm.

The predilection to ask "Why does it make sense?" is the first stepping stone to conceptual understanding of mathematics. Exploring the mathematical reasons underlying algorithms, moreover, led the Chinese teachers to more important ideas of the discipline. For example, the rationale for subtraction with regrouping, "decomposing a higher value unit," is connected with the idea of "composing a higher value unit," which is the rationale for addition with carrying. A further investigation of composing and decomposing a higher value unit, then, may lead to the idea of the "rate of composing and decomposing a higher value unit," which is a basic idea of number representation. Similarly, the concept of place value is connected with deeper ideas, such as place value system and basic unit of a number. Exploring the "why" underlying the "how" leads step by step to the basic ideas at the core of mathematics.

To Justify an Explanation with a Symbolic Derivation

Verbal explanation of a mathematical reason underlying an algorithm, however, seemed to be necessary but not sufficient for the Chinese teachers. As displayed in the previous chapters, after giving an explanation the Chinese teachers tended to justify it with a symbolic derivation. For example, in the case of multidigit multiplication, some of the U.S. teachers explained that the problem 123×645 can be separated into three "small problems": 123×600, 123×40, and 124×5. The partial products, then, are 73800, 4920, and 615, instead of 738, 492, and 615. Compared with most U.S. teachers' emphasis on "lining up," this explanation is conceptual. However, the Chinese teachers gave explanations that were even more rigorous. First, they tended to point out that the distributive law[2] is the rationale underlying the algorithm. Then, as described in chapter 2, they showed how it could be derived from the distributive law in order to

---

[2]In the Chinese mathematics curriculum, the additive versions of commutative and associative laws are first introduced in third grade. The commutative, associative, and distributive laws of multiplication are introduced in fourth grade. They are introduced as alternatives to the standard method. For example, the textbook says of the commutative law of addition, "When two numbers are added, if the locations of the addends are exchanged, the sum remains the same. This is called the commutative law of addition. If the letters a and b represent two arbitrary addends, we can write the commutative law of addition as: $a + b = b + a$. The method we learned of checking a sum by exchanging the order of addends is drawn from this law" (Beijing, Tianjin, Shanghai, and Zhejiang Associate Group for Elementary Mathematics Teaching Material Composing, 1989, pp. 82–83). The textbook illustrates how the two laws can be used as "a way for fast computation." For example, students learn that a faster way of solving $258 + 791 + 642$ is to transform it into $(258 + 642) + 791$, a faster way of solving $1646 - 248 - 152$ is to transform it into $1646 - (248 + 152)$.

illustrate how the distributive law works in this situation and why it makes sense:

$$123 \times 645 = 123 \times (600 + 40 + 5)$$
$$= 123 \times 600 + 123 \times 40 + 123 \times 5$$
$$= 73800 + 4920 + 615$$
$$= 78720 + 615$$
$$= 79335$$

For the topic of division by fractions, the Chinese teachers' symbolic representations were even more sophisticated. They drew on concepts that "students had learned" to prove the equivalence of $1\frac{3}{4} \div \frac{1}{2}$ and $1\frac{3}{4} \times \frac{2}{1}$ in various ways. The following is one proof based on the relationship between a fraction and a division ($\frac{1}{2} = 1 \div 2$):

$$1\frac{3}{4} \div \frac{1}{2} = 1\frac{3}{4} \div (1 \div 2)$$
$$= 1\frac{3}{4} \div 1 \times 2$$
$$= 1\frac{3}{4} \times 2 \div 1$$
$$= 1\frac{3}{4} \times (2 \div 1)$$
$$= 1\frac{3}{4} \times \frac{2}{1}$$

A proof drawing on the rule of "maintaining the value of a quotient" is:

$$1\frac{3}{4} \div \frac{1}{2} = (1\frac{3}{4} \times \frac{2}{1}) \div (\frac{1}{2} \times \frac{2}{1})$$
$$= (1\frac{3}{4} \times \frac{2}{1}) \div 1$$
$$= 1\frac{3}{4} \times \frac{2}{1}$$
$$= 3\frac{1}{2}$$

Moreover, as illustrated in chapter 3, the Chinese teachers used mathematical sentences to illustrate various nonstandard ways to solve the problem $1\frac{3}{4} \div \frac{1}{2}$, as well as to derive these solutions. Symbolic representations are widely used in Chinese teachers' classrooms. As Tr. Li reported, her first-grade students used mathematical sentences to describe their own way of regrouping: $34 - 6 = 34 - 4 - 2 = 30 - 2 = 28$. Other Chinese teachers in this study also referred to similar incidents.

Researchers have found that elementary students in the United States often view the equal sign as a "do-something signal" (see e.g., Kieran, 1990, p. 100). This reminds me of a discussion I had with a U.S. elementary teacher. I asked her why she accepted student work like "3 + 3 × 4 = 12

= 15." She said, "Well, they did the calculational order correctly and got the correct answer, what is wrong?" From the Chinese teachers' perspective, however, the semantics of mathematical operations should be represented rigorously. It is intolerable to have two different values on each side of an equal sign. As my elementary teacher once said to her class, "The equal sign is the soul of mathematical operations." In fact, changing one or both sides of an equal sign for certain purposes while preserving the "equals" relationship is the "secret" of mathematical operations.

The Chinese teachers were skilled in adding and removing parentheses and in changing the order of operations in a mathematical sentence. Drawing on a few simple properties such as the three basic laws, the rule of maintaining the value of a quotient, and the meaning of fractions they developed clever symbolic justifications of the arithmetic algorithms they encountered in the interviews.

As Schoenfeld (1985) indicated, "proof" as a form of explanation is mandatory, an accepted standard of the discipline of mathematics. The Chinese teachers tended to justify mathematical statements both verbally and symbolically. Verbal justification tended to come before symbolic justification, but the latter tended to be more rigorous. After the Chinese teachers reported their investigations of the student's claim, as discussed in chapter 4, they all justified their ideas. All of those who presented an invalid idea only gave verbal justifications. If they had used symbolic representations, I suspect some might have avoided or at least found the pitfalls in their arguments.

Multiple Approaches to a Computational Procedure: Flexibility Rooted in Conceptual Understanding

Although proofs and explanations should be rigorous, mathematics is not rigid. Mathematicians use and value different approaches to solving problems (Pólya, 1973), even arithmetic problems. Dowker (1992) asked 44 professional mathematicians to estimate mentally the results of products and quotients of 10 multiplication and division problems involving whole numbers and decimals. The most striking result of her investigation "was the number and variety of specific estimation strategies used by the mathematicians." "The mathematicians tended to use strategies involving the understanding of arithmetical properties and relationships" and "rarely the strategy of 'Proceeding algorithmically.' "

"To solve a problem in multiple ways" is also an attitude of Chinese teachers. For all four topics, they discussed alternative as well as standard approaches. For the topic of subtraction, they described at least three ways of regrouping, including the regrouping of subtrahends. For the topic of multidigit multiplication, they mentioned at least two explanations of the algorithm. One teacher showed six ways of lining up the partial products. For the division with fractions topic the Chinese teachers demonstrated at least four ways to prove the standard algorithm and three alternative methods of computation.

For all the arithmetic topics, the Chinese teachers indicated that although a standard algorithm may be used in all cases, it may not be the best method for every case. Applying an algorithm and its various versions flexibly allows one to get the best solution for a given case. For example, the Chinese teachers pointed out that there are several ways to compute $1\frac{3}{4} \div \frac{1}{2}$. Using decimals, the distributive law, or other mathematical ideas, all the alternatives were faster and easier than the standard algorithm. Being able to calculate in multiple ways means that one has transcended the formality of an algorithm and reached the essence of the numerical operations—the underlying mathematical ideas and principles. The reason that one problem can be solved in multiple ways is that mathematics does not consist of isolated rules, but connected ideas. Being able to and tending to solve a problem in more than one way, therefore, reveals the ability and the predilection to make connections between and among mathematical areas and topics.

Approaching a topic in various ways, making arguments for various solutions, comparing the solutions and finding a best one, in fact, is a constant force in the development of mathematics. An advanced operation or advanced branch in mathematics usually offers a more sophisticated way to solve problems. Multiplication, for example, is a more sophisticated operation than addition for solving some problems. Some algebraic methods of solving problems are more sophisticated than arithmetic ones. When a problem is solved in multiple ways, it serves as a tie connecting several pieces of mathematical knowledge. How the Chinese teachers view the four basic arithmetical operations shows how they manage to unify the whole field of elementary mathematics.

Relationships Among the Four Basic Operations: The "Road System" Connecting the Field of Elementary Mathematics

Arithmetic, "the art of calculation," consists of numerical operations. The U.S. teachers and the Chinese teachers, however, seemed to view these operations differently. The U.S. teachers tended to focus on the particular algorithm associated with an operation, for example, the algorithm for subtraction with regrouping, the algorithm for multidigit multiplication, and the algorithm for division by fractions. The Chinese teachers, on the other hand, were more interested in the operations themselves and their relationships. In particular, they were interested in faster and easier ways to do a given computation, how the meanings of the four operations are con-nected, and how the meaning and the relationships of the operations are represented across subsets of numbers—whole numbers, fractions, and decimals.

When they teach subtraction with decomposing a higher value unit, Chinese teachers start from addition with composing a higher value unit. When they discussed the "lining-up rule" in multidigit multiplication, they compared it with the lining-up rule in multidigit addition. In representing the meaning of division they described how division models are derived from the meaning of multiplication. The teachers also noted how the introduction of a new set of numbers—fractions—brings new features to arithmetical operations that had previously been restricted to whole num-bers. In their discussions of the relationship between the perimeter and area of a rectangle, the Chinese teachers again connected the interview topic with arithmetic operations.

In the Chinese teachers' discussions two kinds of relationships that connect the four basic operations were apparent. One might be called "derived operation." For example, multiplication is an operation derived from the operation of addition. It solves certain kinds of complicated addition problems in a easier way.[3] The other relationship is inverse op-eration. The term "inverse operation" was never mentioned by the U.S. teachers, but was very often used by the Chinese teachers. Subtraction is the inverse of addition, and division is the inverse of multiplication. These two kinds of relationships tightly connect the four operations. Because all the topics of elementary mathematics are related to the four operations, understanding of the relationships among the four operations, then, be-comes a road system that connects all of elementary mathematics.[4] With this road system, one can go anywhere in the domain.

KNOWLEDGE PACKAGES AND THEIR KEY PIECES: UNDERSTANDING LONGITUDINAL COHERENCE IN LEARNING

Another feature of Chinese teachers' knowledge not found among U.S. teachers is their well-developed "knowledge packages." The four features discussed above concern teachers' understanding of the field of elementary mathematics. In contrast, the knowledge packages reveal the teachers'

---

[3]Although the four interview questions did not provide room for discussion of the relationship between addition and multiplication, Chinese teachers actually consider it a very important concept in their everyday teaching.

[4]The two kinds of relationships among the four basic operations, indeed, apply to all advanced operations in the discipline of mathematics as well. The "road system" of elementary mathematics, therefore, epitomizes the "road system" of the whole discipline.

understanding of the longitudinal process of opening up and cultivating such a field in students' minds. Arithmetic, as an intellectual field, was created and cultivated by human beings. Teaching and learning arithmetic, creating conditions in which young humans can rebuild this field in their minds, is the concern of elementary mathematics teachers. Psychologists have devoted themselves to study how students learn mathematics. Mathematics teachers have their own theory about learning mathematics.

The three knowledge package models derived from the Chinese teachers' discussion of subtraction with regrouping, multidigit multiplication, and division by fractions share a similar structure. They all have a sequence in the center, and a "circle" of linked topics connected to the topics in the sequence. The sequence in the subtraction package goes from the topic of addition and subtraction within 10, to addition and subtraction within 20, to subtraction with regrouping of numbers between 20 and 100, then to subtraction of large numbers with regrouping. The sequence in the multiplication package includes multiplication by one-digit numbers, multiplication by two-digit numbers, and multiplication by three-digit numbers. The sequence in the package of the meaning of division by fractions goes from meaning of addition, to meaning of multiplication with whole numbers, to meaning of multiplication with fractions, to meaning of division with fractions. The teachers believe that these sequences are the main paths through which knowledge and skill about the three topics develop.

Such linear sequences, however, do not develop alone, but are supported by other topics. In the subtraction package, for example, "addition and subtraction within 10" is related to three other topics: the composition of 10, composing and decomposing a higher value unit, and addition and subtraction as inverse operations. "Subtraction with regrouping of numbers between 20 and 100," the topic raised in interviews, was also supported by five items: composition of numbers within 10, the rate of composing a higher value unit, composing and decomposing a higher value unit, addition and subtraction as inverse operations, and subtraction without regrouping. At the same time, an item in the circle may be related to several pieces in the package. For example, "composing and decomposing a higher value unit" and "addition and subtraction as inverse operations" are both related to four other pieces. With the support from these topics, the development of the central sequences becomes more mathematically significant and conceptually enriched.

The teachers do not consider all of the items to have the same status. Each package contains "key" pieces that "weigh" more than other members. Some of the key pieces are located in the linear sequence and some are in the "circle." The teachers gave several reasons why they considered a certain piece of knowledge to be a "key" piece. They pay particular attention to the first occasion when a concept or skill is introduced. For example, the topic of "addition and subtraction within 20" is considered to be such a case for learning subtraction with regrouping. The topic of "multiplication by two-digit numbers" was considered an important step in learning multidigit multiplication. The Chinese teachers believe that if students learn a concept thoroughly the first time it is introduced, one "will get twice the result with half the effort in later learning." Otherwise, one "will get half the result with twice the effort."

Another kind of key piece in a knowledge package is a "concept knot." For example, in addressing the meaning of division by fractions, the Chinese teachers referred to the meaning of multiplication with fractions. They think it ties together five important concepts related to the meaning of division by fractions: meaning of multiplication, models of division by whole numbers, concept of a fraction, concept of a whole, and the meaning of multiplication with whole numbers. A thorough understanding of the meaning of multiplication with fractions, then, will allow students to easily reach an understanding of the meaning of division by fractions. On the other hand, the teachers also believe that exploring the meaning of division by fractions is a good opportunity for revisiting, and deepening understanding of these five concepts.

In the knowledge packages, procedural topics and conceptual topics were interwoven. The teachers who had a conceptual understanding of the topic and intended to promote students' conceptual learning did not ignore procedural knowledge at all. In fact, from their perspective, a conceptual understanding is never separate from the corresponding procedures where understanding "lives."

The Chinese teachers also think that it is very important for a teacher to know the entire field of elementary mathematics as well as the whole process of learning it. Tr. Mao said:

> As a mathematics teacher one needs to know the location of each piece of knowledge in the whole mathematical system, its relation with previous knowledge. For example, this year I am teaching fourth graders. When I open the textbook I should know how the topics in it are connected to the knowledge taught in the first, second, and third grades. When I teach three-digit multiplication I know that my students have learned the multiplication table, one-digit multiplication within 100, and multiplication with a two-digit multiplier. Since they have learned how to multiply with a two-digit multiplier, when teaching multiplication with a three-digit multiplier I just let them explore on their own. I first give them several problems with a two-digit multiplier. Then I present a problem with a three-digit multiplier, and have students think about how to solve it. We have multiplied by a digit at the ones place and a digit at the tens place, now we are going to multiply by a digit at the hundreds place, what can we do, where are we going to put the product, and why? Let them think about it. Then the problem will be solved easily. I will have them, instead of myself, explain the rationale. *On the other hand, I have to know what knowledge will be built on what I am teaching today* (italics added).

ELEMENTARY MATHEMATICS AS FUNDAMENTAL MATHEMATICS

The Chinese teachers' discussion presented a sophisticated and coherent picture of elementary mathematics. It showed that elementary mathematics is not a simple collection of disconnected number facts and calculational algorithms. Rather, it is an intellectually demanding, challenging, and exciting field—a foundation on which much can be built. Elementary mathematics is fundamental mathematics. The term *fundamental* has three related meanings: foundational, primary, and elementary. Mathematics is an area of science that concerns spatial and numerical relationships in which reasoning is based on these relationships. Historically, arithmetic and geometry were the two main branches of the discipline of mathematics. Today, although the number of branches of the discipline has increased and the field of the discipline has been expanded, the foundational status of arithmetic and geometry in mathematics is still unchanged. None of the new branches, whether pure or applied, operates without the basic mathematical rules and computational skills established in arithmetic and geometry. Elementary school mathematics, composed of arithmetic and primary geometry, is therefore the foundation of the discipline on which advanced branches are constructed.

The term *primary* refers to another feature of elementary mathematics. Elementary mathematics contains the rudiments of many important concepts in more advanced branches of the discipline. For instance, algebra is a way of arranging knowns and unknowns in equations so that the unknowns can be made knowable. As we have seen in the previous chapters, the three basic laws with which these equations are solved—commutative, distributive, and associative—are naturally rooted in arithmetic. Ideas of set, one-to-one correspondence, and order are implicit in counting. Set-theoretic operations, like union and Cartesian product, are related to the meaning of whole number addition and multiplication. Basic ideas of calculus are implicit in the rationale of the calculation of area of a circle in elementary geometry.[5]

The foundational and primary features of mathematics, however, are presented in an elementary format. It is elementary because it is at the

---

[5]When teaching the formula for the area of a circle, Chinese teachers bring a paper disc to class. Half of the disc has one color and half has another color. The disc is first cut into two halves. Then the two halves are cut into thin pie-shaped pieces with the edges connected. The two half circles are opened and fit together to form a rectangle-like region: ▨▨▨▨▨▨. Teachers inspire students to imagine subdividing the disc into more slices so that the region more closely approximates a rectangle. Then, drawing on the formula for the area of a rectangle, students learn the rationale for the formula for the area of a circle. This method of approximating the area of a circle was known in the 17th century (see Smith & Mikami, 1914, p. 131).

beginning of students' learning of mathematics. Therefore it appears straightforward and easy. The seemingly simple ideas embedded in students' minds at this stage will last for the duration of their mathematics learning. For example, in their later learning students will never erase their conceptions of equation learned from "$1 + 1 = 2$," although they will be changed and enriched.

From a perspective of attaining mathematical competence, teaching elementary mathematics does not mean bringing students merely to the end of arithmetic or to the beginning of "pre-algebra." Rather, it means providing them with a groundwork on which to build future mathematics learning.

U.S. scholars have claimed that advanced concepts can be presented in an intellectually honest way to elementary students. Three decades ago, Bruner claimed that ideas of advanced mathematics such as topology, projective geometry, probability theory, and set theory could be introduced to elementary school students (Bruner, 1960/1977). His proposal was raised again recently by Hirsch (1996). Kaput, Steen, and their colleagues have suggested a "strand-oriented organization" of school mathematics (Kaput & Nemirovsky, 1995; Steen, 1990). They criticized the traditional "layer-cake" organization of school mathematics because it "picks very few strands (e.g., arithmetic, geometry, and algebra) and arranges them horizontally to form the curriculum" (Steen, p. 4). Instead, they propose a longitudinal structure "with greater vertical continuity, to connect the roots of mathematics to the branches of mathematics in the educational experience of children" (Steen, p. 4) illustrated by a tree with roots that represent strands such as "dimension," "space," "change and variation," etc. (Kaput & Nemirovsky, p. 21).

The elementary teachers with conceptual understanding in this study, however, may not be as radical as Kaput and Steen. As shown in the teachers' interviews, elementary mathematics, constituted of arithmetic and primary geometry, already contains important mathematical ideas. For these teachers, a "horizontally arranged curriculum" may also possess "vertical continuity." Arithmetic can also have "multiple representations," "serious mathematics," and "genuine mathematical conversations."[6] I consider the metaphor that Chinese teachers use to illustrate school mathematics to be more accurate. They believe that elementary mathematics is the foundation for their students' future mathematical learning, and will contribute to their students' future life. Students' later mathematical learning is like a multistoried building. The foundation may be invisible from the

---

[6]"Multiple representations," "genuine mathematical conversations," and "qualitative understanding of mathematical models" are features of mathematical teaching advocated by Kaput and his colleagues (Kaput & Nemirovsky, 1995).

upper stories, but it is the foundation that supports them and makes all the stories (branches) cohere. The appearance and development of new mathematics should not be regarded as a denial of fundamental mathematics. In contrast, it should lead us to an ever better understanding of elementary mathematics, of its powerful potentiality, as well as of the conceptual seeds for the advanced branches.

PROFOUND UNDERSTANDING OF FUNDAMENTAL MATHEMATICS

Indeed, it is the mathematical substance of elementary mathematics that allows a coherent understanding of it. However, the understanding of elementary mathematics is not always coherent. From a procedural perspective, arithmetic algorithms have little or no connection with other topics, and are isolated from one another. Taking the four topics studied as an example, subtraction with regrouping has nothing to do with multidigit multiplication, nor with division by fractions, nor with area and perimeter of a rectangle.

Figure 5.1 illustrates a typical procedural understanding of the four topics. The letters S, M, D, and G represent the four topics: subtraction with regrouping, multidigit multiplication, division with fractions, and the geometry topic (calculation of perimeter and area). The rectangles represent procedural knowledge of these topics. The ovals represent other procedural knowledge related to these topics. The trapezoids underneath the rectangles represent pseudoconceptual understanding of each topic. The dotted outlines represent missing items. Note that the understandings of the different topics are not connected.

In Fig. 5.1 the four topics are essentially independent and few elements are included in each knowledge package.[7] Pseudoconceptual explanations for algorithms are a feature of understanding that is only procedural. Some teachers invented arbitrary explanations. Some simply verbalized the algorithm. Yet even inventing or citing a pseudoconceptual explanation requires familiarity with the algorithm. Teachers who could barely carry out an algorithm tended not to be able to explain it or connect it with other procedures, as seen in some responses to the division by fractions and geometry topics. With isolated and underdeveloped knowledge packages,

---

[7]Given a topic, a teacher tends to see other topics related to its learning. If it is procedural, a teacher may see an explanation for it. If it is conceptual, a teacher may see a related procedure or concept. This tendency initiates organization of a well-developed "knowledge package." So I use the term "knowledge package" here for the group of topics that teachers tend to see around the topic they are teaching.

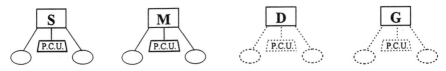

FIG. 5.1. Teachers' procedural knowledge of the four topics.

the mathematical understanding of a teacher with a procedural perspective is fragmentary.

From a conceptual perspective, however, the four topics are connected, related by the mathematical concepts they share. For example, the concept of place value underlies the algorithms for subtraction with regrouping and multidigit multiplication. The concept of place value, then, becomes a connection between the two topics. The concept of inverse operations contributes to the rationale for subtraction with regrouping as well as to the explanation of the meaning of division by fractions. Thus the concept of inverse operations connects subtraction with regrouping and division by fractions. Some concepts, such as the meaning of multiplication, are shared by three of the four topics. Some, such as the three basic laws, are shared by all four topics. Figure 5.2 illustrates how mathematical topics are related from a conceptual perspective.

Although not all the concepts shared by the four topics are included, Fig. 5.2 illustrates how relations among the four topics make them into a network. Some items are not directly related to all four topics. However, their diverse associations overlap and interlace. The three basic laws appeared in the Chinese teachers' discussions of all four topics.

In contrast to the procedural view of the four topics illustrated in Fig. 5.1, Fig. 5.3 illustrates a conceptual understanding of the four topics. The four rectangles at the top of Fig. 5.3 represent the four topics. The ellipses represent the knowledge pieces in the knowledge packages. White ellipses represent procedural topics, light gray ones represent conceptual topics,

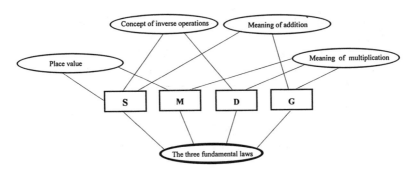

FIG. 5.2. A few shared concepts connect the four topics.

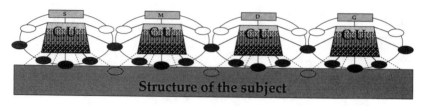

FIG. 5.3. Teachers' conceptual knowledge of the four topics.

dark gray ones represent the basic principles, and ones with dotted outlines represent general attitudes toward mathematics.

When it is composed of well-developed, interconnected knowledge packages, mathematical knowledge forms a network solidly supported by the structure of the subject. Figure 5.3 extends the model of a conceptual understanding of a particular topic given in Fig. 1.4 and illustrates the breadth, depth, connectedness, and thoroughness of a teacher's conceptual understanding of mathematics. Because the four topics are located at various subareas of elementary mathematics, this model also serves as a miniature of a teacher's conceptual understanding of the field of elementary mathematics.

The ellipses with dotted outlines, general attitudes toward mathematics, are usually not included in teachers' knowledge packages for particular topics. However, they contribute significantly to the coherence and consistency of a teacher's mathematical knowledge. Basic attitudes of a subject may be even more penetrating than its basic principles. A basic principle may not support all topics, but a basic attitude may be present with regard to every topic. Basic attitudes toward mathematics mentioned by teachers during interviews, such as "to justify a claim with a mathematical argument," "to know how as well as to know why," "to keep the consistency of an idea in various contexts," and "to approach a topic in multiple ways" pertain to all topics in elementary mathematics.[8]

I call the subject matter knowledge illustrated in Fig. 5.3 profound understanding of fundamental mathematics (PUFM). By profound understanding I mean an understanding of the terrain of fundamental mathematics that is deep, broad, and thorough. Although the term *profound* is often considered to mean intellectual depth, its three connotations, *deep*, *vast*, and *thorough*, are interconnected.

---

[8]Both dimensions of the structure—basic principles and basic attitudes (Bruner, 1960/1977)—are very powerful in making connections. Unfortunately Fig. 5.3 is too simple to well illustrate the one-to-many relationships between general principles or attitudes and mathematical concepts or topics.

Duckworth, a former student and colleague of Jean Piaget, believes we should keep learning of elementary mathematics and science "deep" and "complex" (1987, 1991). Inspired by Piaget's concern for how *far*, instead of how *fast*, learning would go, she proposed the notion of "learning with depth and breadth" (1979). After a comparison between building a tower "with one brick on top of another" and "on a broad base or a deep foundation," Duckworth said:

> What is the intellectual equivalent of building in breadth and depth? I think it is a matter of making connections: breadth could be thought of as the widely different spheres of experience that can be related to one another; depth can be thought of as the many different kinds of connections that can be made among different facets of our experience. I am not sure whether or not intellectual breadth and depth can be separated from each other, except in talking about them. (p. 7)

I agree with Duckworth that intellectual breadth and depth "is a matter of making connections," and that the two are interwoven. However, her definition of intellectual breadth and depth is too general for use in discussing mathematical learning.[9] Moreover, she does not explain what their relationship is.

Based on my research, I define *understanding a topic with depth* as connecting it with more conceptually powerful ideas of the subject. The closer an idea is to the structure of the discipline, the more powerful it will be, consequently, the more topics it will be able to support. *Understanding a topic with breadth*, on the other hand, is to connect it with those of similar or less conceptual power. For example, consider the knowledge package for subtraction with regrouping. To connect subtraction with regrouping with the topics of addition with carrying, subtraction without regrouping, and addition without carrying is a matter of breadth. To connect it with concepts such as the rate of composing or decomposing a higher value unit or the concept that addition and subtraction are inverse operations is a matter of depth. Depth and breadth, however, depend on thoroughness—the capability to "pass through" all parts of the field—to weave them together. Indeed, it is this thoroughness which "glues" knowledge of mathematics into a coherent whole.

---

[9]For educational researchers, the depth of teachers' subject matter knowledge seems to be subtle and intriguing. On one hand, most would agree that teachers' understanding should be deep (Ball, 1989; Grossman, Wilson, & Shulman, 1989; Marks, 1987; Steinberg, Marks, & Haymore, 1985; Wilson, 1988). On the other hand, because the term *depth* is "vague" and "elusive in its definition and measurements" (Ball, 1989; Wilson, 1988), progress in understanding it has been slow. Ball (1989) proposed three "specific criteria" for teachers' substantive knowledge: correctness, meaning, and connectedness to avoid the term *deep*, which she considered a vague descriptor of teachers' subject matter knowledge.

Of course, the reason that a profound understanding of elementary mathematics is possible is that first of all, elementary mathematics is a field of depth, breadth, and thoroughness. Teachers with this deep, vast, and thorough understanding do not invent connections between and among mathematical ideas, but reveal and represent them in terms of mathematics teaching and learning. Such teaching and learning tends to have the following four properties:

Connectedness. A teacher with PUFM has a general intention to make connections among mathematical concepts and procedures, from simple and superficial connections between individual pieces of knowledge to complicated and underlying connections among different mathematical operations and subdomains. When reflected in teaching, this intention will prevent students' learning from being fragmented. Instead of learning isolated topics, students will learn a unified body of knowledge.

Multiple Perspectives. Those who have achieved PUFM appreciate different facets of an idea and various approaches to a solution, as well as their advantages and disadvantages. In addition, they are able to provide mathematical explanations of these various facets and approaches. In this way, teachers can lead their students to a flexible understanding of the discipline.

Basic Ideas. Teachers with PUFM display mathematical attitudes and are particularly aware of the "simple but powerful basic concepts and principles of mathematics" (e.g., the idea of an equation). They tend to revisit and reinforce these basic ideas. By focusing on these basic ideas, students are not merely *encouraged* to approach problems, but are *guided* to conduct real mathematical activity.

Longitudinal Coherence.[10] Teachers with PUFM are not limited to the knowledge that should be taught in a certain grade; rather, they have achieved a fundamental understanding of the whole elementary mathematics curriculum. With PUFM, teachers are ready at any time to exploit an opportunity to review crucial concepts that students have studied previously. They also know what students are going to learn later, and take opportunities to lay the proper foundation for it.

These four properties are interrelated. While the first property, connectedness, is a general feature of the mathematics teaching of one with PUFM,

---

[10]Kaput (1994) used this term to describe curricula, here I use it to describe the corresponding property for teacher knowledge. This property is related to an aspect of what Shulman (1986) called curricular knowledge.

the other three—multiple perspectives, basic ideas, and longitudinal coherence—are the kinds of connections that lead to different aspects of meaningful understanding of mathematics—breadth, depth, and thoroughness.

Unfortunately, a static model like Fig. 5.3 cannot depict the dynamics of these connections. When they teach, teachers organize their knowledge packages according to teaching context. Connections among topics change with the teaching flow. A central piece in a knowledge package for one topic may become a marginal piece in the knowledge package for another, and vice versa.

Conducting interviews for my study made me think of how people know the town or city they live in. People know the town where they live in different ways. Some people—for example, newcomers—only know the place where their home is located. Some people know their neighborhoods quite well, but rarely go farther away. Some people may know how to get to a few places in the town—for example, the place they work, certain stores where they do their shopping, or the cinemas where they go for a movie. Yet they may only know one way to get to these places, and never bother to explore alternative routes. However some people, for example, taxi drivers, know all the roads in their town very well. They are very flexible and confident when going from one place to another and know several alternative routes. If you are a new visitor, they can take the route that best shows the town. If you are in a rush, at any given time of day they know the route that will get you to your destination fastest. They can even find a place without a complete address. In talking with teachers, I noticed parallels between a certain way of knowing school mathematics and a certain way of knowing roads in a town. The way those teachers with PUFM knew school mathematics in some sense seemed to me very like the way a proficient taxi driver knows a town. There may also be a map in development of the town in a taxi driver's mind as well. Yet a teacher's map of school mathematics must be more complicated and flexible.

SUMMARY

This chapter contrasted the Chinese and U.S. teachers' overall understanding of the four topics discussed in the previous chapters. The responses of the two groups of teachers suggest that elementary mathematics is construed very differently in China and in the United States. Although the U.S. teachers were concerned with teaching for conceptual understanding, their responses reflected a view common in the United States—that elementary mathematics is "basic," an arbitrary collection of facts and rules in which doing mathematics means following set procedures step-by-step to arrive at answers (Ball, 1991). The Chinese teachers were concerned with knowing why algorithms make sense as well as knowing how to carry them out. Their attitudes were similar to those of practicing mathematicians. They tended to justify an explanation with a symbolic derivation, give multiple solutions for a problem, and discuss relationships among the four basic operations of arithmetic.

For each of the three interview topics that they taught, the Chinese teachers described a "knowledge package," a network of procedural and conceptual topics supporting or supported by the learning of the topic in question. Items in a knowledge package differed in status; the first occasions when a particular concept was introduced were considered "key pieces" and given more emphasis in teaching. For instance, "addition and subtraction within 20" is considered a key piece of the knowledge package for subtraction with regrouping because it is the first occasion when the concept of composing and decomposing a ten is used.

Elementary mathematics can be viewed as "basic" mathematics—a collection of procedures—or as fundamental mathematics. Fundamental mathematics is elementary, foundational, and primary. It is elementary because it is at the beginning of mathematics learning. It is primary because it contains the rudiments of more advanced mathematical concepts. It is foundational because it provides a foundation for students' further mathematics learning.

Profound understanding of fundamental mathematics (PUFM) is more than a sound conceptual understanding of elementary mathematics—it is the awareness of the conceptual structure and basic attitudes of mathematics inherent in elementary mathematics and the ability to provide a foundation for that conceptual structure and instill those basic attitudes in students. A profound understanding of mathematics has breadth, depth, and thoroughness. Breadth of understanding is the capacity to connect a topic with topics of similar or less conceptual power. Depth of understanding is the capacity to connect a topic with those of greater conceptual power. Thoroughness is the capacity to connect all topics.

The teaching of a teacher with PUFM has connectedness, promotes multiple approaches to solving a given problem, revisits and reinforces basic ideas, and has longitudinal coherence. A teacher with PUFM is able to reveal and represent connections among mathematical concepts and procedures to students. He or she appreciates different facets of an idea and various approaches to a solution, as well as their advantages and disadvantages—and is able to provide explanations for students of these various facets and approaches. A teacher with PUFM is aware of the "simple but powerful" basic ideas of mathematics and tends to revisit and reinforce them. He or she has a fundamental understanding of the whole elementary mathematics curriculum, thus is ready to exploit an opportunity to review concepts that students have previously studied or to lay the groundwork for a concept to be studied later.

Profound Understanding Of Fundamental Mathematics: When And How Is It Attained

At the end of my study I conducted a brief two-part exploration of when and how a teacher attains PUFM. First, in order to have a general idea about when one might attain PUFM, I interviewed two groups of people in China who had not been teachers, using the same questions that had been asked of teachers. One group was a class of 26 preservice teachers. The other group consisted of 20 ninth-grade students.[1] The former were examined for their knowledge at the end of their teacher education program, and the latter were investigated for the kind of knowledge a student might have upon entering a teacher education program.

The second part of the exploration concerned how PUFM is attained. I interviewed three teachers whom I had identified as having PUFM. The interviews explored two main questions: What the teachers thought a teacher's subject matter knowledge of mathematics should be and how they acquired their own knowledge of mathematics. The responses to the question of what a teacher's knowledge of mathematics should be were discussed in the previous chapter. The second part of this chapter discusses the teachers' descriptions of how their working conditions supported and continue to support the growth of their mathematical knowledge and its organization for teaching.

---

[1]Chinese lower secondary (Grades 7–9) schools differ substantially in quality. The students I interviewed were from a mediocre school in Shanghai where at most half of the students were able to pass college entrance examinations.

WHEN IS PROFOUND UNDERSTANDING
OF FUNDAMENTAL MATHEMATICS ATTAINED?:
WHAT THE PRETEACHING GROUPS KNEW
ABOUT THE FOUR TOPICS

Differences Between the two Chinese Preteaching Groups

The two preteaching groups showed no obvious differences in algorithmic competence. All their computations for the problems of subtraction, multiplication, and division by fractions were correct, except for one ninth-grade student who made an error while adding the three partial products for the multidigit multiplication problem. Their explorations of the claim about the relationship between perimeter and area showed that both groups knew the formulas for calculating perimeter and area of a rectangle very well. Fifty-eight percent of the prospective teachers and 60% of the ninth graders thought that the claim "when the perimeter of a figure increases its area increases" would not hold all the time. Most provided a counterexample to disprove it, and a few elaborated the various possible cases.

When representing the concept of division by fractions, however, the two preteaching groups revealed some interesting differences. Prospective teachers tended to provide correct answers, but from a narrower perspective. The students, on the other hand, had a broader perspective, but made more mistakes.

Eighty-five percent of the prospective teachers, but only 40% of the ninth graders, created a conceptually correct story problem to represent the meaning of $1\frac{3}{4} \div \frac{1}{2}$. Of the 22 prospective teachers who provided at least one correct story problem, 20 (91%) represented the partitive model (i.e., finding a whole given that half is $1\frac{3}{4}$). Only two (9%) represented the measurement model (i.e., finding how many halves there are in $1\frac{3}{4}$). Among the eight students who succeeded in creating a representation, however, the models were equally distributed: Four represented the partitive model and the other four represented the measurement model.

All of the prospective teachers who did not provide a story said that they were unable to do it. No stories displaying misconceptions were found among the prospective teachers. The twelve middle school students who failed to provide a conceptually correct representation, however, seemed "braver" and less "cautious." They explored the topic from various directions. Eight created a story representing the meaning of $1\frac{3}{4} \times 2$, a subprocedure in the calculation. Three made a story representing $1\frac{3}{4} \times \frac{1}{2}$, and one said he was unable to make a story.

The difference between the two groups in representing the meaning of division by fractions seemed to reflect the influence of the teacher education program on the mathematical knowledge of the prospective teachers. Their knowledge of the topic seemed to be "cleaned up"—cleared of misconceptions. However, this process may have narrowed their perspectives. Because of their caution about what is correct and incorrect, they tended to not to try alternative ways when they got stuck.

Another difference between the two groups was that the prospective teachers showed concern for teaching and learning when discussing a mathematical topic. They tended to provide an explanation after a calculation, even though most of their explanations were very limited and brief. For example, in responding to the question about the students' error in multidigit multiplication, the ninth graders tended to simply state that the students were wrong and demonstrate the correct calculation. In contrast, the preservice teachers' responses often included three steps. First, the problem was that the students had not lined up the partial products correctly. Second, the prospective teachers said that they would explain the rationale underlying the algorithm to the students. Third, they would have the students do more exercises. Although only one preservice teacher specifically discussed the rationale, and none discussed at length what type of exercises would be provided to the students, the prospective teachers were clearly concerned about teaching and learning.

In summary, although the preservice teachers and ninth-grade students had similar algorithmic competence, they displayed two main differences. First, the prospective teachers seemed to have "cleaned-up" mathematical concepts, while their mathematical approach seemed narrowed. Second, unlike the students, the prospective teachers were concerned about teaching and learning.

Differences Between the U.S. Teachers and the two Chinese Preteaching Groups

Now let us take a look at the difference between the U.S. teachers and the two Chinese preteaching groups. For the topics of subtraction with regrouping and multidigit multiplication, the three groups showed similar success in algorithmic competence. However, the two Chinese preteaching groups displayed more conceptual understanding. For example, in their explanations of the lining-up rule for multidigit multiplication, they all showed an understanding of the rationale underlying the algorithm.

The performance of the two Chinese groups on the two more advanced topics was markedly better than that of the U.S. teachers. All members of the Chinese groups succeeded in computing $1\frac{3}{4} \div \frac{1}{2}$ and knew the formulas for calculating perimeter and area. However, only 43% of the U.S. teachers succeeded in the division by fractions calculation, and 17% of the U.S. teachers reported that they did not know the area and perimeter formulas. For the two more conceptually demanding questions, the difference was even greater. Eighty-five percent of the Chinese prospective teachers and 40% of the Chinese ninth graders created a conceptually correct story

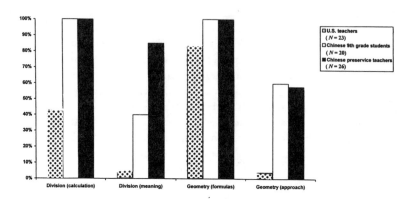

FIG. 6.1. Differences between the U.S. teachers and two Chinese preteaching groups on knowledge of the two advanced topics.

problem to represent the meaning of division by fractions, but only 4%
of the U.S. teachers did. Fifty-eight percent of the Chinese prospective
teachers and 60% of the Chinese students displayed a correct approach
to the relation between perimeter and area of a rectangle. Again, only 4%
of the U.S. teachers did. It appears that the more advanced the topic and
the more conceptual thinking required, the less competently U.S. teachers
performed. Figure 6.1 summarizes these differences for the case of the
two advanced topics.

Differences Between the Chinese Teachers
and the two Preteaching Groups

The differences in mathematical knowledge between the Chinese teachers
and the two Chinese preteaching groups were of another sort. Their algorithmic competence, indicator of mathematical knowledge from a *layperson*'s perspective, was similar. In terms of the features of mathematical
knowledge of a *teacher*, however, the two preteaching groups differed substantially from the group of teachers.

Interviewing prospective teachers and ninth grade students took significantly less time than interviewing teachers, although the interview questions
were the same. Many prospective teachers tended to give explanations for
an algorithm, but their explanations were very brief. The students did not
think of providing explanations, but spent more time on the representation
of division by fractions and the relation between perimeter and area. Neither of the two preteaching groups provided any elaborate discussion of
any of the four topics. Neither of the two groups discussed connections

among mathematical topics, multiple solutions of a problem,[2] or basic ideas of the subject related to the topics.

PUFM as a kind of teachers' subject matter knowledge, however, does not always have clear boundaries. In many cases, it is hard to say that a teacher has or doesn't have PUFM. For example, about one tenth of the Chinese teachers interviewed could be identified as having PUFM. They were all teachers with many years of teaching experience. Most of them had taught all the grades of elementary mathematics. Many had taught all the grades more than once. About one tenth of the Chinese teachers could be categorized as having no PUFM at all. Most of the other teachers, however, fell into a gray area between the two extremes. Some of them showed a broad, deep, and thorough understanding of the subarea of elementary mathematics that they were teaching, but not of the whole field. For example, some teachers were particularly familiar with the content of lower grades and others were particularly familiar with the content of higher grades. They gave elaborate discussions of topics from the areas with which they were familiar, but not of the rest. In fact, during interviews those who gave the most detailed discussions of the first two topics were usually teaching lower grades, and those who discussed the other two topics most elaborately were usually teaching upper grades.

It seems to be that PUFM, which I found in a group of Chinese teachers, was developed after they became teachers—that it developed during their teaching careers. The problem is, then, how did the Chinese teachers develop their PUFM after becoming teachers? To explore this question, I interviewed three teachers whom I considered to have PUFM.

PROFOUND UNDERSTANDING OF FUNDAMENTAL MATHEMATICS: HOW IT IS ATTAINED?

For convenience in data collection, I interviewed Tr. Mao, Tr. Wang, and Tr. Sun, all of whom taught at the same elementary school in Shanghai. They were teaching high, middle, and low grades of elementary mathematics, respectively. Like most of the teachers I interviewed,[3] these teachers taught only mathematics at the time of the interview. (Some teachers switch between subjects but this is infrequent now.) In general, at a school with specialized teachers, a new teacher's specialization is determined by the school's need, the new teacher's scores on teacher education exams, and the teacher's own interests.

Unlike elementary teachers in the United States, Tr. Mao, Tr. Wang, and Tr. Sun taught three to four 45-minute classes per day. When not

---

[2]After being asked to provide more than one story if they could, six prospective teachers provided more than one representation, but all were of a similar partitive model.

[3]The twelve teachers at the rural school taught all subjects.

teaching, they corrected student work or prepared lessons in the offices they shared with their colleagues.

Studying Teaching Materials Intensively

When asked how they had attained their mathematical knowledge in "a systematic way," these teachers referred to "studying teaching materials intensively [*zuanyan jiaocai*] when teaching it":

> First of all, you have to teach it personally, and you have to study teaching materials intensively when you teach it. In normal school you take courses such as "The Content and Teaching Methods for Elementary Mathematics." But that is not nearly enough. You only get a brief and rudimentary idea of what elementary mathematics is but it is not relevant to real teaching. Only through teaching a grade personally can you get to really know what is taught in that grade. Moreover, you should not stick to teaching one single grade but you should teach "round" by "round." People divide elementary school education into several small rounds. In our school we have the first round, which includes first through third grades, and the second round, which includes fourth and fifth grades. In each round, several grades are connected together and cover a subfield of elementary math. If you have taught the first round, you become familiar with the picture of what is taught in the first three grades and how they are connected. If you have taught the second round, you become familiar with the picture of what is taught in the next two grades. If you have taught both of the rounds, you know the whole picture of the curriculum of elementary school mathematics. The more times you have taught a round, the more familiar you become with the content in that round. But merely teaching is not enough. It only makes you know the content, yet not necessarily know it well. To know it well you have to study teaching materials intensively through teaching. (Tr. Sun)

The three elements referred to by Tr. Sun—teaching, teaching round-by-round, and studying teaching materials intensively when teaching—were also mentioned by the other teachers. Teaching and teaching round-by-round may not be hard for an audience outside of China to understand. But we may need more explanation of what these teachers meant by "studying teaching materials intensively [*zuanyan jiaocai*]," a term one hears frequently when talking with a Chinese teacher.

Probably anyone who knows Chinese and English would translate the Chinese term *jiaocai* as "teaching materials" because *jiao* literally means "teaching" and *cai* means "materials." But I would say that in fact *jiaocai* is more like what "curriculum" means in the United States. Generally, when Chinese teachers refer to *zuanyan jiaocai*, the term consists of three main components—the *Teaching and Learning Framework* (*jiaoxue dagang*), textbooks (*keben*), and teacher's manuals (*beike fudao cailiao*).

The *Teaching and Learning Framework* is published by the National Department of Education. It stipulates what students at each grade should
learn and the standards for their learning. It is a document similar in some
ways to the National Council of Teachers of Mathematics' *Standards for
School Mathematics* (NCTM, 1989) or state documents like *Mathematics Framework for California Public Schools* (California Department of Education, 1985,
1992). In China, the textbooks are intended to interpret and embody the
Teaching and Learning Framework. The National Department of Education
once published only one set of textbooks for all its public schools. In the
last decade, several different textbook series have been produced that
interpret the framework in ways that are more relevant for different local
situations. However, the quality of textbooks is still strictly controlled by
the central and local governments and the various versions are actually
very similar. Each set of textbooks comes with a series of teacher's manuals
that provide teachers with backgrounds of the knowledge in the corresponding textbook and with suggestions of how to teach it. Both textbooks
and manuals are carefully composed by experienced teachers and experts
in school curriculum who are recognized throughout the country. Taking
Walker's (1990) definition of curriculum as "the content and purpose of
an educational program together with their organization" (p. 5), we can
say that in some sense the three materials can be considered as the three
components that constitute China's national curriculum.

Chinese teachers study the three kinds of materials in different ways.
During the summer or before the beginning of a semester, teachers usually
study the *Teaching and Learning Framework.* When studying the framework,
particularly the part related to the grade which they are to teach or are
teaching, teachers decide general goals for the school year and each semester. Teachers do not "negotiate" with this document but follow it. They
consider one of their main tasks to be helping students to reach the
learning standards stipulated in the framework.

The textbook is the material on which Chinese teachers spend most of
their time and devote most of their efforts to "study intensively." They
study it constantly throughout the school year when they teach it. First of
all, they work for an understanding of "what it is." They study how it
interprets and illustrates the ideas in the *Teaching and Learning Framework,*
why the authors structured the book in a certain way, what the connections
among the contents are, what the connections are between the content
of a certain textbook and its predecessors or successors, what is new in a
textbook compared with an old version and why changes have been made,
and so on. At a more detailed level, they study how each unit of the
textbook is organized, how the content was presented by the authors, and
why. They study what examples are in a unit, why these examples were
selected, and why the examples were presented in a certain order. They
review the exercises in each section of a unit, the purpose for each exercise

section, and so on. Indeed, they conduct a very careful and critical investigation of the textbook. Although teachers usually find the authors' ideas ingenious and inspiring, they also sometimes find parts of the textbook that from their perspective are unsatisfactory, or inadequate illustrations of ideas in the framework.

Textbooks in China (and some other Asian countries) are quite different from those in the United States. Stevenson and Stigler (1992) described them as

> Separate volumes, seldom containing more than one hundred pages, cover each semester's work in each subject. The covers are attractive, but the inside pages have few illustrations and are devoted primarily to text. Illustrations tend to depict only the central point of the lesson, and there is very little information that is not necessary for the development of the concepts under consideration. They present the essence of the lesson, with the expectation that the teacher will elaborate and supplement the information with other materials. (p.139)

For example, the two textbooks for the two semesters of third grade mathematics each have fewer than 120 pages. Together they weigh only 6 ounces. The eleven topics they cover[4] are very carefully organized, each connected with the other, and "there is very little information that is not necessary for the development of the concepts under consideration." Such a compact

---

[4]The eleven topics (with subtopics in parentheses) are:

1. Division with one-digit divisor (dividing with a one-digit divisor, division when the quotient has zero in or at the end of the number, problems containing continuing division and multiplication, review).
2. Problems with combined operations and word problems (number sentences, word problems, review).
3. Reading and writing of numbers with multiple digits.
4. Addition and subtraction with multidigit numbers (addition with multidigit numbers, commutative law and associative law in addition, subtraction with multidigit numbers, the relationship between addition and subtraction, how the commutative law and associative law can make some operations with addition and subtraction easier, review).
5. Recognition of kilometer.
6. Recognition of ton, kilogram, and gram.
7. Multiplication with two-digit multiplier (multiplying a two-digit multiplier, multiplication when the multiplicand and/or multiplier have zeros at the end, review).
8. Division with two-digit divisors (dividing with a two-digit divisor, relationship between multiplication and division, review).
9. Problems with combined operations and word problems (number sentences, word problems, review).
10. Year, month, and day.
11. Perimeter of rectangles and squares (lines and line segments, angles, features of rectangles and squares, computing the perimeter of rectangles and squares).

After the eleven topics, the textbook has a "Review of the whole year."

but rigorous structure helps teachers to study the content thoroughly and grasp it solidly.

Besides a careful investigation of "what to teach," teachers study "how to teach it," or, using their language, "how to deal with teaching material [*chuli jiaocai*]."[5] Indeed, in the investigation of "what it is," concern for "how to teach it" is always implied and included. After all, a textbook is composed for the purpose of teaching it. Getting straight to the problem of "how to deal with teaching material," teachers consider the textbook from a perspective of how to teach it—how they are going to present the material, explain a topic, design appropriate exercises for students, etc.—in brief, as Tr. Mao said, "how to promote maximal learning in the shortest time, how to benefit all students in a class, advanced ones as well as slow ones, as much as possible." In the process of studying what is in a textbook and how to deal with it interactions between "what to teach" and "how to teach" occur. It is easy to see that through such interactions a teacher's subject matter knowledge would develop, stimulated by concern for how to teach.

Among the three teaching materials described earlier, Chinese teachers take the teacher's manuals least seriously. Though many teachers, particularly new teachers, find them very helpful as an exploration of what to teach and how to teach, it is usually suggested that one should not let oneself rely on a teacher's manual and be confined by it. In practice, teacher's manuals are usually studied as supplements to a textbook.

Teacher's manuals were not a part of the study described in this book. However, like the teachers in my study, I used manuals when I was an elementary teacher. The following description of teacher's manuals is based on that experience.

Teacher's manuals provide background for the mathematics in the corresponding textbooks and suggestions of how to teach it. The introduction of a typical teacher's manual gives an overview of the textbook: its main topics, the rationale for the textbook's organization, the relationship between the topics in the textbook and the topics of the preceding and succeeding volumes. The main body of the manual is a section-by-section discussion of each topic and subtopic of the textbook. The discussion of each topic focuses on these questions:

What is the concept connected with the topic?

What are the difficult points of teaching the concept?

What are the important points of teaching the concept?

What are the errors and confusions that students tend to have when learning this topic?

---

[5]When teachers refer to *chuli jiaocai*, they mean "deal with the textbook." Although in a broad sense *jiaocai* includes textbook, teacher's manual, and *Teaching and Learning Framework*, in practice most time is devoted to the textbook.

After discussion of these questions, suggested solutions for pedagogical problems are sometimes provided. For example, here is part of the discussion of "The meaning and properties of fractions" from the teacher's manual for the Grade 4 textbook (Shen & Liang, 1992). It begins:

> First of all we should let students understand the meaning of fractions— "when a whole '1' is divided evenly into shares, the number expressing one or more of these shares is called a 'fraction.'" Here, the difficult points in students' learning are understanding the concept of a whole "1" and understanding the fractional unit of a fraction. The important point is to explain the concept of "dividing evenly" clearly. (p. 70)

The manual says that teachers should make sure to reveal the concept that a whole "1" does not always represent a single object such as a circle, a rectangle, or an apple. It may also represent a group of objects such as a class of students, a basket of apples, or a pile of books. The manual continues:

> At the beginning of teaching the concept of "dividing evenly," circular shapes are the most appropriate teaching aids because it is easiest to see the relationship between a whole and its parts from an evenly divided circular shape and its sectors. After that, other shapes may be used as teaching aids to strengthen and solidify the concept. For example, you may want to ask students to fold a rectangle evenly into four parts and color one quarter and three quarters of it to help them to build the concept of $\frac{1}{4}$ and $\frac{3}{4}$. Then ask them to cut the rectangle into quarters and stick the quarters on the blackboard to illustrate that $\frac{3}{4}$ is composed of three $\frac{1}{4}$s. The fractional unit of $\frac{3}{4}$ is $\frac{1}{4}$. Using the same approach, one can reveal that $\frac{4}{7}$ is composed of four $\frac{1}{7}$s—the fractional unit of $\frac{4}{7}$ is $\frac{1}{7}$, etc. In this way, the difficult point of teaching "fractional unit" will be solved. (p. 71)

After further discussion of various ways that may be used to help students to grasp the concept of fractional unit, the manual concludes (p. 71):

> If students are able to tell the value of a fraction and its fractional unit, it means that they have a preliminary understanding of the meaning of a fraction. Teachers can then give them a few shapes for further differentiation. For example, ask students which of these shaded parts represent the fraction underneath it correctly, which incorrectly, and why:

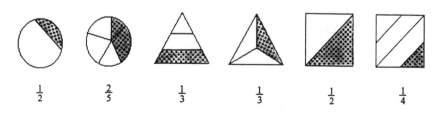

$$\frac{1}{2} \qquad \frac{2}{5} \qquad \frac{1}{3} \qquad \frac{1}{3} \qquad \frac{1}{2} \qquad \frac{1}{4}$$

A few experienced teachers said that they did not use a teacher's manual often because they already "knew what is in it." However, for beginning teachers and even for experienced teachers who teach a particular grade for the first time, the manuals provide a framework for thinking about what they will be teaching and information that is a first stepping stone to a deeper understanding.

The teachers I interviewed all felt that "studying teaching materials intensively" was very important for them:

> To study teaching materials is extremely important. To study teaching materials is to study what we are to teach and how to teach it to our students; in other words, to find links between the knowledge and the students. The student teachers from normal schools doing their student teaching with me usually can't understand why we spend so much time studying teaching materials and what we can learn from studying. For them, it seems to be too simple and too plain to study: there are just several example problems, one of which you can solve in a minute and explain to students in two minutes. But I told them that even after teaching for more than thirty years, every time I study a textbook I see something new. How to inspire students' minds, how to explain in a clear way, how to spend less time and let students benefit more, how to motivate students to learn these topics . . . Your answers for all these questions are supported by a deep and broad understanding of what the teaching material is about. And every time you study it, you get a better idea of what it is and how to teach it. You never will feel you have nothing more to learn from studying teaching materials. (Tr. Mao)

"Studying teaching materials" occupies a significant status in Chinese teachers' work. Sometimes it is used as a synonym for "class planning":

> I always spend more time on preparing a class than on teaching, sometimes, three, even four, times the latter. I spend the time in studying the teaching materials: What is it that I am going to teach in this lesson? How should I introduce the topic? What concepts or skills have the students learned that I should draw on? Is it a key piece on which other pieces of knowledge will build, or is it built on other knowledge? If it is a key piece of knowledge, how can I teach it so students can grasp it solidly enough to support their later learning? If it is not a key piece, what is the concept or the procedure it is built on? How am I going to pull out that knowledge and make sure my students are aware of it and the relation between the old knowledge and the new topic? What kind of review will my students need? How should I present the topic step-by-step? How will students respond after I raise a certain question? Where should I explain it at length, and where should I leave it to students to learn it by themselves? What are the topics that the students will learn which are built directly or indirectly on this topic? How can my lesson set a basis for their learning of the next topic, and for related topics that they will learn in their future? What do I expect the advanced

students to learn from the lesson? What do I expect the slow students to learn? How can I reach these goals? etc. In a word, one thing is to study whom you are teaching, the other thing is to study the knowledge you are teaching. If you can interweave the two things together nicely, you will succeed. We think about these two things over and over in studying teaching materials. Believe me, it seems to be simple when I talk about it, but when you really do it, it is very complicated, subtle, and takes a lot of time. It is easy to be an elementary school teacher, but it is difficult to be a good elementary school teacher. (Tr. Wang)

From the previous statements we can see how the interactions between "what it is" and "how to teach it" occur in the teachers' minds before they teach a lesson or a topic. Through this process, both their knowledge of what to teach and how to teach grow.

The understanding of the rationale of subtraction with regrouping is a striking example of how Chinese teachers improved their knowledge of school mathematics through studying what they call "teaching materials." Although we saw in this study that most of the Chinese teachers explained subtraction with regrouping as "decomposing a higher value unit," in the late 1970s, most Chinese teachers used "borrowing." During her interview on subtraction, one teacher reported that the parents of some of her students were still teaching this concept to their children. However, the version of the *Teaching and Learning Framework* and the textbook series published in the early 1980s eliminated the concept of borrowing and replaced it with the concept of "decomposing a higher value unit," and most teachers now use the latter.

Learning Mathematics From Colleagues

Chinese teachers not only study teaching materials individually, they also do it with their colleagues. There are also interactions between and among colleagues on the understanding of school mathematics.

Chinese teachers are organized in *jiaoyanzu* or "teaching research groups" (for more information see Paine & Ma, 1993). These groups, usually meeting once a week for about one hour, get together formally to share their ideas and reflections on teaching. During this period of time, a main activity is to study teaching materials. In addition, because Chinese teachers do not have their own desks in a classroom, they share an office with their colleagues, usually with other members of their teaching research groups. Teachers read and correct students' work, prepare their lessons, have individual talks with students, and spend their nonteaching time at their offices. Therefore, they have significant informal interactions with officemates outside of the formal meetings of their teaching research groups.

When asked if she had learned any mathematics from her colleagues, Tr. Wang immediately referred to her experience when she started teaching:

I have learned so much math from other teachers. When I first came to the school teacher Xie[6] was my mentor. He was a very good mathematics teacher and now is retired. I liked to listen to Xie and other teachers discussing how to solve a problem. They usually had various ways to solve a problem. I was so impressed that they could use seemingly very simple ideas to solve very complicated problems. It was from them that I started to see the beauty and power of mathematics.

In fact, not only do young teachers learn mathematics through collegiality, experienced teachers also benefit from it. Tr. Mao said:

Discussions with my colleagues are usually very inspiring. Especially when we share about how each of us deals with a certain topic, designs classroom practices, manages the teaching pace, what homework each of us chooses and why, etc. In my teaching research group I am the eldest one and have taught the longest time, yet I learn a lot from my young colleagues. They are usually more open minded than I am in their ways of solving problems. For example, Jianqiang is a young teacher who has taught for only three years. He often solves the problems in his own ingenuous way, very inspiring. Aged people have rich experience, but we usually have a fixed way of solving a problem. How I taught it before may confine my mind. But the young people do not have such fixed ways. They tend to think from various dimensions, so we can stimulate each other.

Tr. Sun had taught in two schools. I asked her to compare collegiality in the two schools.

I came to this school three years ago, when I moved back to Shanghai. Before then I taught in a school in Jiading County, Zhejiang Province. We had had very close relationships in our teaching research group, too. I think a teaching research group is always helpful because you need to be stimulated by someone else when trying to have a better understanding of something. How other teachers interpret the *Teaching and Learning Framework*, how your colleagues understand a certain topic you are to teach, and how they are to teach it, etc. are usually inspiring. Moreover, sharing your ideas with others pushes you to make your ideas clearer and more explicit. I always feel that my ideas would never have gotten sufficiently developed if I had not shared them with my colleagues.

---

[6]This was not the Tr. Xie who participated in the study.

Indeed, as suggested in Tr.Sun's discussion, to learn something specific from one's colleagues is only one of the benefits from collegiality. Another, sharing ideas with colleagues, increases one's motivation to study and make ideas clearer and more explicit. In addition, group discussion is a context where one easily gets inspired. The interactions between "what is it" and "how to teach it" seem to provide the driving force for the growth of the Chinese teachers' knowledge of school mathematics, while collegiality collects momentum for the process.

Learning Mathematics from Students

I had not expected that the teachers would tell me that they had learned mathematics from their students, but they did. The most impressive example was provided by Tr. Mao:

> A good teacher can learn from his or her students to enrich himself. Sometimes the way of solving a problem proposed by a student is one I have never thought about, even though I have taught elementary school for several decades. I can tell you something that happened just a few days ago. We were in the "triangle unit" and I asked my class to try to get the area of the following figure:

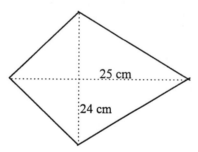

> Most students thought that it was impossible to solve this problem, since neither of the altitudes of the triangles was known. The way I usually teach this is to refer to the formula for the area of a triangle and the distributive property. I usually say to students, "Look, this figure, from top to bottom, consists of two triangles. There is something common in these two triangles. What is it?" Students would find that the two triangles share a common base. Then, from left to right, the figure also consists of two triangles and they also share a common base. "Let's start from the upper and lower triangles. Since we have learned how to use a letter to represent a number, why don't we try to use letters to represent the unknown altitudes. Given that we write the unknown altitude of this upper triangle as h_1, how can we represent the altitude of the lower triangle? h_2. OK, then how can we write out the formula for their areas? A student would say for the area of the upper triangle we would have $25 \times h_1 \div 2$ and for the lower triangle $25 \times h_2 \div 2$. So the area

of the whole figure would be $25 \times h_1 \div 2 + 25 \times h_2 \div 2$. Since we have learned the distributive property; we know that the common factor 25 can be taken out and so can $\div 2$. So we can reorganize the problem this way:

$$25 \times h_1 \div 2 + 25 \times h_2 \div 2 = 25 \times (h_1 + h_2) \div 2$$

At this step, students would suddenly see the light. We know what $h_1 + h_2$ is! It is 24 cm! So the problem would be solved. But this time before my explanation one student raised his hand and said he could solve the problem. He said, "I will draw a rectangle around the figure:

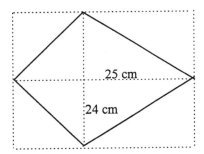

The length of the area is 25 cm and the width is 24 cm. Its area is 25×24. Our original figure at the middle part of the rectangle is exactly half of the rectangle. So I just divide 25×24 by 2 and will know the area of that figure." As you can see, his way was much simpler than my way. I had never even thought of this smart way! But I understood his idea immediately. Most students were still puzzled. I needed to lead them to understand how and why it would work. I said to the class, "This is a very good idea. Please take a look, how many small rectangles are there in this big rectangle?" "Four." "OK." I pointed to one of these small rectangles and asked, "What is this line in this rectangle?" "Diagonal line." "Then how about the area of the two small rectangles divided by the diagonal line?" "They have the same area." Then the students soon found that each small rectangle was divided into two pieces. We had four pieces inside and four pieces outside; the four inside ones, which formed the original figure, were of the same area as that of the four outside ones. Therefore, the area of our original figure was exactly half of the big rectangle . . .

But to catch students' new ideas such as this one in the classroom you have to have a good understanding of mathematics. You have to catch it in a moment with the whole class waiting for your guidance.

Tr. Wang also mentioned that she had learned from students and said that she was convinced that some advanced students were more knowledgeable than she when she first came to teach in the school. Tr. Sun described what she learned from students in the lower grades:

Students are very creative. They have taught me a lot. I used to teach upper level students in another school. In this school they wanted me to teach lower grades. The little ones have surprised me so many times. For example, the problem of subtraction with decomposing about which you interviewed me, I had never thought that it could be solved in so many different ways. It was my students who proposed the nonstandard ways. In fact, their proposals deepened my understanding of the algorithm.

These teachers' discussions about how they had learned from their students reminded me of a conversation I had with another teacher many years ago. She said:

In terms of solving mathematical problems, some of my students are even more capable than I am. Some problems in the math competition of the school district are too complicated for me to solve. But some students in my class can solve them. I am glad that my students can go farther than where I am. But I also know that it is me, my teaching, that has empowered them.

I think she was right. Creative students are fostered in a creative teaching and learning context. Indeed, it is a teacher who creates such a context, who prepares students to become their teacher's teachers.

Learning Mathematics by Doing It

Doing mathematics was a hot topic for these Chinese teachers. "Solving one problem with several ways [yiti duojie]" for them seemed to be an important indicator of ability to do mathematics. Teachers told me that it was one way in which they improved themselves. Tr. Wang said that it was one of the main ways in which her knowledge of mathematics had improved:

My knowledge of mathematics improved substantially after I became a teacher. When I first came to this school in 1980, I had very little knowledge of elementary mathematics. For I had my own elementary and secondary schooling during the Cultural Revolution, when schools did not teach students seriously. At first I was the aide of teacher Xie for his sixth-grade class. My work was to correct students' homework and to help slow students. At that time I felt that many students in Xie's class were smarter than I. I was surprised when I saw how capable the fast students were at solving complicated problems. I couldn't do it at all. Next year I was assigned to teach third grade. Then second grade, then third grade, and then third, third, fourth, fifth, sixth. In recent years I have been teaching higher grades. One way I have improved my mathematical knowledge is through solving mathematical problems, doing mathematics. The smart ways that the experienced teachers like Xie, Pan, and Mao, and even those advanced students, solved mathematics problems really impressed me. To improve myself I first of all did in advance all the problems which I asked my students to do. Then I studied how to explain and analyze the problems for kids. To do more mathematics problems I have looked for books of mathematical problem collections and I do the problems in these books. I don't know how many mathematics problems I have done after I became a teacher, many, many, uncountable. Currently I am studying a collection of problems from mathematics competitions. These problems are more complicated than those we teach in school, but through studying them I feel I have improved. I share the way I solve difficult problems with other teachers, usually with Jianqiang. He also likes to do complicated math problems. We enjoy discussing various ways of solving them.

"Doing mathematics" is the major activity of mathematicians. Lange (1964) writes:

> Most members of the mathematical community—it is a remarkably worldwide community, possessing a universality uncommon in other areas of human enterprise—would prefer to *do* mathematics, not concern themselves excessively with the question of what it is that they are doing. (p. 51)

While mathematicians may "not concern themselves with the question of what it is that they are doing," teachers who teach mathematics cannot ignore the question of what it is that they are teaching. However, a mathematics teacher should keep his or her enthusiasm for doing mathematics as well. It appears that a mathematics teacher should go back and forth between the two: doing mathematics, as well as making clear what it is that he or she is doing or teaching. Through this interaction, one develops a teacher's subject matter knowledge.

In the three teachers' discussions of how they developed their understanding of school mathematics, we see a process with a series of interactions: between considerations of what one should teach and how to teach it; among colleagues; between teachers and students; and between one's interest in mathematics as a teacher and as a layperson or mathematician. Although all these interactions contribute to the development and the construction of a teacher's subject matter knowledge of mathematics, the interaction between the consideration of what to teach and how to teach it seems to be the "axle" that runs the "wheel," while the collegiality among teachers serves as the "spokes" that connect all the pieces.

A teacher's subject matter knowledge of mathematics, which develops under a concern of teaching and learning, will be relevant to teaching and is likely to be used in teaching. In other words, the Chinese teachers develop and deepen their subject matter knowledge of elementary mathematics by preparing for classes, teaching the material, and reflecting on the process. Therefore, what they learn will contribute to and be used in teaching.

SUMMARY

This chapter discussed the results of two brief studies that explored when and how PUFM is attained. In order to investigate when a teacher might attain PUFM, I interviewed two groups of Chinese nonteachers, ninth-grade students and preservice teachers, asking them the same questions that I had asked of teachers. Both groups showed conceptual understanding and algorithmic competence. In contrast with the ninth-grade students, the prospective teachers' responses to the four scenarios showed a concern for teaching and learning. No responses displayed PUFM: there were no discussions of connections among mathematical topics, multiple solutions of a problem, basic principles of mathematics, or longitudinal coherence.

All of the members of the Chinese preteaching groups displayed more conceptual understanding than did the U.S. teachers; for instance, all showed an understanding of the rationale for multidigit multiplication. The Chinese preteaching groups also showed more procedural knowledge: all did calculations correctly (with the exception of one minor error) and all knew the formulas for the area and perimeter of a rectangle. Eighty-five percent of the preservice teachers, but only 40% of the ninth graders, created a story problem that correctly represented the meaning of division by fractions. Fifty-eight percent of the preservice teachers and 60% of the ninth graders reached a correct solution in their discussions of the relationship between area and perimeter of a rectangle. In contrast, 43% of the U.S. teachers succeeded in the division by fractions calculation. Only one of the U.S. teachers (4%) created a story problem that correctly represented the meaning of division by fractions. Only one of the U.S. teachers reached a correct solution in discussing the relationship between area and perimeter of a rectangle and 17% reported that they did not know the area and perimeter formulas.

The second study explored how Chinese teachers attain PUFM. I interviewed three teachers with PUFM, asking them how they had acquired their mathematical knowledge. The teachers mentioned several factors: learning from colleagues, learning mathematics from students, learning mathematics by doing problems, teaching, teaching round-by-round, and studying teaching materials intensively.

During the summers and at the beginning of school terms, Chinese teachers study the *Teaching and Learning Framework*, a document similar in some ways to the National Council of Teachers of Mathematics *Standards for School Mathematics* (NCTM, 1989) or state documents like *Mathematics Framework for California Public Schools* (California Department of Education, 1985, 1992). The most studied material is the textbook. Teachers study and discuss it during the school year as they are teaching. Comparatively little time is devoted to studying teachers' manuals, although new teachers find them helpful.

The two studies suggest that, although their schooling contributes a sound basis for it, Chinese teachers develop PUFM during their teaching careers—stimulated by a concern for what to teach and how to teach it, inspired and supported by their colleagues and teaching materials.

Conclusion

As I said at the beginning of this book, the initial motivation for my study was to explore some possible causes of the unsatisfactory mathematics achievement of U.S. students in contrast to their counterparts in some Asian countries. In concluding, I would like to return to my original concern about the mathematics education of children in the United States. Having considered teachers' knowledge of school mathematics in depth, I suggest that to improve mathematics education for students, an important action that should be taken is improving the quality of their teachers' knowledge of school mathematics.

Although the intent of my study was not to evaluate U.S. and Chinese teachers' mathematical knowledge, it has revealed some important differences in their knowledge of school mathematics. It does not seem to be an accident that not one of a group of above average U.S. teachers displayed a profound understanding of elementary mathematics. In fact, the knowledge gap between the U.S. and Chinese teachers parallels the learning gap between U.S. and Chinese students revealed by other scholars (Stevenson et al., 1990; Stevenson & Stigler, 1992). Given that the parallel of the two gaps is not mere coincidence, it follows that *while we want to work on improving students' mathematics education, we also need to improve their teachers' knowledge of school mathematics.* As indicated in the introduction, the quality of teacher subject matter knowledge directly affects student learning—and it can be immediately addressed.

Teachers' subject matter knowledge develops in a cyclic process as depicted in Fig. 7.1.

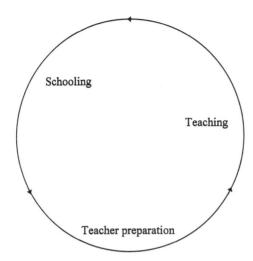

FIG. 7.1.   Three periods during which teachers' subject matter knowledge develops.

Figure 7.1 illustrates three periods during which teachers' subject matter knowledge of school mathematics may be fostered. In China, the cycle spirals upward. When teachers are still students, they attain mathematical competence. During teacher education programs, their mathematical competence starts to be connected to a primary concern about teaching and learning school mathematics. Finally, during their teaching careers, as they empower students with mathematical competence, they develop a *teacher's* subject matter knowledge, which I call in its highest form PUFM.

Unfortunately, this is not the case in the United States. It seems that low-quality school mathematics education and low-quality teacher knowledge of school mathematics reinforce each other. Teachers who do not acquire mathematical competence during schooling are unlikely to have another opportunity to acquire it. The NCRTE (1991) study of teacher education programs indicates that most U.S. teacher preparation programs focus on how to teach mathematics rather than on the mathematics itself. After teacher preparation, teachers are expected to know how and what they will teach and not to require further study (Schifter, 1996a). This assumption is reflected in the U.S. educational structure: The National Commission on Teaching and America's Future (1997) found no system in place to ensure that teachers get access to the knowledge they need. This lack may be an important impediment to reform. In 1996, after two years of intensive study, the commission concluded that "Most schools and teachers cannot achieve the goals set forth in new educational standards, not because they are unwilling, but because they do not know how, and the systems they work in do not support them in doing so" (p. 1).

Reflecting on Chinese mathematics education one may notice that the upward spiral is not there by itself but is cultivated and supported by the solid substance of school mathematics in China. If the subject they taught did not have depth and breadth, how could Chinese teachers develop a profound understanding of it? In fact, there may exist another upward spiral in China—between substantial elementary mathematics and solid mathematics education. This contrasts with the sustained low levels in the United States, where inadequate elementary mathematics ("basic skills," "shopkeeper arithmetic") reinforces and is reinforced by unsatisfactory mathematics education. In the United States, it is widely accepted that elementary mathematics is "basic," superficial, and commonly understood. The data in this book explode this myth. Elementary mathematics is not superficial at all, and any one who teaches it has to study it hard in order to understand it in a comprehensive way.[1]

How can these self-perpetuating relationships—between unsatisfactory student learning and inadequate teacher knowledge, between unsatisfactory mathematics education and inadequate elementary mathematics—be broken? How can the goals of reform be achieved? I conclude with some recommendations.

ADDRESS TEACHER KNOWLEDGE AND STUDENT LEARNING AT THE SAME TIME

First of all, I would like to indicate that although I take the gap in teacher knowledge as a factor in the gap in student learning, I do not regard improvement of teachers' knowledge as necessarily preceding improvement of students' learning. Rather, I believe both should be addressed simultaneously, and that work on each should support the improvement of the other. Because they are interdependent processes, we cannot expect to improve teachers' mathematical knowledge first, and in so doing automatically improve students' mathematics education.

As we saw in the previous chapter, a teacher's subject matter knowledge of school mathematics is a product of the interaction between mathematical competence and concern about teaching and learning mathematics. The quality of the interaction depends on the quality of each component. Given that their own schooling does not yet provide future teachers with sound mathematical competence, their base for developing solid teaching knowledge is weakened. As my data show, the group of Chinese ninth-grade students were more competent in elementary mathematics than the group

---

[1]Other scholars, such as Ball (1988d) have also revealed the falsity of the assumption that elementary mathematics is commonly understood.

of U.S. teachers, and in addition showed more conceptual understanding. This suggests that although Chinese teachers develop PUFM during their teaching careers, their schooling contributes a sound basis for it. Teacher candidates in the United States will not have this sound basis if student learning is not addressed.

The second reason that improving teachers' subject matter knowledge of mathematics cannot be isolated from improving school mathematics teaching is that, as I have revealed, the key period during which Chinese teachers develop a *teacher's* subject matter knowledge of school mathematics is when they teach it—given that they have the motivation to improve their teaching and the opportunity to do so. If this is true, it would be unrealistic to expect U.S. teachers' subject matter knowledge of school mathematics to be improved before mathematics education in school is improved. Improving teachers' subject matter knowledge and improving students' mathematics education are thus interwoven and interdependent processes that must occur simultaneously. What is needed, then, is a teaching context in which it is possible for teachers to improve their knowledge of school mathematics as they work to improve their teaching of mathematics.

ENHANCE THE INTERACTION BETWEEN TEACHERS' STUDY OF SCHOOL MATHEMATICS AND HOW TO TEACH IT

I have indicated that the key period during which Chinese teachers develop their deep understanding of school mathematics is when they are teaching it. However, this finding may not be true of teachers in the United States. The experienced U.S. teachers in this study did not perform better than their new colleagues in terms of subject matter knowledge. This finding agrees with that of the National Center for Research on Teacher Education (NCRTE, 1991). The question then is, Why did teaching mathematics in this country not produce PUFM among teachers?

I have observed that mathematics teaching in the United States lacks an interaction between study of the mathematics taught and study of how to teach it. Several factors hinder teachers from careful study of the school mathematics they teach. One is the assumption that I have already discussed—that elementary mathematics is "basic," superficial, and commonly understood.

Another assumption—that teachers do not need further study of the subject they teach—also hinders teachers' further study of school mathematics. Schifter wrote:

> the notion that even experienced teachers can and should be expected to
> continue learning in their own classrooms contrasts sharply with the tradi-

tional assumption that becoming a teacher marks a sufficiency of learning. It is no great exaggeration to say that, according to the conventions of school culture, teachers, by definition, already know—know the content domain they are to teach, the sequence of lessons they must go through to teach it, and the techniques for imposing order on a roomful of students. (1996a, p. 163)

Even if teachers had the time and inclination for studying school mathematics, what would they study? Ball (1996) wrote, "it is not clear whether most curriculum developers write with teacher learning as a goal." H. Burkhardt (personal communication, May 11, 1998) said, "Professional developers, though they advocate a constructivist approach for kids, are only gradually allowing teachers to learn in a constructive fashion."

Textbook manuals offer teachers little guidance (Armstrong & Bezuk, 1995; Schmidt, 1996, p. 194), possibly because teachers are not expected to read them. Burkhardt (personal communication, May 11, 1998) said:

The math textbook provides a script (with stage directions) for the teacher to use in explaining the topic and guiding the lesson; the students are only expected to read and do the exercises at the end of the chapter. Nobody reads "teachers' guides" except on masters courses.

Although the results of the Third International Mathematics and Science Study indicate that elementary mathematics lessons in the United States tend to be based on the textbook (Schmidt, 1996, p. 104), little research focuses on exactly how teachers use textbooks (Freeman & Porter, 1989, pp. 67–88; Sosniak & Stodolsky, 1993). This research indicates that there may be wide variation in teachers' topic selection, content emphasis, and sequence of instruction. Textbooks are rarely followed from beginning to end (Schmidt, McKnight, & Raizen, 1997). Case studies suggest that teachers' knowledge plays a very important role in how textbook contents are selected and interpreted (Putnam, Heaton, Prawat, & Remillard, 1992). Even the teaching of one topic may have wide variation. As we have seen in the first three chapters of this book, different teachers may construe the same topic very differently.

In China, teaching a course is considered to be like acting in a play. Although an actor has to know a play very well and can interpret it in an original way, he or she is not supposed to write (or rewrite) the play. Indeed, a well-written play will not confine an actor's performance or creativity but will rather stimulate and inspire it.

The same can be true for teachers. Teaching can be a socially cooperative activity. We need good actors as well as good playwrights. A thoughtfully and carefully composed textbook carries wisdom about curriculum that teachers can "talk with" and that can inspire and enlighten them. In China, textbooks are considered to be not only for students, but also for teachers' learning of the mathematics they are teaching. Teachers study textbooks very carefully; they investigate them individually and in groups, they talk about what textbooks mean, they do the problems together, and they have conversations about them. Teacher's manuals provide information about content and pedagogy, student thinking and longitudinal coherence.

Time is an issue here. If teachers have to find out what to teach by themselves in their very limited time outside the classroom and decide how to teach it, then where is the time for them to study carefully what they are to teach? U.S. teachers have less working time outside the classroom than Chinese teachers (McKnight et al., 1987; Stigler & Stevenson, 1991), but they need to do much more in this limited time. What U.S. teachers are expected to accomplish, then, is impossible. It is clear that they do not have enough time and appropriate support to think through thoroughly what they are to teach. And without a clear idea of what to teach, how can one determine how to teach it thoughtfully?

REFOCUS TEACHER PREPARATION

I contend that teacher education is a strategically critical period during which change can be made. As the report of the Conference on the Mathematical Preparation of Elementary School Teachers points out:

> It makes sense to attack the problems of elementary school mathematics education at the college level. All teachers go to college—it's where they expect to learn how to teach. Moreover, the task is almost manageable at the college level. . . . only about a thousand colleges educate teachers. (Cipra, 1992, p. 5)

Although my data do not show that Chinese teachers develop their PUFM during teacher preparation, this does not mean that the role of teacher preparation in improving teachers' knowledge of elementary mathematics should be minimized. On the contrary, in the vicious circle formed by low-quality mathematics education and low-quality teacher knowledge of school mathematics—a third party—teacher preparation may serve as the force to break the circle.

Refocusing teacher preparation, however, creates another important task for educational research—rebuilding a solid and substantial school mathematics for teachers and students to learn. What we should do is to rebuild a substantial school mathematics with a more comprehensive understanding of the relationship between fundamental mathematics and new advanced branches of the discipline. To rebuild a substantial school mathematics for today is a task for mathematics education researchers. Indeed, unless such a school mathematics is developed, the mutual reinforcement of low-level content and teaching will not be undone.

UNDERSTAND THE ROLE THAT CURRICULAR MATERIALS, INCLUDING TEXTBOOKS, MIGHT PLAY IN REFORM

Like textbooks, reform documents such the California *Framework* (1985) and the National Council of Teachers of Mathematics (NCTM) *Standards* (1989) lend themselves to multiple interpretations (Putnam et al., 1992) that depend on the reader's knowledge and beliefs about mathematics, teaching, and learning.

The *Professional Standards for Teaching Mathematics* (NCTM, 1991, p. 32) says that "textbooks can be useful resources for teachers, but teachers must also be free to adapt or depart from texts if students' ideas and conjectures are to help shape teachers' navigation of the content." Ferrucci (1997) pointed out that discontinuing the use of textbooks may be viewed as being consistent with this statement. Others characterize reform teachers as "using the textbook as a supplement to the curriculum" for homework, practice, and review; in contrast, traditional teachers depend on the text to guide the scope and sequence of the curriculum (Kroll & Black, 1993, p. 431).

Because of dissatisfaction with textbooks (Ball, 1993b; Heaton, 1992; Schifter, 1996b) or because they were encouraged to do so in preservice programs (Ball & Feiman-Nemser, 1988), some reform-minded teachers independently organize their own curricula, make their own materials, and implement the lessons they have designed (Heaton, 1992; Shimahara & Sakai, 1995; Stigler, Fernandez, & Yoshida, 1996, p. 216; for narratives from SummerMath teachers, see Schifter, 1996c, 1996d). Ball and Cohen (1996) wrote:

> educators often disparage textbooks, and many reform-oriented teachers repudiate them, announcing disdainfully that they do not use texts. This idealization of professional autonomy leads to the view that good teachers do not follow textbooks, but instead make their own curriculum. . . . This hostility to texts, and the idealized image of the individual professional, have inhibited careful consideration of the constructive role that curriculum might play. (p. 6)

Teachers need not have an antagonistic relationship with textbooks. My data illustrate how teachers can both use and go beyond the textbook. For example, Chinese teachers' knowledge packages are consistent with the national curriculum. But the student's idea that Tr. Mao "caught" (chapter 6) and the nonstandard methods of subtraction with regrouping, multidigit multiplication, and division by fractions described by the Chinese teachers were not in the textbook.

Teacher's manuals can explain curriculum developers' intentions and reasons for the way topics are selected and sequenced. Manuals can also provide very specific information about the nature of students' responses to particular activities (Magidson, 1994 April; Stigler, Fernandez, & Yoshida, 1996). Information about student responses can support teachers who focus on student thinking. However, such information may be useless if teachers do not recognize its significance or do not have time and energy for careful study of manuals (Magidson, 1994 April).

UNDERSTAND THE KEY TO REFORM: WHATEVER THE FORM OF CLASSROOM INTERACTIONS MIGHT BE, THEY MUST FOCUS ON SUBSTANTIVE MATHEMATICS

Like the use of textbooks, the kind of teaching advocated by reform documents is subject to different interpretations. For example, Putnam and his colleagues (1992) interviewed California teachers and state and district mathematics educators. Some thought the primary focus of the 1985 California *Framework* was what to teach—"important mathematical content"; others thought it was how to teach—"a call to use manipulatives and cooperative groups" (p. 214). During 1992 and 1993, the Recognizing and Recording Reform in Mathematics Education Project studied schools across the United States. Project members Ferrini-Mundy and Johnson (1994) noted that superficial efforts can pass for change. "Mathematics classrooms can *appear* to be quite Standards-oriented, with calculators in evidence, students working in groups, manipulatives available, and interesting problems under discussion" (p. 191), but investigators need a deeper understanding of what is happening in these classrooms.

This dicotomy sharpens when we consider Chinese teachers' classrooms. On one hand, mathematics teaching in Chinese classrooms, even by a teacher with PUFM, seems very "traditional"; that is, contrary to that advocated by reform. Mathematics teaching in China is clearly textbook based. In Chinese classrooms, students sit in rows facing the teacher, who is obviously the leader and maker of the agenda and direction in classroom learning. On the other hand, one can see in Chinese classrooms, particularly in those of teachers with PUFM, features advocated by reform—teaching for conceptual understanding, students' enthusiasm and opportunities to express their ideas, and their participation and contribution to their own learning processes. How can these seemingly contradictory features—some protested against and some advocated by reform—occur at the same time? What might this intriguing contrast imply for reform efforts in the United States?

The perspective of Cobb and his colleagues (Cobb, Wood, Yackel, & McNeal, 1992) helps to explain this puzzle. Cobb and his associates view the essence of the current reform as a change of classroom mathematics tradition and contend that traditional and reform instruction differ in "the quality of the taken-to-be-shared or normative meanings and practices of mathematics" rather than in "rhetorical characterizations."

In their case study of two classrooms, one with "a tradition of school mathematics" where knowledge was "transmitted" from the teacher to "passive students" and one with "a tradition of inquiry mathematics" in which "mathematical learning was viewed as an interactive, constructive, problem-centered process," the scholars found that in both the teachers and the students actively contributed to the development of their classroom mathematics tradition, while in both classrooms the teachers expressed their "institutionalized authority" during the process. Cobb and his associates suggest that "meaningful learning" may be mere rhetoric in mathematics education because "the activity of following procedural instructions can be meaningful for students" in certain classroom mathematics traditions. The transmission metaphor that describes traditional mathematics teaching as the attempt to transmit knowledge from the teacher to passive students may be appropriate only "in the political context of reform" (p. 34).

In this sense, although the mathematics teaching in Chinese teachers' classrooms does not meet some "rhetorical characterizations" of the reform, it is actually in the classroom mathematics tradition advocated by the current reform. In fact, even though the classroom of a Chinese teacher with PUFM may look very "traditional" in its form, it transcends the form in many aspects. It is textbook based, but not confined to textbooks. The teacher is the leader, but students' ideas and initiatives are highly encouraged and valued.

On the other hand, from a teacher who cannot provide a mathematical explanation of algorithms for subtraction with regrouping, multidigit multiplication, or division by fractions; from a teacher who cannot provide a correct representation for the meaning of an arithmetical operation such as division by fractions; or from a teacher who is not motivated to explore new mathematical claims, what kind of "teaching for understanding" can we expect?

To make the point more clearly we can think about a classroom like that of Ball (1993a, 1993b, 1996), considered by some to be a model of current reform:

> In the classroom centered on student thinking and discussion—the classroom envisioned by mathematics education reformers—the children regularly disperse into small groups where they work together on problems, while the teacher visits around the classroom listening for significant mathematical issues and considering what types of intervention, if any, are appropriate. And when the children reassemble to compare their ideas and solutions, her questions facilitate discussion. (Schifter, 1996b, p. 3)

That is not at all the way the Chinese classrooms are organized. What I want to point out is, however, that even though they look very different, the difference is superficial. If you look carefully at the kind of mathematics that the Chinese students are doing and the kind of thinking they have been encouraged to engage in, and the way in which the teachers' interactions with them foster that kind of mental and mathematical process, the two kinds of classrooms are actually much more similar than they appear. On the other hand, although the fact that so many U.S. elementary teachers have children in groups facing each other and using manipulatives may mean that their classrooms look more like Ball's classroom when you walk in, nevertheless, neither the mathematics nor the mathematical thinking that the students are doing nor what the teacher is attempting to help them understand are the same. The real mathematical thinking going on in a classroom, in fact, depends heavily on the teacher's understanding of mathematics.

Another point I would like to make is that the change of a classroom mathematics tradition may not be a "revolution" that simply throws out the old and adopts the new. Rather, it may be a process in which some new features develop out of the old tradition. In other words, the two traditions may not be absolutely antagonistic to each other. Rather, the new tradition embraces the old—just as a new paradigm in scientific research does not completely exclude an old one but includes it as a special case.

In real classroom teaching, the two traditions may not be distinguished from each other clearly, or they may not be so "pure" as has been described. For example, my study indicates that teachers with PUFM never ignore the role of "procedural learning" no matter how much they emphasize "conceptual understanding."

Moreover, this research suggests that teachers' subject matter knowledge of mathematics may contribute to a classroom mathematics tradition and its alteration. A "taken-to-be-shared mathematical understanding" that marks a classroom tradition cannot be independent from the mathematical knowledge of people in the classroom, especially that of the teacher who is in charge of the teaching process. If a teacher's own knowledge of the mathematics taught in elementary school is limited to procedures, how could we expect his or her classroom to have a tradition of inquiry mathematics? The change that we are expecting can occur only if we work on changing teachers' knowledge of mathematics.

I would like to end with a quotation from Dewey (1902/1975):

> But here comes the effort of thought. It is easier to see the conditions in their separateness, to insist upon one at the expense of the other, to make antagonists of them, than to discover a reality to which each belongs. (p. 91)

Appendix

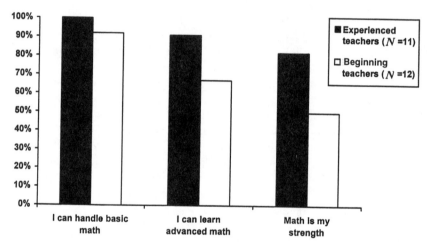

FIG. A.1. The U.S. teachers' view of their own mathematical knowledge.

TABLE A.1
Experienced U.S. Teachers' Years of Teaching Experience

| | Years taught | |
	Elementary school	Middle school
Tr. Baird	14	
Tr. Barbara	5	
Tr. Barry	23	
Tr. Belinda	12	
Tr. Belle	19	
Tr. Bernadette	17	
Tr. Bernice	8	
Tr. Beverly	15	
Tr. Blanche	1	
Tr. Brady	19	
Tr. Bridget	2	14

Note. None of the teachers reported preschool or kindergarten experience.

备课辅导材料	*beike fudao cailiao*	Teacher's manuals
处理教材	*chuli jiaocai*	To deal with teaching material
教研组	*jiaoyanzu*	Teaching research groups
教学大纲	*jiaoxue dagang*	*Teaching and Learning Framework*
借一当十	*jie yi dang shi*	To borrow 1 unit from the tens and regard it as 10 ones
进率	*jin lu*	The rate for composing a higher value unit
进一	*jin yi*	Decomposing a unit of higher value
课本	*keben*	Textbooks
退一	*tui yi*	Decomposing a unit of higher value
一题多解	*yiti duojie*	Solving one problem in several ways
知其然，知其所以然	*zhi qi ran, zhi qi suoyi ran*	"Know how, and also know why."
钻研教材	*zuanyan jiaocai*	To study teaching materials intensively

FIG. A.2.

References

Armstrong, B., & Bezuk, N. (1995). Multiplication and division of fractions: The search for meaning. In J. Sowder & B. Schappelle (Eds.), *Providing a foundation for teaching mathematics in the middle grades* (pp. 85–119). Albany: State University of New York Press.

Ball, D. (1988a). Mount Holyoke College, South Hadley, Massachusetts Summermath for teachers program and educational leaders in mathematics project. In National Center for Research on Teacher Education, *Dialogues in teacher education* (pp. 79–88). East Lansing, MI: National Center for Research on Teacher Education.

Ball, D. (1988b). *Knowledge and reasoning in mathematical pedagogy: Examining what prospective teachers bring to teacher education.* Unpublished doctoral dissertation, Michigan State University, East Lansing.

Ball, D. (1988c). *The subject matter preparation of prospective teachers: Challenging the myths.* East Lansing, MI: National Center for Research on Teacher Education.

Ball, D. (1989). *Teaching mathematics for understanding: What do teachers need to know about the subject matter.* East Lansing, MI: National Center for Research on Teacher Education.

Ball, D. (1990). Prospective elementary and secondary teachers' understanding of division. *Journal for Research in Mathematics Education, 21*(2), 132–144.

Ball, D. (1991). Research on teaching mathematics: Making subject matter knowledge part of the equation. In J. Brophy (Ed.), *Advances in research on teaching* (Vol. 2, pp. 1–48). Greenwich, CT: JAI Press.

Ball, D. (1992). Magical hopes: Manipulatives and the reform of math education. *American Educator, 16*(1), 14–18, 46–47.

Ball, D. (1993a). Halves, pieces, and twoths: Constructing and using representational contexts in teaching fractions. In T. Carpenter, E. Fennema, & T. Romberg (Eds.), *Rational numbers: An integration of research* (pp. 157–195). Hillsdale, NJ: Lawrence Erlbaum Associates.

Ball, D. (1993b). With an eye on the mathematical horizon: Dilemmas of teaching elementary school mathematics. *Elementary School Journal, 93*(4), 373–397.

Ball, D. (1996). Connecting to mathematics as a part of teaching to learn. In D. Schifter (Ed.), *What's happening in math class?: Reconstructing professional identities* (Vol. 2, pp. 36–45). New York: Teachers College Press.

Ball, D., & Cohen, D. (1996). Reform by the book: What is—or what might be—the role of curriculum materials in teacher learning and instructional reform? *Educational Researcher, 25*(9), 6–8, 14.

Ball, D., & Feiman-Nemser, S. (1988). Using textbooks and teachers' guides: A dilemma for beginning teachers and teacher educators. *Curriculum Inquiry, 18,* 401–423.

Beijing, Tianjin, Shanghai, and Zhejiang Associate Group for Elementary Mathematics Teaching Material Composing (1989). *Shuxue, Diwuce* [Mathematics Vol. 5]. Beijing, China: Beijing Publishing House.

Bruner, J. (1960/1977). *The process of education.* Cambridge, MA: Harvard University Press.

California State Department of Education. (1985). *Mathematics framework for California public schools.* Sacramento, CA: California State Department of Education.

California State Department of Education. (1992). *Mathematics framework for California public schools.* Sacramento, CA: California State Department of Education.

Chang, L., & Ruzicka, J. (1986). *Second international mathematics study, United States, Technical report I.* Champaign, IL: Stipes.

Cipra, B. (Ed.). (1992). *On the mathematical preparation of elementary school teachers.* Report of a two-part conference held at the University of Chicago in January and May, 1991.

Cobb, P., Wood, T., Yackel, E., & McNeal, B. (1992). Characteristics of classroom mathematics traditions: An interactional analysis. *American Educational Research Journal, 29*(3), 573–604.

Cohen, D. K. (1991). A revolution in one classroom: The case of Mrs. Oublier. *Educational Evaluation and Policy Analysis, 12,* 311–330.

Coleman, J. S. (1975). Methods and results in IEA studies of effects of school on learning. *Review of Educational Research, 45*(3), 355–386.

Crosswhite, F. J. (1986). *Second international mathematics study: Detailed report for the United States.* Champaign, IL: Stipes.

Crosswhite, F. J., Dossey, J., Swafford, J., McKnight, C., & Cooney, T. (1985). *Second international mathematics study. Summary report for the United States.* Champaign, IL: Stipes.

Dewey, J. (1902/1975). The child and the curriculum. In M. Dworkin (Ed.), *Dewey on education: Selections* (pp. 91–111). New York: Teachers College Press.

Dowker, A. (1992). Computational strategies of professional mathematicians. *Journal for Research in Mathematics Education, 23*(1), 45–55.

Driscoll, M. J. (1981). *Research within reach: Elementary school mathematics.* Reston, VA: National Council of Teachers of Mathematics.

Duckworth, E. (1979, June). *Learning with breadth and depth.* Presented as the Catherine Molony Memorial Lecture, City College School of Education, Workshop Center for Open Education, New York.

Duckworth, E. (1987). Some depths and perplexities of elementary arithmetic. *Journal of Mathematical Behavior, 6,* 43–94.

Duckworth, E. (1991). Twenty-four, forty-two, and I love you: Keep it complex. *Harvard Educational Review, 61,* 1–24.

Ferrini-Mundy, J., & Johnson, L. (1994). Recognizing and recording reform in mathematics: New questions, many answers. *Mathematics Teacher, 87*(3), 190–193.

Ferrucci, B. (1997). Institutionalizing mathematics education reform: Vision, leadership, and the Standards. In J. Ferrini-Mundy & T. Schram (Eds.), The Recognizing and Recording Reform in Mathematics Education Project: Insights, issues, and implications (pp. 35–47). *Journal for Research in Mathematics Education Monograph No. 8.*

Freeman, D. J., & Porter, A. C. (1989). Do textbooks dictate the content of mathematics instruction in elementary schools? *American Educational Research Journal, 26*(3), 403–421.

Fuson, K. C., Smith, S. T., & Lo Cicero, A. M. (1997). Supporting Latino first graders' ten-structured thinking in urban classrooms. *Journal for Research in Mathematics Education, 28*(6), 738–766.

Geary, D., Siegler, R., & Fan, L. (1993). Even before formal instruction, Chinese children outperform American children in mental addition. *Cognitive Development, 8*(4), 517–529.

Greer, B. (1992). Multiplication and division as models of situations. In D. Grouws (Ed.), *Handbook of mathematics teaching and learning* (pp. 276–295). New York: Macmillan.

Grossman, P., Wilson, S., & Shulman, L. (1989). Teachers of substance: Subject matter knowledge for teaching. In M. Reynolds (Ed.), *Knowledge base for the beginning teacher* (pp. 23–36). New York: Pergamon Press.

Heaton, R. (1992). Who is minding the mathematics content?: A case study of a fifth grade teacher. *Elementary School Journal, 93*(2), 153–162.

Hiebert, J. (1984). Children's mathematics learning: The struggle to link form and understanding. *Elementary School Journal, 84*, 497–513.

Hirsch, E. D., Jr. (1996). *The schools we need and why we don't have them.* New York: Doubleday.

Husen, T. (1967a). *International study of achievement in mathematics* (Vol. 1). New York: Wiley.

Husen, T. (1967b). *International study of achievement in mathematics* (Vol. 2). New York: Wiley.

Kaput, J. (1994). Democratizing access to calculus: New routes to old roots. In A. Schoenfeld (Ed.), *Mathematical thinking and problem solving* (pp. 77–156). Hillsdale, NJ: Lawrence Erlbaum Associates.

Kaput, J., & Nemirovsky, R. (1995). Moving to the next level: A mathematics of change theme throughout the K–16 curriculum. *UME Trends, 6*(6), 20–21.

Kieran, C. (1990). Cognitive processes involved in learning school algebra. In P. Nesher & J. Kilpatrick (Eds.), *Mathematics and cognition: A research synthesis by the International Group for the Psychology of Mathematics education* (pp. 96–112). Cambridge, England: Cambridge University Press.

Kroll, L., & Black, A. (1993). Developmental theory and teaching methods: A pilot study of a teacher education program. *Elementary School Journal, 93*(4), 417–441.

Lange, L. (1964). The structure of mathematics. In G. Ford & L. Pugno (Eds.), *The structure of knowledge and the curriculum* (pp. 50–70). Chicago, IL: Rand McNally.

LaPointe, A. E., Mead, N. A., & Philips, G. W. (1989). *A world of differences: An international assessment of mathematics and science.* Princeton, NJ: Educational Testing Service.

Lee, S. Y., Ichikawa, V., & Stevenson, H. W. (1987). Beliefs and achievement in mathematics and reading: A cross-national study of Chinese, Japanese, and American children and their mothers. In D. Kleiber & M. Maehr (Eds.), *Advances in motivation* (Vol. 7, pp. 149–179). Greenwich, CT: JAI Press.

Leinhardt, G. (1987). Development of an expert explanation: An analysis of a sequence of subtraction lessons. *Cognition and Instruction, 4*(4), 225–282.

Leinhardt, G., & Greeno, J. (1986). The cognitive skill of mathematics teaching. *Journal of Educational Psychology, 78*(2), 75–95.

Leinhardt, G., Putnam, R., Stein, M., & Baxter, J. (1991). Where subject matter knowledge matters. In J. Brophy (Ed.), *Advances in research on teaching* (Vol. 2, pp. 87–113). Greenwich, CT: JAI Press.

Leinhardt, G., & Smith, D. (1985). Expertise in mathematics instruction: Subject matter knowledge. *Journal of Educational Psychology, 77*(3), 247–271.

Lindquist, M. (1997). NAEP findings regarding the preparation and classroom practices of mathematics teachers. In P. Kenney & E. Silver (Eds.), *Results from the sixth mathematics assessment of the National Assessment of Educational Progress* (pp. 61–86). Reston, VA: National Council of Teachers of Mathematics.

Lynn, R. (1988). *Educational achievement in Japan: Lessons for the West.* NY: Sharpe.

Magidson, S. (1994, April). *Expanding horizons: From a researcher's development of her own instruction to the implementation of that material by others.* Paper presented at the annual meeting of the American Educational Research Association, New Orleans, LA.

Marks, R. (1987). *Those who appreciate: A case study of Joe, a beginning mathematics teacher* (Knowledge Growth in a Profession Publication Series). Stanford, CA: Stanford University, School of Education.

McKnight, C., Crosswhite, F., Dossey, J., Kifer, E., Swafford, J., Travers, K., & Cooney, T. (1987). *The under-achieving curriculum: Assessing U.S. schools from an international perspective.* Champaign, IL: Stipes.

Miura, I., & Okamoto, Y. (1989). Comparisons of American and Japanese first graders' cognitive representation of number and understanding of place value. *Journal of Educational Psychology, 81,* 109–113.

National Center for Education Statistics. (1997). *Pursuing excellence: A study of U.S. fourth-grade mathematics and science achievement in international context* (NCES 97-255). Washington, DC: U.S. Government Printing Office.

National Center for Research on Teacher Education. (1988). *Dialogues in teacher education.* East Lansing, MI: National Center for Research on Teacher Education.

National Center for Research on Teacher Education. (1991). *Findings from the teacher education and learning to teach study: Final report.* East Lansing, MI: National Center for Research on Teacher Education.

National Commission on Teaching and America's Future. (1997). *Doing what matters most: Investing in quality teaching.* New York: Author.

National Council of Teachers of Mathematics. (1989). *Curriculum and evaluation: Standards for school mathematics.* Reston, VA: National Council of Teachers of Mathematics.

National Council of Teachers of Mathematics. (1991). *Professional standards for teaching mathematics.* Reston, VA: Author.

Paine, L., & Ma, L. (1993). Teachers working together: A dialogue on organizational and cultural perspectives of Chinese teachers. *International Journal of Educational Research, 19*(8), 675–718.

Pólya, G. (1973). *How to solve it: A new aspect of mathematical method.* Princeton NJ: Princeton University Press (2nd printing).

Putnam, R. (1992). Teaching the "hows" of mathematics for everyday life: A case study of a fifth-grade teacher. *The Elementary School Journal, 93*(2), 163–177.

Putnam, R., Heaton, R., Prawat, R., & Remillard, J. (1992). Teaching mathematics for understanding: Discussing case studies of four fifth-grade teachers. *Elementary School Journal, 93*(2), 213–228.

Resnick, L. B. (1982). Syntax and semantics in learning to subtract. In T. Carpenter, P. Moser, & T. Romberg (Eds.), *Addition and subtraction: A cognitive perspective* (pp. 136–155). Hillsdale, NJ: Lawrence Erlbaum Associates.

Robitaille, D. F., & Garden, R. A. (1989). *The IEA study of mathematics II: Contexts and outcomes of school mathematics.* New York: Pergamon.

Schifter, D. (1996a). Conclusion: Throwing open the doors. In D. Schifter (Ed.), *What's happening in math class?: Reconstructing professional identities* (Vol. 2, pp. 163–165). New York: Teachers College Press.

Schifter, D. (1996b). Introduction: Reconstructing professional identities. In D. Schifter (Ed.), *What's happening in math class?: Reconstructing professional identities* (Vol. 2, pp. 1–8). New York: Teachers College Press.

Schifter, D. (Ed.). (1996c). *What's happening in math class?: Envisioning new practices through teacher narratives* (Vol. 1). New York: Teachers College Press.

Schifter, D. (Ed.). (1996d). *What's happening in math class?: Reconstructing professional identities* (Vol. 2). New York: Teachers College Press.

Schmidt, W. (Ed.). (1996). *Characterizing pedagogical flow: An investigation of mathematics and science teaching in six countries.* Boston: Kluwer.

Schmidt, W., McKnight, C., & Raizen, S. (1997). *A splintered vision: An investigation of U.S. science and mathematics education.* Boston: Kluwer.

Schoenfeld, A. (1985). *Mathematical problem solving.* Orlando, FL: Academic Press.

Schram, P., Nemser, S., & Ball, D. (1989). *Thinking about teaching subtraction with regrouping: A comparison of beginning and experienced teachers' responses to textbooks.* East Lansing, MI: National Center for Research on Teacher Education.

Shen, B., & Liang, J. (1992). *Xiao xue shu xue jiao xue fa* [Teaching elementary mathematics—A teacher's manual]. Shanghai, Beijing: The Press of East China Normal University.

Shimahara, N., & Sakai, A. (1995). *Learning to teach in two cultures: Japan and the United States.* New York: Garland Publishing.

Shulman, L. (1986). Those who understand: Knowledge growth in teaching. *Educational Researcher, 15,* 4–14.

Simon, M. (1993). Prospective elementary teachers' knowledge of division. *Journal for Research in Mathematics Education, 24*(3), 233–254.

Smith, D., & Mikami, Y. (1914). *A history of Japanese mathematics.* Chicago: Open Court Publishing Company.

Sosniak, L., & Stodolsky, S. (1993). Teachers and textbooks: Materials use in four fourth-grade classrooms. *Elementary School Journal, 93*(3), 2549–275.

Steen, L. (1990). Pattern. In L. Steen (Ed.), *On the shoulders of giants* (pp. 1–10). Washington, DC: National Academy Press.

Stein, M., Baxter, J., & Leinhardt, G. (1990). Subject matter knowledge and elementary instruction: A case from functions and graphing. *American Educational Research Journal, 27*(4), 639–663.

Steinberg, R., Marks, R., & Haymore, J. (1985). *Teachers' knowledge and structure content in mathematics* (Knowledge Growth in a Profession Publication Series). Stanford, CA: Stanford University, School of Education.

Stevenson, H. W., Azuma, H., & Hakuta, K. (Eds.). (1986). *Child development and education in Japan.* New York: W. H. Freeman.

Stevenson, H. W., Lee, S., Chen, C., Lummis, M., Stigler, J., Fan, L., & Ge, E. (1990). Mathematics achievement of children in China and the United States. *Child Development, 61,* 1053–1066.

Stevenson, H. W., & Stigler, J. W. (1992). *The learning gap.* New York: Summit Books.

Stigler, J. W., Fernandez, C., & Yoshida, M. (1996). Cultures of mathematics instruction in Japanese and American elementary classrooms. In T. Rohlen & G. LeTendre (Eds.), *Teaching and learning in Japan* (pp. 213–247). Cambridge, England: Cambridge University Press.

Stigler, J. W., Lee, S. Y., & Stevenson, H. W. (1986). Mathematics classrooms in Japan, Taiwan, and the United States. *Child Development, 58*(5), 1272–1285.

Stigler, J. W., & Perry, M. (1988a). Cross-cultural studies of mathematics teaching and learning: Recent findings and new direction. In D. Grouws & T. Cooney (Eds.), *Perspectives on research on effective mathematics teaching* (Vol. 1). Reston, VA: National Council of Teachers of Mathematics.

Stigler, J. W., & Perry, M. (1988b). Mathematics learning in Japanese, Chinese, and American classrooms. *New directions for child development, 41,* 27–54.

Stigler, J. W., & Stevenson, H. W. (1991). How Asian teachers polish each lesson to perfection. *American Educator, 14*(4), 13–20, 43–46.

Walker, D. (1990). *Fundamentals of curriculum.* Santiago, Chile: Harcourt Brace Jovanovich.

Wilson, S. (1988). *Understanding historical understanding: Subject matter knowledge and the teaching of U.S. history.* Unpublished doctoral dissertation, Stanford University, Stanford, CA.

Author Index

Subject Index

A

abacus, 8
addition
  with carrying, 8, 16, 17
  with composing, 16, *see also* with
    carrying
  within 10, 18, 19
  within 20, 17
algorithm, xxiii, 12, 21, 108, 111,
  112, 119
associative law, 39, 109

B

basic attitudes, xxiii, 24, 25, 103,
  104, 120
  conditionality, 94-96, 100
  confidence, 24, 63, 81, 98, 99
  examples, role of, 86, 87
  justification with symbolic
    derivation, 109-111
  justification, 40, 41, 52, 59, 81,
    105, 111
  know how and also know why,
    xxiii, 108
  multiple solutions, 64, 111, 112
  promoting discussion, 24
  proof, 24, 81, 92, 93, 111
  simple solutions, 64
basic ideas, 11, 24, 25, 122, *see also*
  basic attitudes, basic principles
basic principles, xxiii, 23-25, 97, 120
  associative law, 39, 109
  commutative law, 39, 109
  composing a higher value unit, 45
  distributive law, 39-41, 97, 109
  equivalence of fraction and
    division, 64

fundamental laws, 81, 111, 116
inverse operation, 23, 113
order of operations, 64
rate of composing a higher value
  unit, 23
beike fudao cailiao, 130, *see also*
  teachers' manuals
borrowing, 2-4, 9, 136
breadth, 121-123

C

calculus, 116
chuli jiaocai, 133
collegiality, 136-138, 141
commutative law, 39, 109
composing a higher value unit, 45
composition of 10, 19
concept knot, 78, 81, 82, 115
conditionality, 94-96, 100
confidence, 24, 63, 81, 98, 99
connectedness, 122
connections, 21, 81, 82, 112, 119
curriculum
  China
    area formulas, 91, 116
    closed figure, 84
    division, 58, 60, 132
    fractions, 58, 61
    fundamental laws, 39, 109,
      132
    Grade 3, 109, 132
    Grade 4, 58, 109
    Grade 6, 58
    inverse operations, 59
    maintaining value of a
      quotient, 60
    secondary, 84